my **revision** notes

Pearson Edexcel GCSE (9–1)

# HISTORY

## FOUR UNITS IN ONE

Sam Slater
John Wright
Steve Waugh

HODDER EDUCATION
AN HACHETTE UK COMPANY

The Publishers would like to thank the following for permission to reproduce copyright material.

**Photo credits: p43** © The Print Collector/HIP/TopFoto; **p45** © Granger, NYC/TopFoto; **p50** © TopFoto; **p135** © INTERFOTO/Alamy Stock Photo; **p140** © Munich Putsch, 1940 (oil on canvas), Schmitt, H. (f l.1940)/Private Collection/Peter Newark Pictures/Bridgeman Images; **p145** © Punch Limited; **p157** © Everett Collection Historical/Alamy Stock Photo; **pp161**, **163** © ullsteinbild/TopFoto; **p166** © Glasshouse Images/Alamy Stock Photo.

**Acknowledgements:** mark schemes reproduced by kind permission of Pearson Education Ltd



Orders: please contact Bookpoint Ltd, 130 Milton Park, Abingdon, Oxon OX14 4SE. Telephone: +44 (0)1235 827827. Fax: +44 (0)1235 400401. Email education@bookpoint.co.uk Lines are open from 9 a.m. to 5 p.m., Monday to Saturday, with a 24-hour message answering service. You can also order through our website: www.hoddereducation.co.uk

ISBN: 978 1 5104 6944 0



First published in 2017
This combined edition published 2019 by
Hodder Education
An Hachette UK Company
Carmelite House, 50 Victoria Embankment
London EC4Y 0DZ

www.hoddereducation.co.uk

Impression number 10 9 8 7 6 5 4 3 2 1
Year 2023 2022 2021 2020 2019



Cover photo © Gábor Páll/Alamy Stock Photo
Illustrations by Gray Publishing
Produced and typeset in Bembo by Gray Publishing, Tunbridge Wells, Kent with revisions by Integra Software Services Ltd
Printed in Spain

A catalogue record for this title is available from the British Library.

# How to get the most out of this book

This book will help you revise for the following options:

**Paper 1: Thematic study and historic environment**
Medicine in Britain, c1250–Present and the British Sector of the Western Front, 1914–18

**Paper 2: British depth study**
Early Elizabethan England 1558–88

**Paper 2: Period study**
Superpower relations and the cold war 1941–91

**Paper 3: Modern depth study**
Weimar and Nazi Germany 1918–39

Use the revision planner on pages 3–10 to track your progress, topic by topic. Tick each box when you have:

1 revised and understood each topic
2 completed the activities
3 checked your answers online.

The content in the book is organised into a series of double-page spreads which cover the specification's content. The left-hand page on each spread has the key content for each topic, and the right-hand page has one or two activities to help you with exam skills or to learn the knowledge you need. Answers to these activities can be found online at www.hoddereducation.co.uk/myrevisionnotes. Quick multiple-choice quizzes to test your knowledge of each topic can be found on the website.

At the end of the unit is an exam focus section which gives you guidance on how to answer each exam question type.

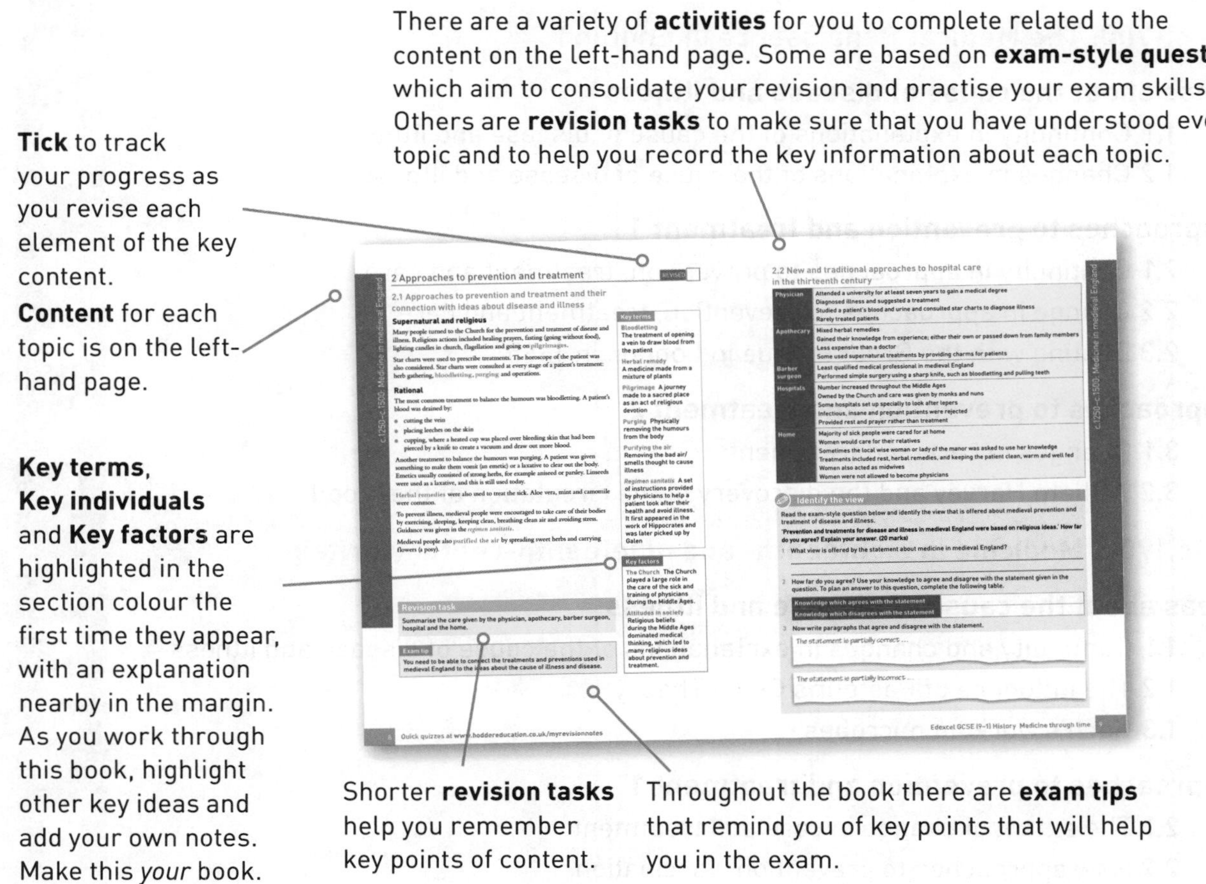
There are a variety of **activities** for you to complete related to the content on the left-hand page. Some are based on **exam-style questions** which aim to consolidate your revision and practise your exam skills. Others are **revision tasks** to make sure that you have understood every topic and to help you record the key information about each topic.
**Tick** to track your progress as you revise each element of the key content.
**Content** for each topic is on the left-hand page.
**Key terms**, **Key individuals** and **Key factors** are highlighted in the section colour the first time they appear, with an explanation nearby in the margin. As you work through this book, highlight other key ideas and add your own notes. Make this *your* book.
Shorter **revision tasks** help you remember key points of content.
Throughout the book there are **exam tips** that remind you of key points that will help you in the exam.

# Contents and revision planner

## Paper 1: Medicine in Britain c1250–Present and the British Sector of the Western Front, 1914–18

### Part 1: Medicine in Britain, c.1250–present

REVISED

## Paper 2: Early Elizabethan England 1558–88

### Key topic 1: Queen, government and religion, 1558–69

REVISED



### Key topic 2: Challenges to Elizabeth at home and abroad, 1569–88

## Key topic 3: Elizabethan society in the Age of Exploration, 1558–88

REVISED



## Exam focus

## Paper 2: Superpower relations and the Cold War 1941–91

### Key topic 1: The origins of the Cold War, 1941–58

REVISED



### Key topic 2: Cold War crises, 1958–70

## Key topic 3: The end of the Cold War, 1970–91

REVISED



## Exam focus

## Weimar and Nazi Germany 1918–39

### Key topic 1: The Weimar Republic, 1918–29



### Key topic 2: Hitler's rise to power, 1919–33



### Key topic 3: Nazi control and dictatorship, 1933–39

REVISED

# MEDICINE IN BRITAIN

## c.1250–PRESENT & THE BRITISH SECTOR OF THE WESTERN FRONT, 1914–18

# Part 1 Medicine in Britain, c.1250–present

## An overview of medicine from c.1250

REVISED

Medicine in Britain is a development study. It is important that you have a secure chronological understanding of the content – what happened, and when. You also need to be able to identify change and continuity in the understanding of the cause of disease and illness, and in the methods of prevention and treatment.

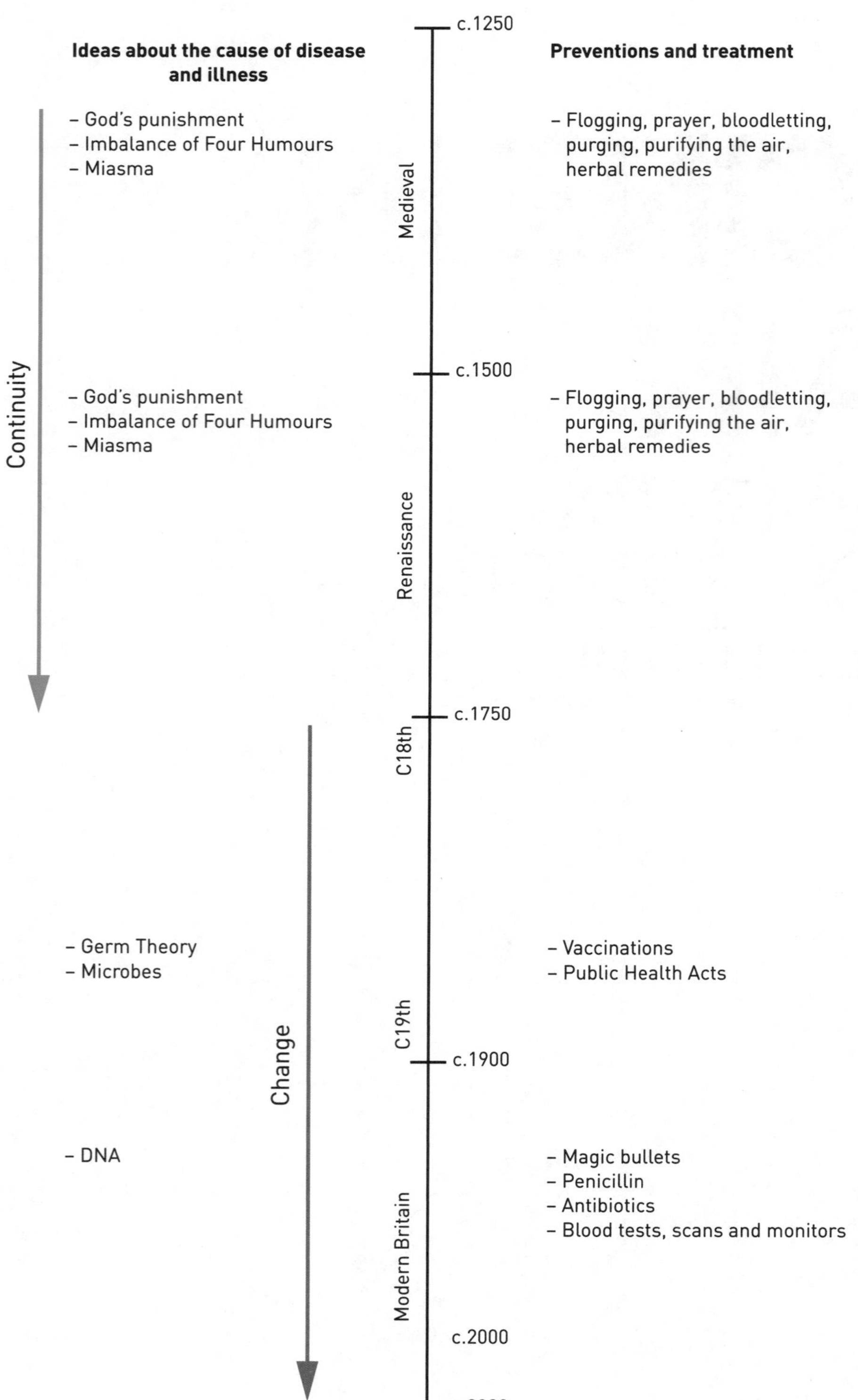


### Revision task

Create your own medicine timeline by copying this timeline. Make it bigger. You could use a roll of lining paper. As you work through this book, add key events, individuals and discoveries.

### Exam tip

You need to be aware of what changed and continued in medicine from c.1250 to the present day. Look for patterns, trends and turning points.

## The role of factors

REVISED

Factors are things that influenced medicine in the following ways:

- They helped to cause change: for example, the factor science and technology led to Pasteur discovering germs after experimenting with milk in 1860.
- They helped to prevent change: for example, the factor of the Church hindered any advance in medical knowledge during the medieval period because the Church protected the ideas of Galen and did not allow them to be challenged.

The main factors that you could be asked about in your exam are shown in the diagram below, with an explanation of what they mean.

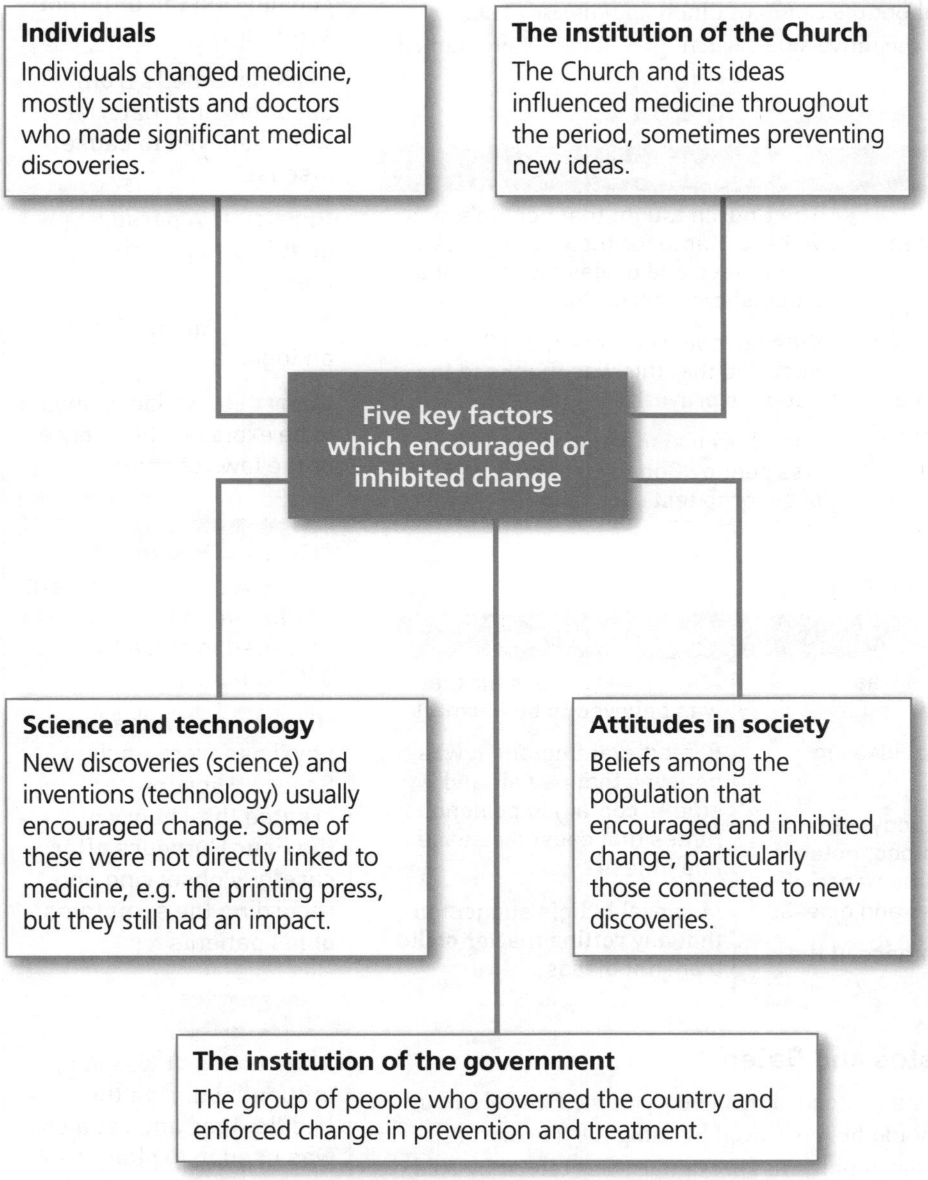

**Revision task**

Create a table of the factors in each time period that led to a change in medical understanding of the cause of disease and illness and new preventions and treatment. Repeat this for the care provided within the community.

**Five key factors which encouraged or inhibited change**

**Individuals**
Individuals changed medicine, mostly scientists and doctors who made significant medical discoveries.

**The institution of the Church**
The Church and its ideas influenced medicine throughout the period, sometimes preventing new ideas.

**Science and technology**
New discoveries (science) and inventions (technology) usually encouraged change. Some of these were not directly linked to medicine, e.g. the printing press, but they still had an impact.

**Attitudes in society**
Beliefs among the population that encouraged and inhibited change, particularly those connected to new discoveries.

**The institution of the government**
The group of people who governed the country and enforced change in prevention and treatment.

**Exam tip**

You need to be aware of what and how each factor contributed to medical developments during each time period. Look at what factors caused change and continuity. Look for patterns and trends.

# c.1250–c.1500: Medicine in medieval England

The Church and religious beliefs had a great influence over medicine during this period, leading to a continuation of ideas about cause, preventions and treatments.

## 1 Ideas about the cause of disease and illness

REVISED

Medieval England was a religious society. The majority of people followed the teachings of the Catholic Church and attended services regularly. The cause of disease and illness was unknown due to the lack of scientific knowledge. The majority of people in medieval England could not read or write and would learn from what they heard in church about the causes of illness and disease. The Church controlled education and the universities, where **physicians** were trained.

### 1.1 Supernatural and religious explanations

| Supernatural explanation | Religious explanations |
|---|---|
| Astrology, the alignment of the planets and stars, was used when diagnosing illness<br>Star charts (map of the night sky) would be consulted by looking at when a patient was born and when they fell ill to help provide a **diagnosis** of what was wrong with them | The Church taught that people's sins were to blame for their illnesses and that illness and disease were sent as a punishment from God<br>When people recovered, the Church declared that this was thanks to the patient's prayers<br>The Church also taught that disease was sent by God to cleanse the soul of sin or to test your faith |

### 1.2 Rational explanations

| Theory of the Four Humours | Miasma Theory |
|---|---|
| The Theory of the Four Humours was developed in Ancient Greece by **Hippocrates**<br>It continued to influence medical ideas in medieval England<br>This theory suggested that the body was made up of four liquids (humours) – blood, phlegm, black and yellow bile – and an imbalance of these substances caused illness and disease<br>It was believed that an equal balance of the humours led to good health | A **miasma** was bad air that was believed to be harmful<br>In medieval England it was believed that bad air and smells contained poisonous fumes that caused disease and illness<br>Medieval beliefs suggested that any rotting matter could transmit disease |

### The influence of Hippocrates and Galen

**Galen**, a physician in Ancient Rome, extended the Theory of the Four Humours by suggesting that the humours should be rebalanced by using the Theory of Opposites. He suggested that too much phlegm, for example, was caused by cold and the 'opposite' should be used, such as hot chillies and peppers to rebalance the humour. Galen also believed in the idea of the soul, which fitted with the teachings of the Church. This led to the Church promoting the ideas of Galen, and doctors widely using the Theory of the Four Humours, throughout the period c.1250–c.1500.

#### Key terms

**Diagnosis** Identifying the nature of an illness after considering the different symptoms

**Miasma** Smells from decomposing material were believed to cause disease

**Physician** A person qualified to practise medicine

**Rational** An idea based on logic

**Supernatural** Ideas unable to be explained by science or the laws of nature

#### Key individuals

**Galen** A doctor in Ancient Rome. Galen had his ideas recorded in more than 350 books

**Hippocrates** A leading physician from Ancient Greece. Hippocrates created the Theory of the Four Humours after carefully observing and recording the symptoms of his patients

#### Key factors

**The Church** It was very influential during the Middle Ages and religion was used to explain the causes of illness.

**Attitudes in society** Religious beliefs in the Middle Ages dominated medical thinking. Galen's ideas continued as the Church accepted them.

## Memory map

Create a memory map to show the different ideas that people in medieval England had about the cause of disease. Add some key words from the information on page 6 and your own knowledge to the diagram below. Use two different colours to show whether they are religious and supernatural explanations or rational explanations. To help you remember the information, you could add small drawings.

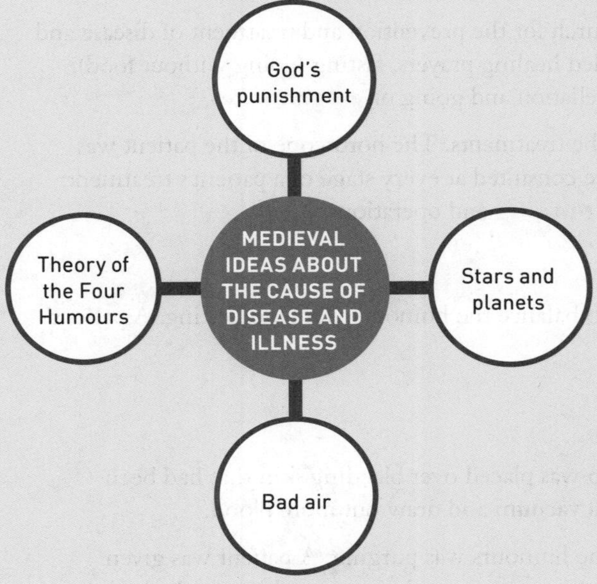

## Eliminate irrelevance

Here is an exam-style question:

**Explain why there was continuity in ideas about the cause of disease during the period c.1250–c.1500. (12 marks)**

**You may use the following in your answer:**

- **The Church**
- **Galen**

**You must also use information of your own.**

Below is a paragraph which is part of an answer to the question above. Some parts of the answer are not relevant to the question. Identify these and draw a line through the information that is irrelevant, justifying your deletions in the margin.

In medieval England there were religious and supernatural explanations for the cause of illness. The Church was very powerful and controlled education throughout the period, which led to the continuity of ideas. The Church taught that God was responsible for illness and disease. The Church taught that God sent disease as a punishment for sin or to cleanse the soul. As a result of this, many people would also turn to the Church for treatments and preventions. Religious believers would attend church and pray, pay for a special mass to be said to remove their sin and also fast. Some believers would go on a pilgrimage and during the Black Death in 1348 flagellants across Europe would whip themselves to show God how sorry they were for their sins and to show that they did not need to be punished with the disease. These beliefs continued throughout the period c.1250–c.1500 because the Church remained in control of education and continued to teach these ideas. Due to the power that the Church held in society, there was no challenge of the religious explanations, treatments and preventions for disease and illness.

# 2 Approaches to prevention and treatment

REVISED

## 2.1 Approaches to prevention and treatment and their connection with ideas about disease and illness

### Supernatural and religious

Many people turned to the Church for the prevention and treatment of disease and illness. Religious actions included healing prayers, fasting (going without food), lighting candles in church, flagellation and going on **pilgrimages**.

Star charts were used to prescribe treatments. The horoscope of the patient was also considered. Star charts were consulted at every stage of a patient's treatment: herb gathering, **bloodletting**, **purging** and operations.

### Rational

The most common treatment to balance the humours was bloodletting. A patient's blood was drained by:

- cutting the vein
- placing leeches on the skin
- cupping, where a heated cup was placed over bleeding skin that had been pierced by a knife to create a vacuum and draw out more blood.

Another treatment to balance the humours was purging. A patient was given something to make them vomit (an emetic) or a laxative to clear out the body. Emetics usually consisted of strong herbs, for example aniseed or parsley. Linseeds were used as a laxative, and this is still used today.

**Herbal remedies** were also used to treat the sick. Aloe vera, mint and camomile were common.

To prevent illness, medieval people were encouraged to take care of their bodies by exercising, sleeping, keeping clean, breathing clean air and avoiding stress. Guidance was given in the ***regimen sanitatis***.

Medieval people also **purified the air** by spreading sweet herbs and carrying flowers (a posy).

#### Key terms

**Bloodletting** The treatment of opening a vein to draw blood from the patient

**Herbal remedy** A medicine made from a mixture of plants

**Pilgrimage** A journey made to a sacred place as an act of religious devotion

**Purging** Physically removing the humours from the body

**Purifying the air** Removing the bad air/smells thought to cause illness

***Regimen sanitatis*** A set of instructions provided by physicians to help a patient look after their health and avoid illness. It first appeared in the work of Hippocrates and was later picked up by Galen

#### Key factors

**The Church** The Church played a large role in the care of the sick and training of physicians during the Middle Ages.

**Attitudes in society** Religious beliefs during the Middle Ages dominated medical thinking, which led to many religious ideas about prevention and treatment.

#### Revision task

Summarise the care given by the physician, apothecary, barber surgeon, hospital and the home.

#### Exam tip

You need to be able to connect the treatments and preventions used in medieval England to the ideas about the cause of illness and disease.

## 2.2 New and traditional approaches to hospital care in the thirteenth century

| | |
|---|---|
| **Physician** | Attended a university for at least seven years to gain a medical degree<br>Diagnosed illness and suggested a treatment<br>Studied a patient's blood and urine and consulted star charts to diagnose illness<br>Rarely treated patients |
| **Apothecary** | Mixed herbal remedies<br>Gained their knowledge from experience; either their own or passed down from family members<br>Less expensive than a doctor<br>Some used supernatural treatments by providing charms for patients |
| **Barber surgeon** | Least qualified medical professional in medieval England<br>Performed simple surgery using a sharp knife, such as bloodletting and pulling teeth |
| **Hospitals** | Number increased throughout the Middle Ages<br>Owned by the Church and care was given by monks and nuns<br>Some hospitals set up specially to look after lepers<br>Infectious, insane and pregnant patients were rejected<br>Provided rest and prayer rather than treatment |
| **Home** | Majority of sick people were cared for at home<br>Women would care for their relatives<br>Sometimes the local wise woman or lady of the manor was asked to use her knowledge<br>Treatments included rest, herbal remedies, and keeping the patient clean, warm and well fed<br>Women also acted as midwives<br>Women were not allowed to become physicians |

### Identify the view

Read the exam-style question below and identify the view that is offered about medieval prevention and treatment of disease and illness.

**'Prevention and treatments for disease and illness in medieval England were based on religious ideas.' How far do you agree? Explain your answer. (16 marks, with a further 4 marks available for spelling, punctuation and grammar.)**

1 What view is offered by the statement about medicine in medieval England?

______________________________

______________________________

2 How far do you agree? Use your knowledge to agree and disagree with the statement given in the question. To plan an answer to this question, complete the following table.

| | |
|---|---|
| **Knowledge which agrees with the statement** | |
| **Knowledge which disagrees with the statement** | |

3 Now write paragraphs that agree and disagree with the statement.

*The statement is partially correct ...*

*The statement is partially incorrect ...*

## 3 Case study: Dealing with the Black Death, 1348–49

REVISED

The Black Death was an outbreak of the **bubonic plague** that first broke out in China and reached England in 1348. It is believed to have killed 40 per cent of the population of England. It was unlikely a victim would survive the disease once they caught it; they would die within three to five days. We know little about the treatments because its victims died so quickly.

### Beliefs about the causes

Beliefs about the causes related to medieval views about the world, including:

- God had sent the disease as a punishment for sins.
- An unusual alignment of the planets Mars, Jupiter and Saturn in 1345.
- An imbalance of the four humours (see page 14) or the existence of evil humours within the body.
- Bad air (miasma) which had corrupted the body's humours. This poisonous air was believed to have been released from a volcano or an earthquake.

### Approaches to treatment

Treatments for the Black Death related to the ideas about its causes:

- People prayed, confessed sins, donated and asked God for forgiveness.
- Holy charms were worn to show one's religious beliefs.
- Bleeding, purging and treatments based on Galen's Theory of Opposites (see page 14) were used to rebalance the four humours.
- A victim would sniff strong herbs, such as myrrh, in order to replace the bad air in their body.
- Many victims would light fires to remove the bad air and replace it with the smoke and fumes from the fire.
- Because some victims survived once the pus was released, victims would lance the buboes in the hope that this would cure them of the disease.

### Attempts to prevent its spread

Ways to prevent the Black Death from spreading centred around religion, keeping the streets clean to prevent bad air and isolating its victims.

- Many would pray to God in the hope of avoiding punishment.
- The king and bishops ordered processions in every church at least once a day.
- People went on pilgrimages and made sacrifices to God, such as fasting.
- **Flagellants** whipped themselves to ask for God's forgiveness.
- People carried posies of sweet-smelling herbs and flowers.
- Rakers cleared animal dung from the streets to stop creating bad air.
- Fines for throwing litter were increased to keep the streets cleaner.
- To reduce the waste on the streets, butchers had to use segregated areas to butcher animals or face punishment.
- Ringing bells and birds were used to keep the air moving.
- New quarantine laws were issued to prevent the movement of people. Those new to an area had to remain isolated for 40 days, to ensure they were not infected.
- The authorities **quarantined** houses of victims.

#### Key terms

**Bubonic plague** A contagious and fatal epidemic disease caused by bacteria and characterised by chills, fever, vomiting and buboes

**Flagellants** Religious believers who whipped themselves to show God that they repented their sins and to ask for his forgiveness to avoid the plague

**Quarantine** Separating the sick to stop the spread of disease. Those with the disease were isolated in the quarantined area

#### Exam tip

You need to be able to explain the link between what people did to treat and prevent the Black Death and the medieval beliefs that existed about the cause of disease.

## Organising knowledge

Use the information on page 10 to complete the table below to show the links between cause, treatment and prevention of the Black Death.

| Black Death | Religion | Rational | Supernatural |
|---|---|---|---|
| Beliefs about cause | | | |
| Treatment | | | |
| Prevention | | | |

## Analysing factors

You need to understand the role that factors had on the medieval ideas about the cause of disease and the treatments and preventions that they used. Make a copy of the concentric circles. Rank order the factors in the box that explain the ideas that existed about cause, treatment and prevention, beginning with the most important in the middle to the least important on the outside. Explain your decisions by annotating the diagram.

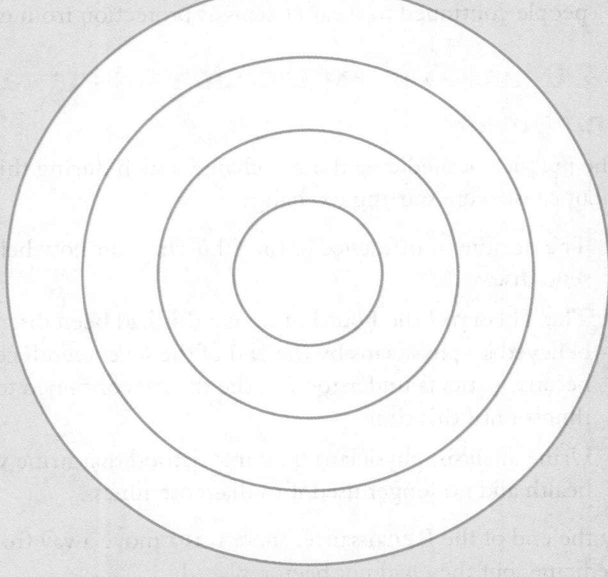

For example, if you believe that the religious ideas about cause, treatment and prevention were the most influential, write 'The Church' in the centre circle. You can then annotate this with details of the religious ideas, such as it was believed that God sent the Black Death as a punishment for sins.

**FACTORS**

- government
- individuals
- attitudes in society
- the Church
- science and technology.

For a reminder about each factor see page 13.

# c.1500–c.1700: The Medical Renaissance in England

Ideas about the causes of disease and illness were starting to change during the **Renaissance**. However, this led to very little change in methods of prevention and treatment. The Renaissance did see the introduction of science and technology improving medicine.

## 1 Ideas about the cause of disease and illness

REVISED

During the Medical Renaissance new ideas began to influence medicine and slowly replace old beliefs. As **Protestantism** spread across Europe, the Catholic Church was less able to promote its beliefs and control medicine. As a more **secular** society developed, scientific ideas were discovered both in medicine, and beyond.

### 1.1 Continuity in explanations of the cause of disease and illness

- Miasma Theory (see page 14): this idea continued and became more widespread during **epidemics**.
- The influence of the Church: during epidemics, such as the Great Plague, religious causes were still influential.
- Supernatural: from 1500, astrology was less popular, but during epidemics people continued to wear charms as protection from evil spirits.

### 1.2 Changes in explanations of the cause of disease and illness

The practice of medicine did not change much during this time, but the ideas about cause were starting to change:

- The decline in influence of the Church: most now believed that God did not send disease.
- The Theory of the Four Humours: this had been discredited and was not believed by physicians by the end of the seventeenth century. However, because patients understood it, the theory continued to be used to diagnose illness until this time.
- Urine analysis: physicians now understood that urine was not linked to ill health and no longer used it to diagnose illness.

By the end of the Renaissance, there was a move away from old ideas about medicine, but they had not been replaced.

#### Animalcules

A new idea that little animals were the cause of illness developed after they could be seen by newly invented, more powerful microscopes. These images were not very clear.

#### The work of Thomas Sydenham

**Thomas Sydenham** was important in moving medicine away from the ideas of Hippocrates and Galen. Sydenham believed in closely observing the symptoms of a patient, noting these down in detailed descriptions and then looking for remedies to treat the disease, rather than relying on medical books.

**Key terms**

**Epidemic** A widespread occurrence of an infectious disease in a community at a particular time

**Printing press** A machine for reproducing text and pictures

**Protestantism** The practice of the Protestant Church

**Renaissance** A revival of ideas from 1500 to 1700

**Secular** Not connected with religious or spiritual matters

**Key individual**

**Thomas Sydenham**
A well-respected doctor in London during the 1660s and 1670s. He was given the nickname of the 'English Hippocrates' because, like the Greek doctor, he placed great importance on observing a patient. His book *Observationes Medicae* was used for two centuries

## The influence of the printing press

In the fifteenth century, the first printing press was invented. It enabled medical information to spread further and more quickly; and contributed to the decline in influence of the Church. Now physicians were able to publish books that criticised Galen.

## The Royal Society

The Royal Society was founded in London in 1660 to discuss new ideas in astronomy, medicine and science. It was important in the development of new medical ideas because it made it possible for scientists and physicians to study one another's work. The Royal Society also sponsored scientists and assisted them with the publication of their ideas.

**Key factor**

**Science and technology**
Science began to play a significant role in medicine during the Renaissance. Physicians and doctors started to question the old ideas and look to science for new explanations for the cause of disease and illness. New technology was developed that assisted the development of medicine; the printing press and microscopes.

## Organising knowledge

Use the information on page 12 to complete the table below to show the old and new ideas that existed during the Renaissance in England about the cause of disease and illness.

| Ideas about the cause of disease and illness during the medical Renaissance in England | |
|---|---|
| **New ideas** | **Old ideas** |
| | |

## Making comparisons

Look at the exam-style question below and the two answers. Which answer is better for comparing the key features of medical understanding? Why?

**Explain one way in which ideas about the causes of disease were similar in the fourteenth and seventeenth centuries. (4 marks)**

**ANSWER 1**

Ideas about the causes of disease in the fourteenth and seventeenth centuries were similar because at both times illness was believed to have been caused by bad air.

**ANSWER 2**

In the fourteenth and seventeenth centuries disease was believed to have a rational cause, for example bad air (miasma). During the Great Plague, like the Black Death, people believed that bad air (miasma) was caused by rotting waste and a movement of the planets. They believed that this led to an imbalance of the four humours and so disease in the form of the plague.

# 2 Approaches to prevention and treatment 1

REVISED

## 2.1 Continuity in approaches to prevention, treatment and care

Many of the preventions and treatments used during medieval England continued throughout the Renaissance because there was little change in the ideas about the cause of illness. These included:

- bloodletting, purging and sweating
- herbal remedies
- the practice of *regimen sanitatis* (see page 16)
- the removal of bad air
- treatment of the sick by apothecaries and surgeons for those who could not afford a physician
- women cared for the sick who did not go to hospital.

**Key terms**

**Pomander** A ball that contained perfumed substances

**Transference** Belief that an illness or disease could be transferred to something else. For example, people believed that if you rubbed an object on a boil the disease would transfer from the person to the object

## 2.2 Changes in approaches to prevention, treatment and care

The move towards scientific thinking also led to new preventions and treatments:

- People started to believe in **transference**.
- People began to look for chemical cures for diseases rather than relying on herbs and bloodletting.
- Ideas that the weather conditions were the cause of disease became more popular and so people would relocate to avoid a disease.
- Renaissance hospitals began to treat people with wounds and curable diseases such as fevers.
- Hospitals that specialised in one particular disease were new in this period. These became known as pest houses, plague houses or poxhouses.

**Revision task**

Summarise the continuity in the prevention and treatment of disease and illness in the period c.1250–c.1700. Try to make this visual by creating a mind map.

**Exam tip**

You need to know the similarities and differences between the preventions and treatments during the Great Plague in 1665 those used during the Black Death in 1348.

## 2.3 Dealing with the Great Plague in London in 1665

The plague returned to England throughout the seventeenth century. The Great Plague was the last major epidemic of the plague to hit England.

| Idea about cause | Prevention and treatment |
|---|---|
| Astrology: an unusual alignment of the planets<br>Punishment from God to cleanse man of his sins<br>An imbalance of the four humours<br>Miasma: bad air caused by foul-smelling rubbish<br>Person to person by touch | Prayers were recited<br>Plague victims were quarantined for 28 days and the door was painted with a cross alongside the words 'Lord have mercy upon us'<br>People were encouraged to carry a **pomander** to drive away the bad air<br>Fasting took place and some changed their diet to include a lot of garlic<br>Plague doctors treated patients wearing a birdlike mask (because birds were believed to attract disease away from the patient), with sweet-smelling herbs inside to ward off miasma<br>Smoking tobacco to ward off miasma<br>Local authorities tried to prevent the plague from spreading by:<br>• banning public meetings, funerals and fairs<br>• closing theatres<br>• sweeping streets clean<br>• burning barrels of tar and sweet-smelling herbs to ward off miasma<br>• killing cats and dogs<br>• appointing searchers to monitor the spread of the disease and clear victims' bodies from towns |

## Organising knowledge

Study the Black Death in 1348 (page 10) and the Great Plague in 1665 (page 14). Complete the table below to show the similarities and differences between these two outbreaks.

| Similarities | Differences |
|---|---|
| Ideas about the cause: | Ideas about the cause: |
| Preventions and treatments: | Preventions and treatments: |

## You're the examiner

Below is an exam-style question.

**Explain why there was continuity in the way disease and illness were prevented and treated in the period c.1250–c.1700. (12 marks)**

**You may use the following information in your answer:**
- **Great Plague**
- **Attitudes in society**

1 Below are a mark scheme and a paragraph which is part of an answer to the question. Read the paragraph and the mark scheme. Decide which level you would award the paragraph. Write the level below, along with a justification for your choice.

Remember that for the higher levels you must:
- explain three reasons
- focus explicitly on the question
- support reasons with precise details.

| Mark scheme | |
|---|---|
| **Level** | |
| 1 | A simple or generalised answer is given, lacking development and organisation |
| 2 | An explanation is given, showing limited analysis and with only an implicit link to the question |
| 3 | An explanation is given, showing some analysis, which is mainly directed at the focus of the question |
| 4 | An analytical explanation is given which is directed consistently at the focus of the question |

### STUDENT ANSWER

*People tried to prevent catching the Great Plague by placing those who had the disease in quarantine for 28 days, by carrying a pomander to drive away the miasma because they believed it was caused by the bad air, and by eating a diet heavy with garlic. Some healers advised smoking tobacco to also ward off the miasma. Local government also took action by banning public meetings and fairs, and closing theatres. Fires were lit and barrels of tar were burned. These actions took place because the local government wanted to prevent the spread of the disease by contagion and miasma. Here we can see a similarity with the Black Death during the Middle Ages as this epidemic was also believed to have been spread by bad air and contagion.*

Level ☐ Reason ____________________

2 Now suggest what the student has to do to achieve a higher level.

3 Try and rewrite this paragraph at a higher level.

4 Now try and write the rest of the answer to the question.

# 3 Approaches to prevention and treatment 2

REVISED

## 3.1 Changes in care and treatment

The new approach to medicine and knowledge developed during the Renaissance led to a change in medical training and care of the sick.

### Improvements in medical training

Apothecaries and surgeons were better educated between 1500 and 1700:

- Wars were being fought with new technology, which led to new wounds that required more surgery.
- The increase in available chemicals led to new ingredients being available for apothecaries.

Physicians continued to train at universities with little change. Due to the decline in power of the Church, **dissection** was legalised but it was difficult to get a supply of fresh corpses to work on. This meant that physicians continued to train from books, such as those of Galen. Training did advance as physicians were inspired to challenge the old teachings and investigate for themselves (see below, Vesalius and Harvey). The printing press made books more widely available for physicians to study.

### The influence in England of the work of Vesalius

In 1543, **Vesalius** published his most famous book, *On the Fabric of the Human Body*. Vesalius had been able to dissect a large number of executed criminals.

| Learning of Vesalius | Impact of Vesalius |
|---|---|
| Vesalius found around 300 mistakes in the anatomical work of Galen, which included:<br>• the human lower jaw has one bone, not two<br>• the human breastbone has three parts, not seven<br>• men do not have one fewer pair of ribs than women<br>• the human liver does not have five separate lobes<br>Vesalius corrected these mistakes and encouraged other doctors to base their work on dissection rather than old books. Vesalius explained these mistakes by pointing out that Galen had dissected animals, rather than humans | **Anatomy** became central to the study of medicine, and doctors were encouraged to carry out dissections for themselves<br>Vesalius' work was heavily copied and appeared in other medical texts<br>His work inspired other anatomists. After Vesalius' death, Fabricius went on to discover valves in human veins and shared his discovery with William Harvey<br>Vesalius caused a lot of controversy because he had challenged the ideas of Galen. This angered traditional physicians who argued that the human body had not changed since the ideas of Galen |

#### Key terms

**Anatomy** The branch of science concerned with the bodily structure of humans

**Dissection** Cutting up a body to study its internal parts

#### Key individuals

**William Harvey** Studied medicine at Cambridge and then at the famous medical school in Padua. In 1615, he became a lecturer in anatomy at the College of Physicians before becoming a doctor to King James I

**Andreas Vesalius** The most famous anatomist of this period. He was a lecturer in surgery at the University of Padua and had a deep interest in the human body

#### Key factor

**Individuals** The work of individuals became important during the medical Renaissance in England. What they discovered about the human body is important, but also the influence that they had.

#### Revision task

Summarise in no more than ten words the changes in medical training and treatment as a result of the work of Vesalius and Harvey.

## 3.2 William Harvey and the discovery of the circulation of the blood

**Harvey** had a keen interest in dissection and observing the human body to improve his knowledge of human anatomy.

| Discovery of the circulation of the blood | Impact of Harvey |
|---|---|
| Harvey's research involved dissecting human corpses and cutting open cold-blooded animals because they had a slower heartbeat and this enabled their blood to be observed while they were still alive<br><br>Harvey's research proved that arteries and veins were linked together in one system<br><br>Harvey's theory was that blood must pass from arteries to veins through tiny passages invisible to the naked eye. Today we know these to be capillaries<br><br>Harvey corrected Galen and showed that only the veins carried blood and that the heart acted as a pump | Harvey's theory encouraged other scientists to experiment on actual bodies<br><br>However, his discovery had little practical use in medical treatment and led to very little change<br><br>Some openly criticised Harvey because he did not have a powerful enough microscope to prove that capillaries existed. He was said to be mad |

### Support or challenge

Below is an exam-style question which asks how far you agree with a specific statement. Below this are a series of general statements which are relevant to the question. Using your own knowledge and the information throughout this key topic, decide whether these statements support or challenge the statement in the question and tick the appropriate box.

**'Individuals had the most significant impact on medical training between c.1500 and c.1700.' How far do you agree? Explain your answer. (16 marks, with a further 4 marks available for spelling, punctuation and grammar.)**

**You may use the following in your answer:**
- **Vesalius**
- **The Royal Society**

**You must also use some information of your own.**

| Statement | Support | Challenge |
|---|---|---|
| More powerful microscopes were being developed and, in 1683, one allowed for the observation of tiny 'animalcules' | | |
| The Royal Society first met in 1660 to share scientific knowledge and encourage new ideas | | |
| The Theory of the Four Humours was starting to be rejected by physicians | | |
| Doctors and anatomists were starting to observe the human body themselves rather than relying on old books | | |
| Thomas Sydenham encouraged doctors to observe their patients and note down their symptoms | | |
| The newly developed printing press allowed for medical information to be spread quickly and accurately | | |
| Vesalius dissected human corpses and proved around 300 ideas of Galen incorrect | | |
| Harvey discovered that blood circulated around the body and that the heart acted as a pump | | |
| Without a microscope, Harvey was unable to prove that capillaries existed and so many physicians ignored his ideas | | |

Once you have completed this table, write an answer to this question.

# c.1700–c.1900: Medicine in eighteenth- and nineteenth-century Britain

From 1700, the Church began to lose its influence over disease and illness as there was a focus on scientific explanations. This period saw the growth of cities, which brought threatening diseases such as smallpox, tuberculosis and typhus.

## 1 Ideas about the cause of disease and illness

REVISED

Intellectual movements such as the **Enlightenment** encouraged others to think for themselves to find answers – including about disease and illness.

### 1.1 Continuity and changes in explanations of the cause of disease and illness

Ideas about the cause of disease had not changed by the eighteenth century and people still believed in the Theory of the Four Humours and miasma, but this theory was losing popularity. Scientific thinking led to a change in medical understanding at the end of this period when the **Germ Theory** was developed.

#### Spontaneous generation theory

Microscopes had improved so that scientists could see **microbes** on decaying matter. This led some scientists to develop the theory of spontaneous generation in the early eighteenth century. They argued that the microbes were a product of the decay, rather than the cause of it, and that they spread by miasma.

### 1.2 The influence of Pasteur's Germ Theory

In 1861, **Louis Pasteur** published his discovery of the Germ Theory. He proved that germs were causing liquids to decay. This disproved the spontaneous generation theory. This discovery led him to the theory that germs might cause disease in the human body.

#### Impact

- Little immediate impact on medicine because doctors and surgeons could not see Pasteur's microbes.
- Some impact on the work of Joseph Lister, who linked the Germ Theory to infection in his patients (see page 28). Unfortunately, Lister's ideas were doubted as he could not prove his theory. With the presence of microbes in the organs of healthy people, it seemed impossible to some that they could be the cause of disease and illness.
- In the long term, Pasteur's discovery led to changes in preventing disease with vaccinations and the introduction of antiseptic and aseptic surgery.

### 1.3 Koch's work on microbes

**Robert Koch** developed the work of Pasteur by successfully identifying the different microbes that caused common individual diseases:

- 1876: Koch discovered the bacteria that caused anthrax.
- 1882: Koch went on to discover the bacteria that caused tuberculosis and typhoid.
- 1883: Koch discovered cholera.
- Koch's co-workers also went on to discover the microbes for diphtheria, pneumonia, meningitis, the plague and tetanus.

**Key terms**

**Enlightenment** A European intellectual movement of the late seventeenth and eighteenth centuries that emphasised reason and individualism rather than tradition

**Germ Theory** The theory that germs cause disease, often by infection through the air

**Microbes** A living organism that can only be seen with a microscope. Microbes include bacteria

**Key individuals**

**Robert Koch** A German doctor who identified specific bacteria that caused disease in humans

**Louis Pasteur** A French chemist who discovered germs before going on to develop vaccines

**Key factors**

**Attitudes in society**
The Enlightenment encouraged questioning and new theories about medicine to develop

**Science and technology**
Scientific experiment, microscopes, the swan-neck flask and the Petri dish were all vital instruments in the discovery of germs and development of vaccines

| Koch's influence in Britain | |
|---|---|
| **Positive** | **Negative** |
| Koch made it easier to see microbes by developing a dye that would stain them<br>Koch's new method of growing microbes enabled other scientists to study specific diseases<br>Koch's work inspired other scientists to look for the microbes responsible for other diseases | The discovery of germs and different bacteria alone did not have an impact on medical treatment. It took time for cures and vaccines to be developed<br>Initially the British government rejected the idea of the Germ Theory. Even when Koch went to Calcutta and proved that cholera was caused by microbes in the drinking water, they ignored this and continued to believe in miasma |

## Revision task

Create a timeline showing the development of the Germ Theory. Include the work of Pasteur and Koch.

## Analysing factors

You need to understand the role that factors had on the ideas about cause of disease and illness in the eighteenth and nineteenth centuries. Copy and complete the diagram below. For each factor in the diagram, explain how it led to advances in the understanding of the cause of disease and illness during this period. If a factor contributed in multiple ways, you will want to have more than one explanation.

Once you have completed the diagram, decide which factor you think was the most significant and why.

For a reminder about each factor see page 13.

**Ideas about the cause of disease and illness, 1700–1900**

- **Individuals**
- **Government**
- **Science and technology**
- **Attitudes in society**

## Complete the paragraph

Below are an exam-style question and a paragraph which is part of an answer to this question. The paragraph gives an argument for agreeing with the statement and some historical support but does not go on to develop the explanation.

1 Rewrite the paragraph with extra precise supporting knowledge and a full explanation linking back to the statement.

2 Complete the answer to this question.

**'There was complete change in ideas about the cause of disease and illness in the period c.1700–c.1900.' How far do you agree? Explain your answer. (16 marks, with a further 4 marks available for spelling, punctuation and grammar.)**

**You may use the following information in your answer.**

- **Germ Theory**
- **Robert Koch**

**You must also use information of your own.**

*There was complete change in the ideas about the cause of disease and illness in the period c.1700–c.1900 because science prevailed and microbes were identified and understood. In 1861, Louis Pasteur discovered and published his Germ Theory. Although Pasteur had only proven that microbes caused decay in liquids, he inspired other scientists to look for a similar cause to explain disease in the human body. Robert Koch followed Pasteur and identified the microbes that caused anthrax, tuberculosis and cholera.*

# 2 Approaches to prevention and treatment 1

REVISED

## 2.1 The extent of change in care and treatment

| | |
|---|---|
| **Hospital care** | From the eighteenth century more people were treated in a hospital, but this led to less sanitary conditions<br>**Florence Nightingale** trained as a nurse in Germany and Paris before being sent by the government to the Crimea to improve hospitals during the Crimean War<br>Nightingale noticed the high death rate among soldiers<br>Alongside 38 nurses, Nightingale made changes. The wards were cleaned of any dirt, organisation was improved and patients were given clean bedding and meals. Within six months the death rate fell from 40 per cent to 2 per cent<br>Nightingale returned to Britain, campaigning for cleaner hospitals and improved training for nurses. In 1859 she wrote *Notes on Nursing*. In 1860 she set up the Nightingale School for Nurses<br>Nightingale also influenced the way hospitals were designed. By 1900 they looked very different; they were built from materials that could easily be cleaned and had separate wards |
| **Surgery** | Surgery in the eighteenth century was dangerous. Patients faced the problems of pain, infection and bleeding<br>In 1847, **James Simpson** discovered chloroform as an **anaesthetic**<br>Doctors had to be careful using chloroform because the dosage had to be carefully controlled. In 1848, Hannah Greener died from an overdose during an operation to have her toenail removed<br>Chloroform continued to be used and was given a royal blessing in 1853 when Queen Victoria used it during the birth of her son<br>The problem of infection was overcome in 1865 by **Joseph Lister**<br>Lister used carbolic acid to clear bacteria from the wounds of patients. This became known as **antiseptic surgery**<br>Unfortunately, Lister's ideas faced opposition because the medical profession took time to understand the Germ Theory. The carbolic spray was unpleasant to use; it dried out the skin of surgeons and left an odd smell. From 1890, **aseptic surgery** was performed |

## 2.2 New approaches to prevention: vaccination

Throughout the eighteenth century, smallpox epidemics threatened Britain. Smallpox spread quickly and killed many. There was no understanding about its cause or how to prevent it.

Initially, **inoculation** was used to prevent the spread of smallpox. It was expensive and only available to the rich. Inoculation was dangerous as some patients died from the dose that they were given.

**Edward Jenner**, a country doctor, observed that milkmaids who had previously suffered from cowpox did not catch smallpox during the epidemics. He believed the two were connected and went on to test his theory in 1796. He gave James Phipps a dose of cowpox and six weeks later infected him with smallpox, but Phipps did not catch it. Jenner repeated his experiment with the same success before publishing his findings.

### Key terms

**Anaesthetic** A chemical used to make a patient unconscious during surgery and so remove pain

**Antiseptic surgery** The removal of bacteria from an operation. Lister used carbolic acid to wash a surgeon's hands, soak bandages and ligatures, and spray the air directly around the wound

**Aseptic surgery** Surgery that takes place in a strictly controlled germ-free environment

**Inoculation** Deliberately infecting oneself with a disease in order to become immune and avoid catching a more severe form later on

### Key individuals

**Edward Jenner** A country doctor who developed the smallpox vaccine following careful observation of milkmaids

**Joseph Lister** A surgeon who discovered that carbolic acid can be used in the operating theatre to remove germs; known as antiseptic surgery

**Florence Nightingale** A British nurse in the Crimean War who encouraged better hygiene in hospitals and improved training of nurses to reduce the death rate

**James Simpson** A surgeon and professor of midwifery who discovered that chloroform can be used as an anaesthetic

It took some time before Jenner's **vaccination** was accepted:

- People opposed the vaccine because Jenner was unable to explain how or why it worked. Pasteur did not publish his Germ Theory until 1861 and so Jenner did not know that bacteria caused disease.
- The idea of infecting someone with an animal disease was considered strange and unacceptable. Many religious believers thought it was against God's law to give people an animal disease.
- Inoculators were against it because their business was under threat.
- The Royal Society refused to publish Jenner's findings because it was thought that his ideas were too revolutionary.
- The Anti-Vaccine Society was set up in 1866 to oppose vaccination. It did this by publishing cartoons to scare people into not trusting the vaccine. One such cartoon showed people who had the vaccine turning into cows.

In 1852, the British government made the smallpox vaccination compulsory, and smallpox was eradicated as a disease in 1980. Jenner's work inspired other scientists, like Pasteur and Koch, to develop vaccines. Pasteur went on to develop vaccines for chicken cholera, anthrax and rabies.

**Key term**

**Vaccination** The injection into the body of killed or weakened organisms to give the body resistance against disease. The smallpox vaccine was the only one to use a different disease and so is known as a 'dead-end' vaccine

**Key factor**

**Individuals** The work of Nightingale, Simpson, Lister and Jenner in the nineteenth century was crucial to the prevention and treatment of disease and illness.

## Revision task

Summarise the contributions of the following individuals to medical advances during the eighteenth and nineteenth centuries:

- Jenner
- Nightingale
- Simpson
- Lister.

## Understand the chronology

The events of the eighteenth and nineteenth centuries that led to a change in the prevention and treatment of disease and illness are very complex. Using pages 18 and 20, place the events listed below in the correct chronological sequence in the timeline.

A Nightingale set up the Nightingale School of Nurses
B Koch identified the microbe for anthrax
C Simpson discovered that chloroform was an anaesthetic
D Jenner developed the smallpox vaccine
E Queen Victoria used chloroform during childbirth
F The British government made the smallpox vaccine compulsory
G Nightingale wrote *Notes on Nursing*
H Hannah Greener died from a chloroform overdose
I Koch identified the microbes for tuberculosis and typhoid
J Lister used the carbolic spray in the operating theatre
K Nightingale went to the Crimea to improve hospitals
L Louis Pasteur published his Germ Theory.

| Date | Event |
|---|---|
| 1796 | |
| 1847 | |
| 1848 | |
| 1852 | |
| 1853 | |
| 1854 | |
| 1859 | |
| 1860 | |
| 1861 | |
| 1865 | |
| 1876 | |
| 1882 | |

# 3 Approaches to prevention and treatment 2

REVISED

## 3.1 New approaches to prevention: fighting cholera

Cholera was a terrible disease that caused sickness and diarrhoea and was usually fatal. Doctors were unable to treat it because they did not know its cause. It was still believed that disease was caused by miasma and so local councils took steps to clean cities.

In 1854, cholera broke out in Soho, London. People tried to prevent its spread by:

- burning barrels of tar to remove the bad air
- smoking cigars to protect against the bad air
- praying and burning the clothes and bedding of victims.

The 1854 outbreak of cholera prompted **John Snow** to investigate.

- Snow created a spot map to show the deaths from cholera that occurred around Broad Street in the Soho district of London.
- This led Snow to notice a pattern; that the deaths were all connected to the water pump.
- Snow removed the handle of the water pump and prevented people from using it.
- There were no more deaths in the Broad Street area from cholera.
- Snow inspected the well underneath the water pump and found that it was close to a cesspit with a cracked lining. This caused waste to seep into the water and spread cholera.

Snow was able to prove that cholera was spread by dirty water and he presented his evidence to the House of Commons. Snow's evidence and the **Great Stink** led the government to agree to a new sewer system, which was planned by Joseph Bazalgette. By 1865, 1300 miles of sewers had been built in London and this project was completed in 1875.

Snow had no scientific evidence to explain the cause of cholera so many rejected his work. It would need Pasteur's Germ Theory and Koch's identification of the cholera microbe before Snow's theory could be explained.

## 3.2 New approaches to prevention: Public Health Acts

In the early nineteenth century, the British government had a *laissez-faire* attitude and believed it was not their role to intervene in the health of the people. However, during the century this attitude began to change. This was as a result of a variety of reasons, including:

- Cholera continued to return to Britain and it killed more people. The government listened to Snow (see above) and Pasteur (see page 26).
- In 1842, Edwin Chadwick published his *Report on the Sanitary Conditions of the Labouring Classes*. Chadwick had spent years researching the lives of the poor in Britain's cities. He concluded that people living in the cities had a lower life expectancy because of the filthy conditions. He believed all cities should have a Board of Health that ensured the supply of clean water and disposal of sewage. Initially, there was opposition to Chadwick's ideas due to the need to increase taxes and for the government to get involved in local matters.
- The British government did very little at first, but as more scientific evidence emerged that showed clean water was important for a healthy population, the government took more action.
- 1866–67 saw the last cholera epidemic in Britain and it had a lower death count than previous cholera epidemics.

**Key individual**

**John Snow** A surgeon who lived in Soho, London, and became one of the city's leading anaesthetists. He was popular and well respected. During the 1848 cholera epidemic, he observed and concluded that the disease was caused by drinking dirty water

**Key terms**

**Great Stink** The hot, dry summer of 1858 caused an awful smell from the exposed sewage on the banks of the River Thames in London. This became known as the Great Stink

***Laissez-faire*** From the French for 'leave alone' and is used to describe the British government's attitude to public health in the early nineteenth century

**Key factor**

**Government** During the nineteenth century, the British government became more supportive and increased their role in the prevention of disease and illness. This was as a consequence of the increase in scientific evidence and understanding.

**Exam tip**

It is important that you can explain government action during this period. Link cause and consequence directly.

| The first Public Health Act in 1848 | The second Public Health Act in 1875 |
|---|---|
| Cities were encouraged to set up Boards of Health and provide clean water supplies. However, because it was not compulsory many did not | Cities were now forced to improve sanitary conditions by:<br>• providing clean water to stop the spread of disease<br>• disposing of sewage to avoid pollution<br>• building public toilets<br>• employing a public officer of health to monitor conditions and outbreaks of disease<br>• creating street lighting |

## RAG: Rate the timeline

Below are an exam-style question and a timeline. Read the question, study the timeline and, using three coloured pens, put a red, amber or green star next to the events to show:

**Red:** events that have **no** relevance to the question

**Amber:** events that have **some** significance to the question

**Green:** events that have **direct** relevance to the question

**Explain why the government increased its role in preventing disease and illness during the period c.1700–c.1900. (12 marks)**

**You may use the following in your answer:**
- **Cholera**
- **Public Health Acts**

**You must also use information of your own.**

**1796** Edward Jenner discovered the smallpox vaccine

**1842** Edwin Chadwick published his *Report on the Sanitary Conditions of the Labouring Classes*

**1847** Simpson discovered chloroform as an anaesthetic

**1848** First Public Health Act

**1852** Government made the smallpox vaccine compulsory

**1854** Cholera epidemic

**1854** John Snow proved that cholera was caused by dirty water

**1858** The Great Stink

**1859** Nightingale wrote *Notes on Nursing*

**1861** Pasteur published his Germ Theory

**1875** Second Public Health Act

**1883** Koch discovered the microbe that caused cholera

## Spot the mistakes

Below is a paragraph which is part of an answer to the question above. However, the paragraph has a series of factual mistakes. Once you have identified the mistakes, rewrite the paragraph.

In 1846 the British government passed the first Public Health Act. This was because the deadly disease typhoid returned to Britain. The government had listened to the advice from John Snow and passed an Act that would provide vaccinations to its citizens. Unfortunately, it had little impact because the measures were too expensive. When typhoid returned in 1854, Florence Nightingale was able to prove that it was spread by sour milk. But she was unable to explain how or why. In 1861, Robert Koch published his Germ Theory. He did this after experimenting with mice. The new understanding of the cause of disease and illness led to the government passing the second Public Health Act in 1865. This Act was compulsory and shows the change in attitudes towards the individual's role in public health.

# c.1900–present: Medicine in modern Britain

The twentieth century saw great changes in medical diagnosis, treatment and prevention as a result of advancing science and technology. After accepting its responsibility for the health of the people, the government adopted a major role in providing medical care.

## 1 Ideas about the cause of disease and illness

REVISED

### 1.1 The influence of genetic factors on health

By 1900, it was clear to scientists that microbes did not cause all disease and illness. The causes of **hereditary diseases** were still unknown. The puzzle of hereditary diseases was solved in 1953 when **DNA** was discovered. It is now understood that Down's syndrome and cystic fibrosis are hereditary diseases.

| The discovery of the human gene | Mapping of the human genome |
| --- | --- |
| In 1953, James Watson and Francis Crick saw the X-rays of DNA created by Rosalind Franklin and Maurice Wilkins<br>Watson and Crick built their own model of DNA. Franklin corrected it and Wilkins shared clearer images with the team<br>This helped Crick and Watson to understand the structure of DNA: that it was shaped as a double helix<br>One gene | Once the structure of DNA was understood, scientists were able to break it apart and look at the parts that caused hereditary diseases such as **haemophilia**<br>The Human Genome Project began in 1990 and was completed in 2000. Scientists all over the world worked to decode and map the human **genome**. This map is used to look for mistakes in the human genome of people suffering from genetic conditions |
| **Impact of the discovery**<br>The understanding of DNA has not led to the treatment of genetic conditions. However, it has given options to prevent diseases after the identification of particular genes. An example of this is breast cancer. Women can have their breasts removed if the gene linked to the disease is identified in their DNA in order to prevent them from possibly developing cancer | |

### 1.2 The influence of lifestyle factors on health

Our understanding of how lifestyle is linked to disease and illness has improved:

- Smoking is linked to a range of diseases including high blood pressure, cancers and heart disease.
- Diet has a huge impact on our health and we are advised to maintain a healthy food intake. For example, too much sugar can lead to type 2 diabetes and too much fat can lead to heart disease.
- Drinking too much alcohol can lead to liver disease and kidney problems.
- The sharing of bodily fluids, for example by having unprotected sex, can lead to the spread of certain diseases.
- Skin cancer can be caused by too much exposure to the sun without sunscreen.

**Key terms**

**DNA** Short for deoxyribonucleic acid. DNA carries genetic information about a living organism. DNA information determines characteristics such as hair and eye colour

**Key terms**

**Genome** The complete set of genes (DNA) in a particular organism. Every human being has unique DNA, unless they are identical twins

**Haemophilia** A medical condition in which the ability of the blood to clot is severely reduced, causing the sufferer to bleed severely from even a slight injury

**Hereditary diseases** Disease and illness caused by genetic factors and passed on from parents to their children

## 1.3 Improvements in diagnosis

The development of technology has enabled doctors to understand and diagnose illness and disease more quickly and accurately. Some examples include:

| Technology | Description | Examples of use |
|---|---|---|
| X-ray | To see inside the human body without cutting it open | Diagnose broken bones |
| CT and MRI scans | Detailed imaging of internal organs | Diagnose internal damage, tumours and other growths |
| Ultrasound | A medical image produced from sound | Diagnose kidney stones, image an unborn baby |
| ECG | Electrocardiograms that measure heart activity | Measure irregular heart movement |
| Endoscope | A camera on the end of a thin tube used to see inside the body | Investigate digestive problems |
| Blood testing | Samples of blood are checked | Diagnose illness |
| Blood pressure monitor | Measures blood pressure | Diagnose high and low blood pressure |

**Key factor**

**Science and technology**

The development of machines and computers since 1900 has improved diagnosis and allowed for more targeted treatment. Technology is advancing all of the time and so is the way that doctors diagnose disease and illness.

**Revision task**

Create a mind map of all of the ways that technology has advanced the diagnosis of illness since 1900.

## Choosing a third cause

Below is an exam-style question. To answer it you need to explain three causes. It is sensible to make use of the two given points. However, you need to explain a third cause. In the spaces below the question, write down your choice and the reasons behind it.

**Explain why there have been changes in understanding the causes of illness during the twentieth century. (12 marks)**

**You may use the following in your answer:**
- **DNA**
- **Lifestyle**

**You must also use information of your own.**

Reason: ______________________

Why I have chosen this reason: ______________________

Details to support this reason: ______________________

## Complete the paragraph

Below is a paragraph which is part of an answer to the question in the 'Choosing a third cause' activity above. The paragraph gives a cause for change and some historical support but does not go on to develop the explanation.

1 Rewrite the paragraph with extra precise supporting knowledge and a full explanation linking back to the statement.

2 Complete the answer to this question.

*Understanding of the cause of illness has changed in the twentieth century as scientists and doctors have increased their understanding of the link between lifestyle and disease and illness. It is now accepted that smoking, diet, alcohol and tanning are the causes of disease. It is now accepted that smoking causes a variety of diseases, such as high blood pressure, a wide range of cancers and heart disease.*

# 2 Approaches to prevention and treatment 1

REVISED

## 2.1 Advances in medicines

### The magic bullet

**Magic bullet** is used to describe a chemical cure that attacks microbes which cause a particular disease, without side-effects. For example:

- The first magic bullet, Salvarsan 606, was developed in 1909 by Paul Ehrlich as a treatment for syphilis.
- Gerhard Domagk followed in 1932 with the discovery of Prontosil. Prontosil was a cure for blood poisoning.

### Antibiotics

In the early twentieth century, the first **antibiotic** was developed as a result of the development of penicillin.

**Key terms**

**Antibiotic** A medicine that destroys or limits the growth of bacteria in the human body

**D-Day** The day (6 June 1944) in the Second World War on which Allied forces invaded northern France by means of beach landings in Normandy

**Magic bullet** A chemical that kills certain bacteria without harming the body, for example Salvarsan 606 and Prontosil

## 2.2 Fleming, Florey and Chain's development of penicillin

| | |
|---|---|
| **Discovery** | The development of penicillin revolutionised how infection was treated. Alexander Fleming, a British doctor, was researching substances that would cure simple infections. In 1928, Fleming noticed a mould on a dirty Petri dish that had killed the harmful staphylococcus bacteria that was growing in the dish. This mould was penicillin. Fleming published his findings in an article but did not pursue this any further |
| **Development** | In 1939, Howard Florey and Ernst Chain were researching antibiotics and they used Fleming's article. They grew their own penicillin mould and began experimenting<br>In 1940, Florey and Chain tested penicillin on infected mice. The penicillin cured the infection<br>In 1941, Florey and Chain had a human patient; a policeman who was suffering from blood poisoning. They began their experiment despite only having a small amount of penicillin. The policeman began to recover<br>Because penicillin was difficult to make in large quantities they did not have enough to treat him for longer, and he died<br>However, Florey and Chain had proven that penicillin could fight infection in a human |
| **Mass production** | Florey and Chain needed a factory that could mass produce penicillin and went to the USA for help. The US government funded 21 pharmaceutical companies to mass produce it. By **D-Day**, in June 1944, enough penicillin had been produced to treat all Allied casualties – over 2.3 million doses |
| **Uses of penicillin and antibiotics** | Penicillin is used to treat diseases caused by a certain family of bacteria. It is also used to prevent infection<br>The development of other antibiotics followed and these are used daily to treat infections, such as streptomycin to treat tuberculosis and tetracycline to treat skin infections |

## 2.3 High-tech medical and surgical treatment

The development of new machinery since 1900 has improved the treatment in hospitals. New high-tech medical and surgical treatments include:

- Radiotherapy and chemotherapy to target and shrink tumours growing inside the body.
- Dialysis to 'wash' the blood of patients with kidney failure.
- Prosthetic limbs to replace those lost, for example by soldiers in war.
- Transplant surgery, for example transplanting the kidneys, liver and heart.
- Keyhole surgery to prevent cutting into a patient's body.

**Revision task**

Create a timeline showing the main developments in the treatment of disease and illness since 1900.

## Organising knowledge

Use the information on page 26 to complete the table below to show the factors that contributed to the development of penicillin in the twentieth century. First, cross out the factor(s) that did not contribute. Second, explain the role that each remaining factor played. For a reminder about each factor see page 13.

| | |
|---|---|
| Individuals | |
| The Church | |
| The government | |
| Science and technology | |
| Attitudes in society | |

## Identify the view

Read the exam-style question below and identify the view that is offered about the development of penicillin in the early twentieth century.

**'The main reason that penicillin was developed in the early twentieth century was because of the work of individuals.' How far do you agree? Explain your answer. (16 marks, with a further 4 marks available for spelling, punctuation and grammar.)**

1 What view is offered by the statement about the development of penicillin?

___

___

2 How far do you agree? Use your knowledge to agree and disagree with the statement given in the question. To plan an answer to this question, complete the following table.

| | |
|---|---|
| Knowledge which agrees with the statement | |
| Knowledge which disagrees with the statement | |

3 Now write paragraphs that agree and disagree with the statement.

*The statement is partially correct ...*

*The statement is partially incorrect ...*

c.1900–present: Medicine in modern Britain

# 3 Approaches to prevention and treatment 2

REVISED

## 3.1 Change in care and treatment

The British government introduced the National Health Service (NHS) in 1948 to provide medical care for all people. It was the largest intervention by the government in medical care, and marked the end of its *laissez-faire* approach (see page 30).

With the NHS, the government aims to provide care for all people 'from the cradle to the grave' through:

- hospitals
- **general practitioners (GPs)**
- dentists
- ambulance services
- health visitors.

Throughout the 1960s, the British government made improvements to the NHS, such as:

- ensuring that hospitals were available across the whole of Britain
- giving GPs incentives to ensure they were up to date with medical developments.

## 3.2 New approaches to prevention

### Mass vaccinations

The government introduced compulsory vaccinations throughout the twentieth century, including diphtheria in 1942 and polio in 1950. These vaccination campaigns were funded by the government to ensure that they were widespread.

### Government legislation

The government has passed laws to ensure healthy living conditions. For example:

- The Clean Air Acts of 1956 and 1968 were passed to prevent **smog** caused by air pollution.
- As part of the Health Act of 2006, it was made illegal to smoke in all enclosed workplaces.

### Government lifestyle campaigns

The government aims to help people prevent illness themselves through education and by promoting healthier lifestyles. Some examples of this are:

- advertising campaigns that warn against the dangers to health from binge drinking and drug use
- encouraging people to eat more healthily and get more exercise, such as the Change4Life campaign.

**Exam tip**

You need to be aware of how science and technology has improved all stages of the fight against lung cancer in the twenty-first century.

**Key terms**

**Bronchoscope** A fibre-optic cable that is passed into the windpipe in order to view the bronchi

**General practitioner (GP)** A community-based doctor who treats minor illnesses. A GP will refer more serious cases of illness to a hospital

**PET-CT scan** A CT scan creates a detailed picture of the inside of the body. A PET-CT scan is similar, but it contains a small amount of radioactive material that is injected instead of dye

**Smog** A heavy fog caused by air pollution. Although smog is no longer a problem, the government continues to pass laws to protect people from air pollution

**Key factors**

**Science and technology** A range of scientific approaches and technology have been developed throughout the twentieth century that diagnose, prevent and treat disease and illness.

**Government** Throughout the twentieth century, the government has taken a more active role in the prevention and treatment of disease and illness; more recently the focus has been on education and prevention.

## 3.3 The fight against lung cancer in the twenty-first century

Lung cancer is the second most common cancer in the UK and the number of deaths from this illness have risen throughout the twentieth century.

| | |
|---|---|
| **Diagnosis** | By the time the disease is detected it is often too far advanced and so difficult to treat. Technology has enabled improvements. Doctors use a **PET-CT scan** or a dye to identify the cancerous cells. A **bronchoscope** can also be used to collect a sample of the cells |
| **Treatment** | If the cancer is detected early an operation to remove the tumour and the infected part of the lung can be carried out. Other treatments include:<br>• transplants – cancerous cells can be replaced with those from a healthy donor<br>• radiotherapy – waves of radiation are aimed at the tumour to shrink it<br>• chemotherapy – patients are injected with different drugs to shrink the tumour before surgery to prevent the recurrence of cancer or to relieve the symptoms when surgery is not possible |
| **Prevention** | Evidence that cigarette smoking was linked to lung cancer was first published in 1950, but the government was slow to respond. As the death rate became too high to ignore, the government took the following action:<br>• banned smoking in all public places in 2007, extended to cars carrying children in 2015<br>• raised the legal age for buying tobacco from 16 to 18 in 2007<br>• banned tobacco advertising in 1965, and banned cigarette advertising entirely in 2005<br>• removed cigarette products from display in shops in 2012<br>• introduced stop smoking campaigns and insisted on plain packaging<br>Each year there is an increase in the taxation on tobacco products to encourage people to stop smoking |

### The comparison question

Look at the exam-style question below and the two answers. Which answer is better for comparing the key features of medical understanding? Why?

**Explain one way in which the prevention of disease and illness was different in the nineteenth and twenty-first centuries. (4 marks)**

**ANSWER 1**

In the nineteenth century, the British government took a *laissez-faire* approach to preventing disease and illness, believing it was not its responsibility. However, by the twenty-first century, the British government no longer had a *laissez-faire* approach to the health of its people and took action in preventing disease and illness by educating the people so that they could take control. This can be seen in the government-encouraged campaigns making the population aware of the dangers of smoking, binge drinking and drug use. It can also be seen in the Change4Life campaign.

**ANSWER 2**

In the nineteenth century, the British government did not take action preventing and treating disease and illness as it did not believe it was its responsibility. However, by the twenty-first century, the British government no longer had this approach and believed that it should educate the people so that they could take control. This can be seen in the government-encouraged campaigns making the population aware of the dangers of smoking, binge drinking and drug use.

# Part 2 The British sector of the Western Front, 1914–18: injuries, treatment and the trenches

## 1 The context of the British sector of the Western Front

REVISED

### Flanders and northern France

| The Ypres Salient | The Somme |
|---|---|
| The scene of many battles during the First World War because it was on the way to the Channel ports of Calais and Dunkirk. The Germans wanted to capture these ports to cut off supplies to the British army<br>The **Ypres Salient** was vulnerable because the Germans had the advantageous position on higher ground. The German army could see the Allied movements and build stronger defences<br>Tunnelling and mines were used by the British at Hill 60, a man-made hill captured by the Germans, to regain control in April 1915<br>The first Battle of Ypres took place between October and November 1914<br>The second Battle of Ypres (April to May 1915) saw the first use of chlorine gas by the Germans<br>The third Battle of Ypres took place in July to November 1917 | The Battle of the Somme lasted from July to November 1916 and took place along the River Somme<br>It is remembered for its high casualty rate. On the first day of the battle the British army suffered nearly 60,000 casualties and 20,000 dead<br>In total there were over 400,000 Allied casualties. This put enormous pressure on the medical services on the Western Front |
| **Arras** | **Cambrai** |
| The Battle of Arras took place in April 1917<br>Before the battle, Allied soldiers had dug a network of tunnels below Arras. The tunnelling was made easy by the chalky ground. New tunnels joined with existing tunnels, caves and quarries. Rooms were created with running water and electricity. There was also a hospital (see page 42). These tunnels were used for safety and to allow troops to the front in secrecy | The Battle of Cambrai took place in October 1917<br>During this battle over 450 large-scale tanks were used by the Allies to launch a surprise assault on the German front line. Unfortunately, the tanks did not have enough infantry support. The British lost the ground they had taken |

### The trench system

The **trenches** dug in 1914 developed into an effective defensive network from 1915. The trenches were about 2.5 metres deep. They were dug in a zig-zag pattern and contained dugouts for men to take protective cover in when needed.

| | |
|---|---|
| **The front line** | The trench nearest the enemy where the soldiers would shoot from |
| **The command trench** | 10–20 metres behind the firing line |
| **The support trench** | 200–500 metres behind the front line |
| **The reserve trench** | At least 100 metres behind the support trench. Reserve troops would be here ready to mount a counterattack if the enemy entered the front line |
| **The communication trench** | Linked the front line with the command, support and reserve trenches |

**Key terms**

**No Man's Land** The land between the Allied and German trenches in the First World War

**Trenches** Long, narrow ditches dug during the First World War in which soldiers fought

**Ypres Salient** An area around Ypres in Belgium where many of the battles took place in the First World War

## The impact of the terrain on helping the wounded

The trench system was complicated and made it hard to move the wounded from the trenches to the hospitals. This was because:

- It was difficult to move through the trench system because it contained equipment and men.
- Communication about the wounded was difficult, especially during major battles.
- It was hard to move around at night.
- Collecting the wounded from **No Man's Land** was dangerous because it was frequently done under fire.
- No Man's Land and the trenches were often deep in mud, which made movement difficult.
- Stretcher bearers found it difficult to move around the corners.
- Transport of the wounded was difficult because of these conditions (see page 42).

### Revision task

Draw and label your own copy of the trench system.

### Exam tip

You need to be able to explain the impact that the terrain of the Western Front had on the care and treatment of the wounded.

### Eliminate irrelevance

Here is an exam-style question:

**Describe two features of the trench system on the Western Front. (4 marks)**

Below is an answer to this question. Read the answer and identify parts that are not relevant to the question. Draw a line through the information that is irrelevant and justify your deletions in the margin.

The trench system used in the First World War by the British began in 1914 and was improved from 1915. The trenches were dug quickly and so were very simple to start with. There was the front line trench, which was closest to the enemy and is where soldiers would fire and mount an attack from. Behind the front line trench was the command trench. The reserve line trench was the furthest away from the front line. It was here that soldiers would be mobilised from for a counterattack should the enemy make it into the front line trenches. Between the British and German trenches was an area of unoccupied land called No Man's Land.

## 2 Conditions requiring treatment on the Western Front

REVISED

### Ill health

| Complaint | Cause | Symptoms | Treatment and prevention | Impact |
|---|---|---|---|---|
| **Trench fever** | Transmitted by body lice | Flu-like symptoms; high temperature, severe headaches, shivering and aching muscles | **Treatment:** drugs were trialled, such as quinine and Salvarsan, but without success. Passing an electric current through the affected area was used effectively<br>**Prevention:** by 1918, the cause had been identified as lice:<br>• clothes were disinfected with repellent gel<br>• delousing stations were set up | Affected nearly half a million men on the Western Front |
| **Trench foot** | Soldiers stood in the mud and waterlogged trenches, which caused painful swelling in their feet | Tight boots added to the problem because they restricted the blood flow. Later, **gangrene** would set in | **Treatment:** soldiers were advised to clean and dry their feet. In the worst cases, amputation<br>**Prevention:**<br>• changing socks and keeping feet dry<br>• rubbing whale oil into feet to protect them | During the winter of 1914 and 1915, over 20,000 Allied men were affected |
| **Shell-shock** | Stressful conditions of war | Tiredness, nightmares, headaches, uncontrollable shaking and a mental breakdown | The condition was not well understood during the war<br>**Treatment:**<br>• mainly consisted of rest<br>• some soldiers received treatment back in Britain | It is estimated that 80,000 British troops experienced shell-shock. Some men were accused of cowardice. Punishments for this included being shot |

### Weapons of war

- *Rifles*: loaded from a cartridge case which created automatic rapid fire, rather than one bullet at a time. Bullets were pointed so that they drove deeper into the body.
- *Machine guns*: had more speed than rifles and could fire 500 rounds a minute. They devastated attacking forces advancing over No Man's Land. Bullets, from machine guns and rifles, would pierce organs and fracture bones.
- *Artillery*: throughout the war, cannons grew bigger and became more powerful, such as the British howitzer which could send 900-kilogram shells. Bombardments were continuous and in some cases lasted weeks and months. Artillery fire caused half of all casualties.
- *Shrapnel*: **shrapnel** caused maximum damage as it exploded mid-air above the enemy. It was most effective against troops advancing across No Man's Land, while shells targeted soldiers in the trenches. An exploded shell or shrapnel could immediately kill or injure a soldier. Together these were responsible for 58 per cent of wounds. In most cases, shrapnel injured the arms and legs of soldiers.

Soldiers experienced an increased number of head injuries as a result of all of the above weapons. In 1915, a steel helmet replaced the soft caps of soldiers. In a trial, it was estimated that the helmet reduced fatal head injuries by 80 per cent.

**Key terms**

**Gangrene** When body tissue decomposes due to a loss of blood supply

**Shrapnel** A hollow shell that was filled with steel balls or lead, together with gunpowder and a timer fuse

**Revision task**

Summarise the weapons and wounds of war:

- rifles
- machine guns
- artillery
- shrapnel.

## Gas attacks

| Chlorine | Phosgene | Mustard |
|---|---|---|
| First used by Germans in 1915<br>Led to death by suffocation<br>In July 1915, gas masks were given to all British troops. Before this soldiers would urinate on handkerchiefs and hold these to their faces to prevent the gas getting into their lungs | First used by Germans in 1915<br>Faster acting than chlorine, but with similar effects<br>Could kill an exposed person within two days | First used by Germans in 1917<br>An odourless gas that worked in 12 hours<br>Caused blisters and could burn the skin through clothing |

It was hard to target a particular place with gas and so it was not used regularly as a weapon in the First World War. Gas was the cause of fewer than five per cent of British deaths. The effects of gas attacks – blindness, loss of taste and smell and coughing – only lasted for a few weeks. Sufferers were given oxygen and had their skin cleansed.

**Exam tip**

You need to be able to make links between the nature of fighting in the First World War and the illnesses that soldiers suffered from.

## You're the examiner

Below is an exam-style question.

**Describe two features of the gas attacks on the Western Front. (4 marks)**

1 Below are a mark scheme and an answer to this question. Read the answer and the mark scheme. Decide how many marks it would get. Write the mark along with a justification for your choice below.

| Mark scheme |
|---|
| Award 1 mark for each valid feature identified up to a maximum of two features. The second mark should be awarded for supporting information. |

**STUDENT ANSWER**

*Chlorine gas was used in the Western Front by the Germans in 1915. Chlorine gas led to death by suffocation after attacking a victim's lungs.*

Mark ☐ Reason ______________________________

______________________________

2 Now suggest what the student has to do to achieve more marks.

3 Write an answer that would achieve more marks.

# 3 Helping the wounded on the Western Front

REVISED

## The evacuation route

Survival depended on the speed of treatment and so the aim was to treat all soldiers quickly.

| | | |
|---|---|---|
| **Stage 1** | Stretcher bearers | Stretcher bearers would advance on No Man's Land at night or during a break in fighting to collect the dead and wounded. Each battalion had sixteen stretcher bearers and it took four men to carry a stretcher |
| **Stage 2** | Regimental Aid Post (RAP) | The RAP was always close to the front line. The battalion regimental medical officer was in the RAP. He identified those who were lightly wounded and those soldiers who needed more medical attention |
| **Stage 3** | Field Ambulance and Dressing Station | A Field Ambulance was a large mobile medical unit with medical officers, support staff and, from 1915, some nurses. The Dressing Station was where emergency treatment was given to the wounded. They were about a mile behind the front line. Here a system of **triage** was set up, where the more and less seriously wounded were separated |
| **Stage 4** | Casualty Clearing Station (CCS) | The CCS was the first large well-equipped medical unit that the wounded would experience. The CCS contained X-ray machines and wards with beds. They were located in tents or huts about ten miles from the fighting |
| **Stage 5** | Base Hospitals | The Base Hospital was usually a civilian hospital or a converted building. Soldiers would arrive by train, motor ambulance or by canal because the journey was less uncomfortable. They had operating theatres, X-ray departments and specialist areas for gas poisoning. From the Base Hospital, most patients were sent back to Britain in hospital trains, which had been converted |

Soldiers received better care as the war progressed. In 1914, there were no motor ambulances, and the horse-drawn ambulances were unable to cope with the great number of casualties. By November 1915, there were 250 motor ambulances in France. Ambulance trains were also introduced to carry up to 800 casualties. Ambulance barges were also used to carry the wounded along the River Somme.

## The underground hospital at Arras

During the Battle of Arras, 160,000 soldiers were killed; and over 7000 were wounded in the first three days. Despite this, the evacuation route here worked well. In 1916, the existing tunnels and quarries were extended. They created an underground town for soldiers to live in with running water and electricity. This location also included a hospital with 700 beds and operating theatres.

## RAMC

All medical officers belonged to the **RAMC**. The membership increased from 9000 in 1914 to 113,000 in 1918 as the number of wounded grew. Doctors had to learn quickly about conditions and wounds they had never faced before.

## FANY

Initially the nurses on the front line were the well-trained Queen Alexandra's nurses. The government turned away volunteer nurses. However, this attitude changed as the number of casualties increased. The work of volunteers involved professional nursing in operating theatres to scrubbing floors. Women of the **FANY** helped the wounded as ambulance drivers and nurses once the British army changed their policy towards volunteers in 1916. FANY units also carried supplies to the front and drove motorised kitchens to supply food.

### Key terms

**FANY** First Aid Nursing Yeomanry. Founded in 1907 by a soldier who hoped they would be a nursing cavalry to help the wounded in battle

**RAMC** Royal Army Medical Corps. This organisation organised and provided medical care. It consisted of all ranks from doctors to ambulance drivers and stretcher bearers

**Triage** A system of splitting the wounded into groups according to who needed the most urgent attention

### Revision task

Summarise the part played in treatment of the wounded by the following: stretcher bearers, horse-drawn and motor ambulances, train and canal ambulances.

## The utility question

Look at the two sources, the exam-style question and the two answers below. Which answer is the best answer to the question and why? You could look at page 42 for guidance on how to answer the utility question to help you make your judgement.

**SOURCE A**

*Stretcher bearers removing a wounded officer.*

**SOURCE B**

*An extract from an article in the Journal of the Royal Army Medical Corps, 1915.*

Admirable as was the organisation of the large base hospitals, the transport of the wounded from the fighting line seems to have been very badly managed during the advance of the Germans through Belgium and northern France. The supply of motor ambulances proved totally inadequate and the slightly wounded had to shift for themselves and squeeze into goods trains.

**How useful are Sources A and B for an enquiry into the problems that faced those helping the wounded on the Western Front? (8 marks)**

**ANSWER 1**

Source A is useful for this enquiry because it shows the stretcher bearers in the First World War having to walk with the wounded through narrow and crowded trenches. Source B is useful for the same enquiry because it tells us that there were not enough motor ambulances and so the wounded had to squeeze into trains.

**ANSWER 2**

Source A is useful for an enquiry into the problems faced in helping the wounded during the First World War because it shows the stretcher bearers in the First World War having to walk with the wounded through narrow and crowded trenches. From my own knowledge, I know that the stretcher bearers would also have had to collect the wounded from No Man's Land during a break in fighting or at night. This caused problems because they were unable to see the wounded soldiers. The stretcher bearer would have to carry the wounded across shell-craters, which was also dangerous because they were difficult to see, and avoid, at night. Source B is useful for the same enquiry because it tells us that there were not enough motor ambulances and so the wounded had to squeeze into trains. From my own knowledge, I know that trains were converted into hospitals and used to transport the wounded back to Britain, as well as canal boats.

Which answer is better?

________________________________________

Why?

________________________________________

# 4 The impact of the Western Front on medicine and surgery 1

REVISED

## Treating wounds and infection

By 1900, most operations were carried out using aseptic methods, but it was not possible to carry out aseptic surgery (see page 28) on the Western Front because treatment needed to be portable. This led to problems treating infections caused by **gas gangrene**, and other treatments had to be found.

- Wound incision or **debridement** – this needed to be done quickly and the wound closed to prevent the spread of infection.
- The Carrel–Dakin method – this involved using a sterilised salt solution in the wound through a tube. However, the solution only lasted six hours and so had to be made as it was needed, which was difficult at times of high demand.
- Amputation – if neither of the above had worked, the only option left to surgeons was to remove the wounded limb. By 1918, 240,000 men had lost limbs.

## The Thomas splint

Men with a gunshot or shrapnel wound only had a twenty per cent chance of survival in 1915. This was because the wounds created a **compound fracture**. This was particularly dangerous when the thigh bone (femur) was fractured because it damaged the muscle and caused major bleeding into the thigh.

The splint that was being used to transport wounded men did not keep the leg rigid. From 1916, the Thomas splint was used, which stopped two joints moving and increased the survival rate from this type of wound to 82 per cent.

## X-rays

In 1895, William Röntgen, a German physicist, discovered X-rays. From 1896, **radiology departments** were opening in a number of hospitals. British hospitals applied X-rays to a medical setting. X-rays enabled a surgeon to carry out a diagnosis before an operation took place and would prove useful on the Western Front.

X-rays were used from the start of the war to locate bullets and shrapnel. These needed to be removed from wounds to prevent infection. Overall, the use of X-rays was success. However, there were some problems:

- X-rays could not detect all objects in the body. Some items, such as clothing, went unnoticed until doctors looked for them during the operation.
- A wounded soldier had to remain still for several minutes for an X-ray to be taken.
- The tubes used in an X-ray were fragile and overheated quickly. This meant that X-ray machines could only be used for an hour and then had to be left to cool down. During an offensive this was a major problem. The solution was to use three machines in rotation.

## The use of mobile X-ray units

There were six **mobile X-ray units** operating in the British sector of the Western Front. These were used to locate shrapnel and bullet wounds. They were transported around the Western Front in a truck, enabling more soldiers to be treated quickly. The mobile X-ray unit could go to the location of a battle, rather than wait for soldiers to be transported. The quality of X-rays taken by the mobile units was not as good, but proved sufficient to locate bullets and shrapnel.

### Key terms

**Compound fracture** An injury where the broken bone pierces the skin and increases the risk of infection

**Debridement** The cutting away of dead, damaged and infected tissue around the wound

**Gas gangrene** An infection that produces gas in gangrenous wounds. Infection was more likely as the soldiers' wounds were exposed to soil containing fertiliser

**Mobile X-ray unit** A portable X-ray unit that could be moved around the Western Front in a truck

**Radiology department** The hospital department where X-rays are carried out

### Revision task

Summarise the following developments in surgery during the First World War:

- treating infection
- the Thomas splint
- mobile X-ray units.

## Complete the answer

Below is an exam-style question and an answer to this question. The answer identifies two features, but does not develop them with any supporting knowledge. Annotate the answer to complete it by adding the support.

**Describe two features of the treatment of wounds on the Western Front. (4 marks)**

The Thomas splint was used in surgery on the Western Front. Mobile X-ray units were also used on the Western Front.

## The utility question

Look at the two sources, the exam-style question and the two answers below. Which answer is the best answer to the question and why? You could look at page 42 for guidance on how to answer the utility question to help you make your judgement.

**How useful are Sources A and B for an enquiry into surgery and the treatment of wounds on the Western Front? (8 marks)**

### SOURCE A

*From 'A report on Gas Gangrene' by Anthony Bowlby, Consulting Surgeon to the British Army, October 1914.*

The gangrene found amongst our wounded soldiers is directly due to infection introduced at the time of the wound, and this is likely to occur if muddy clothing has been carried by the projectile, or if earth has been carried by the explosion.

### SOURCE B

*French medics locating a bullet with an X-ray machine at a French field hospital during the First World War.*

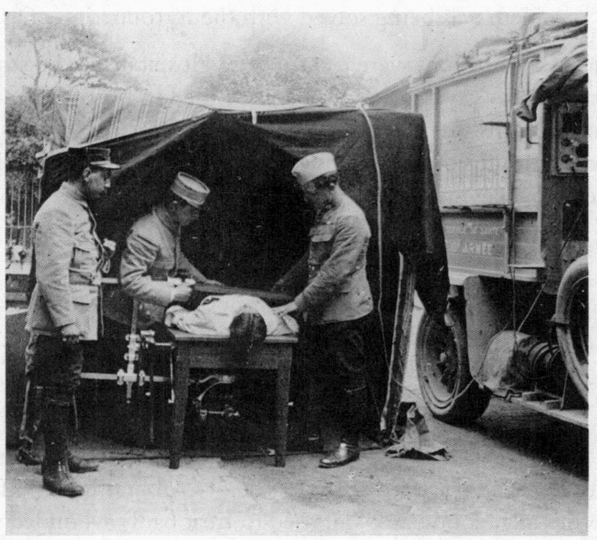

### ANSWER 1

Source A is useful for an enquiry into surgery and the treatment of wounds on the Western Front because it tells us about gas gangrene and how it was caused by an infected wound. From my own knowledge, I know that this problem was made worse during the First World War because many soldiers' wounds were exposed to soil that was full of fertiliser.

### ANSWER 2

Source A is useful for an enquiry into surgery and the treatment of wounds on the Western Front because it is from an official contemporary report published in October 1914 by Anthony Bowlby, a consulting surgeon. Bowlby would have seen first-hand the conditions on the Western Front facing the surgeons and had experience in the number of soldiers whose wounds developed gas gangrene. From my own knowledge, I know that this problem was made worse during the First World War because many soldiers' wounds were exposed to soil that was full of fertiliser.

# 5 The impact of the Western Front on medicine and surgery 2

REVISED

## The development of blood transfusions and the storage of blood

Blood loss was a major problem in surgery before the twentieth century. The first experiments in **blood transfusion** were performed in 1819 by James Blundell. As blood could not be stored, it had to be used as soon as possible. Transfusions were carried out with the donor (the person giving the blood) being directly connected by a tube to the recipient (the person receiving the blood).

There were problems with the early use of blood transfusions:

- Blood clots as soon as it leaves the body and so the tube became blocked up.
- The blood of the donor was sometimes rejected by the recipient because they were not compatible. Blood groups were discovered by Karl Landsteiner in 1901.
- There was a danger of infection from unsterilised equipment. However, this problem was being solved with the introduction of aseptic surgery.

Blood transfusions were used at Base Hospitals by the British on the Western Front from 1915. A syringe and tube were used to transfer the donor blood to the patient. This was extended to Casualty Clearing Stations from 1917. A portable blood transfusion kit was used close to the front line, designed by a doctor called Geoffrey Keynes.

**Key terms**

**Blood transfusion** Blood taken from a healthy person and given to another person

**General anaesthetic** Putting a patient to sleep during an operation

**Local anaesthetic** The area being operated was numbed to prevent pain, but the patient remained awake during the operation

## The blood bank at Cambrai

- In 1915, it was discovered that by adding sodium citrate to blood the need for donor-to-recipient transfusion was removed as blood could be stored and clotting prevented.
- In 1916, it was discovered that adding a citrate glucose solution to blood allowed it to be stored for up to four weeks.

Stored blood was used at the Battle of Cambrai in 1917. Blood was stored in glass bottles at a blood bank and used to treat badly wounded soldiers throughout the battle.

## Other new techniques in the treatment of wounds

- *Brain surgery*: new techniques for dealing with brain injuries were developed for the Western Front that included using a magnet to remove metal fragments from the brain. A **local anaesthetic** was used in operations rather than a **general anaesthetic**. This prevented the brain from swelling and decreased the risks in an operation.
- *Plastic surgery*: a New Zealand doctor, Harold Gillies, was sent to the Western Front in 1915. Gillies became interested in facial reconstruction – replacing and restoring parts of the face that had been destroyed by the weapons of war. Skin grafts were developed, where skin was taken from another part of the patient's body and used to repair the wound.

## Organising knowledge

Study the advances in surgery during the First World War on pages 36 and 38. Make a copy of the table below. Complete it to show the progress made as a result of the war.

| Factor | Before First World War | During First World War |
|---|---|---|
| War wounds | | |
| Infection | | |
| X-rays | | |
| Blood transfusions | | |
| Plastic surgery | | |

## Organising knowledge

Study the different types of sources available to a historian when enquiring into the Western Front in the table below. Complete the table. For each type of source explain what aspects of injuries, treatment and the trenches covered in this book it would be useful for and explain the advantages of using it. For example, hospital records would be useful in providing the number of soldiers treated during an offensive. This information would not have been produced for propaganda and so would give the historian reliable, accurate figures.

| Types of sources | Useful for ... | Advantages |
|---|---|---|
| National army records for individual soldiers | | |
| National newspaper reports | | |
| Government reports on aspects of the war | | |
| Medical articles by doctors and nurses who took part in the war | | |
| Personal accounts of medical treatments by soldiers, doctors, nurses or others who were involved | | |
| Photographs | | |
| Hospital records | | |
| Army statistics | | |

# Exam focus

Your History GCSE is made up of three exams:

- For Paper 1 you have one hour and 15 minutes to answer questions on a thematic study and historic environment, in your case Medicine through time, c1250–present and The British sector of the Western Front, 1914–18: injuries, treatments and the trenches.
- In Paper 2 you have one hour and 45 minutes to answer questions on a period study and a British depth study.
- In Paper 3 you have one hour and 20 minutes to answer questions on a modern depth study.

For Paper 1 you have to answer the following types of questions. Each requires you to demonstrate different historical skills:

- **Question 1** is a key features question in which you have to describe two features and characteristics of the period.
- **Question 2** includes two sub-questions on a source enquiry which test your source analysis skills as well as your ability to frame a historical question.
- **Question 3** is a key features question in which you have to describe the similarity or difference in medicine between two time periods.
- **Question 4** is a causation question which asks you to explain why something happened.
- **Questions 5 and 6** are analytical questions that ask you to evaluate change, continuity and significance in medicine.

The table below gives a summary of the question types for Paper 1 and what you need to do.

| Question number | Marks | Key words | You need to ... |
|---|---|---|---|
| 1 | 4 | Describe two features of ... | • Identify two features<br>• Add supporting information for each feature |
| 2(a) | 8 | How useful are Sources A and B for an enquiry into ... ?<br>Explain your answer, using Sources A and B and your knowledge of the historical context | • Ensure that you explain the value of the contents of each of the sources<br>• Explain how the provenance of each source affects the value of the contents<br>• You need to support your answer with your knowledge of the given topic |
| 2(b) | 4 | How could you follow up Source B to find out more about ...<br>In your answer you must give the question you would ask and the type of source you could use | • Select a detail from Source B that could form the basis of a follow-up enquiry<br>• Write a question that is linked to this detail and enquiry<br>• Identify an appropriate source for the enquiry<br>• Explain how the source might help answer your follow-up question |
| 3 | 4 | Explain one way in which ... were similar/different in the ... and ... centuries | • Identify a similarity or difference<br>• Support the comparison with specific detail from both periods |
| 4 | 12 | Explain why ... You may use the following in your answer: [two given points].<br>You **must** also use information of your own | • Explain at least three causes – you can use the points in the question but must also use at least one point of your own<br>• Ensure that you focus the causes on the question |
| 5/6 | 20 | 'Statement'. How far do you agree? Explain your answer. You may use the following in your answer: [two given points]. You **must** also use information of your own | • Ensure you agree and disagree with the statement<br>• Use the given points and your own knowledge<br>• Ensure you write a conclusion giving your final judgement on the question<br>• There are up to 4 marks for spelling, punctuation, grammar and the use of specialist terminology |

## Question 1: Key features

Below is an example of a key features question which is worth 4 marks.

**Describe two features of the weapons used on the Western Front.**

Feature 1: ______

______

Feature 2: ______

______

### How to answer

You have to identify two features and add supporting information for each. For each of the two features you are given space to write. Remember you need to identify **two** different features.

Below is a sample answer to this key features question with comments around it.

Feature 1:

Machine guns were used by soldiers on the Western Front. Machine guns could fire 500 rounds a minute and devastated the attacking forces.

The first feature is identified.

Supporting information is added.

Feature 2:

Artillery was also used by armies on the Western Front. This included cannons, such as the British howitzer which could send 900-kilogram shells.

The second feature is identified.

Supporting information is added.

### Complete the answer

**Describe two features of the evacuation route on the Western Front.**

Here is the first part of an answer to this question.

Feature 1:

The wounded were first collected by a stretcher bearer. Each battalion had sixteen stretcher bearers and it took four men to carry a stretcher.

1 Highlight the following:
  - Where the feature has been identified.
  - Where supporting information has been added.
2 Now add a second feature.

  Feature 2: ______

  ______

## Question 2: Source analysis

Question 2 is divided into two parts.

- Question 2(a) is a utility question on two sources. You have to explain how useful each source is to a historical enquiry.
- Question 2(b) is an analysis question that asks you to use sources – you have to explain a follow-up enquiry and the source that you would use.

## Question 2(a): Utility

Below is an example of a utility question which is worth 8 marks. The sources will be labelled Source A and Source B.

**Study Sources A and B. How useful are Sources A and B for an enquiry into the impact of the terrain on the transport of the wounded on the Western Front? Explain your answer, using Sources A and B and your own knowledge of the historical context. (8 marks)**

### SOURCE A

*No Man's Land on the Western Front, 1917.*

### SOURCE B

*From the recorded memories of William Easton, East Anglian Field Ambulance. He was eighteen years old in 1916. Here he described conditions near Ypres in 1917.*

Up at Ypres we used to go up the line and we'd be waist deep in mud. We were carrying the wounded down near a place called Hooge, where had been a terrible amount of fighting. One trip down a trench in those conditions and you would all be all in – exhausted. If you got two or three wounded men down in a day, that was all you could expect to do. We had to carry men in fours there and we had to be very careful because you could do more damage to a man than the shell if you jolted him too much or he fell off the stretcher. To make carrying easier we had slings which we put round our shoulders and over the stretcher's handles.

## How to answer

- Explain the value and limitations of the contents of each source and try to add some contextual knowledge when you make a point.
- Explain the value and limitations of the **provenance** of each source and try to add some contextual knowledge when you make a point.
- In your conclusion give a final judgement on the relative value of each source. For example, one source might provide one view of an event, the other source a different view.

**Key term**

**Provenance** Who wrote or created the source, when, and for what purpose. This can have a big impact on what the source tells us.

Below is part of a sample Level 3 answer to this question in which is explained the utility of Source A. Read it and the comments around it.

Source A is useful because it suggests that the shell holes throughout No Man's Land caused an obstacle to the stretcher bearers who were collecting the dead and wounded. This was the case because stretcher bearers would often go into No Man's Land at night or during a break in the fighting. At these times it would have been difficult for them to see the shell holes. The usefulness of Source A is further enhanced by its provenance. It is a photograph taken in 1917 and so it shows exactly what No Man's Land would have looked like at this point in time and could not have been altered. However, a historian must be careful because it may not be typical of No Man's Land throughout the Western Front and may not have looked the same at all locations along the line of the trenches.

A judgement is made on the value of the content of the source.

Own knowledge is used to support this judgement.

The provenance of the source is taken into account when making a judgement on its utility.

### Analysing provenance

Now write your own Level 3 answer on Source B. Remember to take into account how the provenance affects the usefulness of the source content.

## Question 2(b): Framing a historical question

Below is an example of a source question requiring you to frame an enquiry. This is worth 4 marks.

**How could you follow up Source B to find out more about the impact of the terrain on the transport of the wounded on the Western Front? In your answer, you must give the question you would ask and the type of source you could use.**

### How to answer

You have to identify a follow-up enquiry and explain how you would carry this out. For each of the questions you are given space to write. Below is a sample answer to this question with comments around it.

Detail in Source B that I would follow up:

I would follow up on what Easton says about the further damage that stretcher bearers and the conditions could cause wounded men.

The follow-up enquiry is identified.

Question I would ask:

What wounds were made worse by jolts whilst on the stretcher?

The linked question is asked.

What type of source I could use:

Hospital records.

An appropriate source is identified.

How this might help answer my question:

Hospital records could detail the nature of wounds that soldiers arrived with and whether they were caused by the fighting or the conditions while on the stretcher.

An explanation of how the source would help with the follow-up enquiry.

## Question 3: Similarity or difference

Below is an example of a key features question which is worth 4 marks.

**Explain one way in which understanding of the causes of illness was different in the late nineteenth and twentieth centuries.**

### How to answer

- Explain the difference between the two time periods.
- Use specific information from both time periods to support the comparison, showing good knowledge and understanding.

Below is a sample answer to this with comments around it.

In the late nineteenth century, disease and illness was explained by germs. Louis Pasteur had published his Germ Theory in 1861 to prove this. His theory was further developed by Robert Koch, who went on to identify the specific bacteria that caused tuberculosis and anthrax. However, by the twenty-first century it was also understood that disease could also be hereditary and not caused by bacteria. DNA was discovered in 1953 by Crick and Watson. Since DNA was first discovered, scientists have been able to show that specific genes pass on disease such as Down's syndrome and cystic fibrosis.

The belief about the cause of disease in the nineteenth century is identified.

Own knowledge is used to support this.

The change in belief about the cause of disease in the twentieth century is identified.

Own knowledge is used to support this.

## Develop the detail

Below is a question and part of an answer. Read the answer and develop the detail.

**Explain one way in which ideas about the cause of disease were different in the seventeenth and nineteenth centuries.**

*In the seventeenth century it was believed that miasma (bad air) was the cause of disease. However, by the nineteenth century scientists had discovered that germs were the cause of disease.*

## Question 4: Causation

Below is an example of a causation question which is worth 12 marks.

**Explain why there was so much opposition to Jenner's vaccination against smallpox.**

**You may use the following in your answer.**

- **Inoculation**
- **The Royal Society**

**You must also include information of your own.**

### How to answer

- You need to explain at least three causes. This could be the two mentioned in the question and one of your own. You don't have to use the points given in the question, you could decide to make more points of your own instead.
- You need to fully explain each cause and support your explanation with precise knowledge, ensuring that each cause is fully focused on the question.

Below is part of an answer to the question.

*There was a lot of opposition to Jenner's smallpox vaccination at the beginning of the nineteenth century. Doctors were used to giving inoculations and did not want to change their approach. The Royal Society did not help when they said that Jenner's idea was too revolutionary and refused to publish his book. The Anti-Vaccine Society was set up to oppose the vaccination. They did this by publishing cartoons that made fun of the vaccine and tried to scare people into not trusting and therefore not having the vaccination. One such cartoon showed people who had the vaccine turning into cows. Many religious believers thought it was against God's law to give people an animal disease.*

Opposition is described. However, there is no explicit focus on the question.

The supporting evidence is not precise enough.

The answer is losing focus on the question.

## Make an improvement

Try improving the answer. An example of a better answer to this question is on page 45 for you to check your own answer against.

Your point is a short answer to the question. You then back this up with lots of examples to demonstrate all the knowledge you have learned during your studies: this is the section that proves you have studied and revised, rather than just guessing. Finally, you will link that knowledge to the question by explaining it in a final sentence.

- Point: passing my GCSE History exam will be very helpful in the future.
- Example: for example, it will help me to continue my studies next year.
- Explain: this will help me to get the job I want in the future.

**Exam tip**

Writing a good paragraph to explain an answer to something is as easy as PEEing: Point, Example, Explain.

Below is a sample Level 4 answer to the causation question on page 44 with comments around it.

There was a lot of opposition to Jenner's smallpox vaccination at the beginning of the nineteenth century. One cause of the opposition was a lack of acceptance from the medical profession. Doctors were used to giving inoculations and did not want to change their approach. The Royal Society did not help when they said that Jenner's idea was too revolutionary and refused to publish his book.

There was also opposition from the religious community. The Anti-Vaccine Society was set up to oppose the vaccination. They did this by publishing cartoons that made fun of the vaccine and tried to scare people into not trusting and therefore not having the vaccination. One such cartoon showed people who had the vaccine turning into cows. The Anti-Vaccine Society was set up in 1866. Many religious believers thought it was against God's law to give people an animal disease. It was believed that smallpox was sent as a punishment for sin and that only prayer and living a godly life could cure the disease.

Jenner's inability to explain how his smallpox vaccine worked did not help to reduce the opposition. Pasteur did not publish his Germ Theory until 1861, so Jenner did not know that bacteria caused disease. This meant that he did not know exactly how vaccination worked and Jenner wasn't able to explain it to others. The longer term consequence of this was that it was not possible to learn from this discovery how to prevent the spread of other diseases. Without a clear explanation, the opposition to the smallpox vaccine continued.

The first cause is introduced and immediately focuses on the question.

The supporting evidence is precise and relevant to the question.

The second cause is introduced and linked to the first cause and immediately focuses on the question.

The supporting evidence is precise and relevant to the question.

The third cause is introduced and linked to the second cause and immediately focuses on the question. Notice that this is a cause not mentioned in the question.

The supporting evidence is precise and relevant to the question.

## Now have a go

**Explain why some changes took place in medical knowledge during the period *c.*1500–*c.*1700.**

**You may use the following in your answer:**
- **The Royal Society**
- **Vesalius**

**You must also use information of your own.**

## Question 5 and 6: A judgement about change, continuity and significance

Below is an example of question 5 and 6, which asks you to make a judgement about how far you agree with the statement. It is worth 20 marks (4 of these are for spelling, punctuation, grammar and the use of specialist terminology).

**You may use the following in your answer.**
- **1848 Public Health Act**
- **John Snow**

**You must also include information of your own.**

**'Edwin Chadwick's Report was the main reason why public health in towns improved during the nineteenth century.' Do you agree? Explain your answer.**

## How to answer

You need to give a balanced answer which agrees and disagrees with the statement using evidence from the bullet points as well as your own knowledge. Here is one way you could approach this:

- agree with the view with evidence from a bullet point and your own knowledge
- disagree with the view with evidence, possibly from the other bullet point and your own knowledge
- agree/disagree with the view (depending on statement) with another point from your own knowledge
- make a final judgement on whether you agree or disagree with the statement.

Below is part of an answer to this question which agrees with the view given in the statement.

The public health in towns did improve during the nineteenth century and one reason for this was due to Edwin Chadwick's report. In 1842, Edwin Chadwick wrote his 'Report on the Sanitary Conditions of the Labouring Classes'. In this report, Chadwick showed that the poor lived in dirty, overcrowded conditions which caused a huge amount of illness. Due to this, many people were too sick to work and so became poorer still. This had an effect on the richer people because they had to pay more taxes to help the poor. Chadwick suggested that taxes should be cut and money should be saved in the long run by improving drainage and sewers, removing refuse from streets and houses, providing clean water supplies and appointing medical officers in each area to check on these reforms. Initially, there was opposition to Chadwick's ideas due to the initial need to increase taxes and for the government to get involved in local matters. However, after an outbreak of cholera in 1848, the government passed the 1848 Public Health Act which led to many towns improving their public health. This shows that Chadwick was important because he pushed the government to act in 1848 for the first time.

> The answer immediately focuses on the question.

> Support is provided from own knowledge.

> Explanation is provided using the first bullet point.

### Now have a go

1. Have a go at another paragraph by disagreeing with the view given in the statement and using the second bullet point.
2. Write another paragraph that disagrees or agrees with the statement using another point from your own knowledge.
3. Write a conclusion giving your final judgement on the question.

# EARLY ELIZABETHAN ENGLAND

1558–88

# **Key topic 1** Queen, government and religion, 1558–69

Elizabeth faced numerous challenges on her accession and in the early years of her reign. She overcame some of them but, by 1569, there remained religious problems and the issue of Mary, Queen of Scots.

## 1 The situation on Elizabeth's accession

REVISED

When Elizabeth became queen on the death of Mary in 1558, she had to contend with urgent problems, most importantly the fear of invasion, financial concerns and religious challenges. In addition, she was considered to be vulnerable because of her gender and this raised issues of security at home and abroad.

### 1.1 Elizabethan England in 1558

The structure of society in England was **hierarchical** and this was also seen in the way that the country was governed. Each group in society knew its place and obeyed those who were above them in the hierarchy.

#### Society and government

- The queen was the head of society and government and was seen as deriving her position and power from God. She made all the major decisions.
- The Royal court was the centre of all political power in Elizabeth's reign. Her chief advisers and key government officials all attended the court.
- Elizabeth was advised by a small group of leading nobles who had great power and helped to run the government by means of the **Privy Council**.
- Elizabeth appointed nineteen men to her Privy Council. The Council met several times a week and offered advice to the queen.
- The nobles numbered about 100 and they were expected to deal with crime and social unrest in their lands. Nobles would be army commanders in time of war.
- Beneath the nobles were the gentry, that is the lesser nobles, knights and lawyers. They helped to run local government and acted as judges and sheriffs.
- There was also a growing class of merchants. These various groups of people helped to run local government.
- There was a large class of yeomen who owned their land and tenant farmers who rented theirs. Many yeomen had servants and the yeomen could vote in elections to Parliament if they could prove ownership of their land.
- **Parliament** was called only occasionally. It met when Elizabeth called it. The main motive for calling Parliament was usually financial. Elizabeth needed Parliament to grant money from taxes to pay for the running of and defence of the country.
- Parliament was in session only nine times in the years 1558–88. In each session, taxes were granted.
- Parliament was comprised of the House of Lords, which consisted of about 100 Lords, bishops and judges, and the **House of Commons**, which was the lower house of Parliament. There were about 450 MPs in the Commons who were elected by wealthy landowners. Members were mainly merchants, men from the gentry and lawyers.
- At the base of the hierarchy were the craftspeople: labourers, servants and the poor. They had no say in the running of the country.

**Key terms**

**Hierarchical** Classified into successive levels

**House of Commons** The lower house of Parliament. There were about 450 MPs who were elected by wealthy landowners. Members were mainly merchants, gentlemen and lawyers

**Parliament** The representative law-making body consisting of the monarch, the House of Lords and the House of Commons

**Privy Council** A committee of ministers appointed by Elizabeth to advise her

**Exam tip**

You will need to know the situation in 1558, in terms of government and society.

## How important

Complete the table below.

Explain the importance of each of the following in society and government when Elizabeth became queen. Give a brief explanation for each choice.

| Group | Key features | Important | Quite important |
|---|---|---|---|
| Nobles | | | |
| Gentry | | | |
| Royal court | | | |
| Yeomen | | | |
| Merchants | | | |
| Privy Council | | | |

## Giving explanations

Below is a table of suggested reasons why Elizabeth called Parliament only occasionally. Complete the table by **explaining** whether the reason is weak or strong.

| Reason | Weak/strong |
|---|---|
| Groups might plot together in Parliament | |
| Elizabeth may seem weak | |
| May not grant taxes | |
| The House of Lords might expect greater consultation | |
| The House of Commons might expect greater consultation | |
| May lose power to groups in Parliament | |

# 1 The situation on Elizabeth's accession (cont.)

REVISED

## 1.2 The Virgin Queen

Elizabeth faced problems because of who and what she was: young, an unmarried female, seen as **illegitimate** and lacking experience.

### Elizabeth's personal problems

- Many **Catholics** believed Elizabeth was illegitimate because her parents' marriage had been illegal and thus she had no claim to the throne.
- Many felt that as a single woman she could not offer a strong, effective monarchy. If she married, it would deter would-be English usurpers and foreign rulers. A female ruling alone would be seen as weak and vulnerable.
- Marriage would hopefully lead to an heir and this would settle the issue of succession in the event of Elizabeth's death.
- There was a fear that Elizabeth would not choose her advisers wisely.

### Elizabeth's strengths and character

- She was brought up as a **Protestant**.
- She was well educated with a sharp mind.
- She endured the execution of her mother and imprisonment by her half-sister.
- She was cautious and had seen political intrigue for most of her life.

## 1.3 Challenges at home and from abroad

- Tudor monarchs were expected to pay for the costs of running England. If the ruler needed more money, then Parliament had to be called. Rulers did not like to do this because it seemed to give Parliament too much power.
- In 1558, England was at war with France and the threat of invasion was great.
- The war against France had been costly and meant that Elizabeth inherited a debt of £300,000.
- Government spending was high when Elizabeth became queen and despite being in debt, Elizabeth spent £100,000 on arms and munitions.
- Royal land had not produced sufficient rent to keep the **Exchequer's** books balanced.
- Many in France believed that Mary, Queen of Scots should be ruler of England. Mary was Elizabeth's heir; she was a Roman Catholic and was married to the son of the French king.

### Key terms

**Catholic** A member of the Roman Catholic Church, a religion headed by the Pope

**Exchequer** The department of state in England that dealt with the collection and management of royal revenue

**Illegitimate** A child born of parents not lawfully married to each other

**Protestant** A member of any of the Churches that separated from the Roman Catholic Church

### Revision task

What factors were increasing the importance of Parliament in Elizabeth's reign?

### Exam tip

You will need to know the situation in 1558, in terms of Elizabeth's personal, domestic and foreign challenges.

## Organising knowledge

Use the information on page 6 to complete the table below to show the reasons why Elizabeth faced problems when she became queen.

| | |
|---|---|
| A female ruler | |
| Marriage | |
| Religion | |
| Finance | |

## Complete the paragraph

Below is a question about Elizabeth's accession. The first sentence has been started for you. Complete the first sentence by clearly explaining what you think was the most worrying problem. You will then have to write more sentences to ensure that your answer is explained fully.

**Which do you think was the most worrying problem for Elizabeth when she became queen? Explain your answer.**

**ELIZABETH'S MOST WORRYING PROBLEM WAS ...**

**BECAUSE ...**

## 2 The 'settlement' of religion

REVISED

Religion had been the source of many problems since Henry VIII divorced Catherine of Aragon in 1533. Elizabeth did not want to antagonise the Protestants and Catholics but creating a solution would be difficult and religion continued to be a thorny issue for much of her reign.

### 2.1 Religious divisions in England in 1558

Queen Mary had reintroduced Roman **Catholicism** when she became ruler and this caused great resentment among Protestants but pleased the Catholics. Elizabeth was a Protestant and the Protestants hoped for a change in religion in 1558.

#### Roman Catholics and Protestants

- Protestants had rebelled against Queen Mary's reintroduction of Catholicism. Mary burned 300 Protestants who refused to change their religion.
- Elizabeth was a Protestant and sought to restore England to Protestantism, but was aware that forcing people to change religion could cause a civil war.
- Many of Elizabeth's newly appointed advisers were Protestants.
- Elizabeth did not want to surrender authority to the Pope.
- There were some Protestants – the **Puritans** – who wished to follow their own strict brand of religion without any remnants of the Catholic faith and they were strident in their demands.

### 2.2 Elizabeth's religious settlement, 1559

- Elizabeth tried to create a settlement that would satisfy all religious groups.
- The **Acts of Supremacy and Uniformity** re-established Protestantism and made Elizabeth Supreme Governor of the Church of England. Most Catholics accepted this because it seemed to accept the Pope as overall Head of the Church.
- All government officials and **clergy** had to swear an oath to Elizabeth. Only a few refused to take the oath.
- Church services had to be in English. Some Catholics objected to this and Latin masses were held in secret. A new **Prayer Book** was to be used and the Bible was to be in English.
- Some Catholic features were retained, for example candles, crosses and vestments.
- Services included prayers for the queen, and priests were told what to say in sermons.
- Clergy were allowed to marry.
- Failure to attend church services meant a fine of one shilling (equivalent to five pence – a large amount at that time). These were called recusancy fines.
- The settlement did not cause any immediate rebellions or widespread anti-Elizabeth sentiment.

### 2.3 The Church of England: its role in society

- The vast majority of people went to church at least once per week.
- People's lives revolved around the church: baptism, marriage, death, harvests.
- The church ran schools and organised social occasions for local communities and hence the **parish** clergy were important members of the community.
- Leading a good life with the church would lead to everlasting life after death.

**Key terms**

**Act of Supremacy** The Act which made Elizabeth Head of the Church

**Act of Uniformity** The Act specified the form of church service which people had to follow throughout England

**Catholicism** The faith system of the Roman Catholic Church

**Clergy** People who have been trained and approved for carrying out religious services in the Church

**Parish** An area that has its own local church and priest

**Prayer Book** The official service book of the Church of England

**Puritans** English Protestants of the late sixteenth and seventeenth centuries who regarded the Reformation of the Church under Elizabeth I as incomplete and sought to purify the Church of all Roman Catholic practices

**Revision task**

Do you think Elizabeth's religious settlement was a fair compromise?

**Exam tip**

The religious settlement is complex. You will need to understand how Elizabeth tried to satisfy each contending group.

## You're the examiner

Below is an exam-style question.

**Explain why most people in England accepted Elizabeth's religious settlement of 1559.**

**You may use the following in your answer:**
- **Elizabeth made Supreme Governor of the Church**
- **Some Catholic features were retained in churches**

**You must also use information of your own.**

1 Below are a mark scheme and a paragraph which is part of an answer to the question. Read the paragraph and the mark scheme. Decide which level you would award the paragraph. Write the level below, along with a justification for your choice.

| Mark scheme | | |
|---|---|---|
| Level | Mark | |
| 1 | 1–3 | A simple or generalised answer is given, lacking development and organisation |
| 2 | 4–6 | An explanation is given, showing limited analysis and with implicit links to the question |
| 3 | 7–9 | An explanation is given, showing some analysis, which is mainly directed at the focus of the question |
| 4 | 10–12 | An analytical explanation is given which is directed consistently at the focus of the question |

Remember that for the higher levels, students must:
- explain at least three reasons
- focus explicitly on the question
- support their reasons with precise details.

### STUDENT ANSWER

*Queen Mary had been quite a devout Roman Catholic and had brought back Catholicism after her brother Edward had died. Some people objected and she killed those people who objected to the reintroduction. Several hundred people were burnt because they refused to turn to Catholicism. England had had so many changes to religion since Henry VIII.*

Level ☐ Reason ____________________

2 Now suggest what the student has to do to achieve a higher level.

____________________

3 Try and rewrite this paragraph at a higher level.

4 Now try and write the rest of the answer to the question.

## 3 Challenges to the religious settlement

REVISED

Elizabeth had to establish a compromise with the religious settlement and this meant treading carefully between the strict Protestants (Puritans) and Catholics. She adopted a 'middle way' between the two groups. She also had to ensure that any religious changes did not antagonise any Catholic foreign powers. The eventual settlement gained acceptance among Puritans and Catholics in the first decade of her reign, but dissatisfaction grew after 1569.

### 3.1 The Puritan challenge

- Puritans were happy that Elizabeth reintroduced Protestantism once more but did not like some of the remaining traces of the Catholic Church such as decorations in church, altars, music and robes (vestments) worn by the clergy.
- In the **Communion service**, Puritans felt that the presence of Jesus was spiritual, not physical.
- Some Puritans remained as bishops and together with some Puritan MPs tried to persuade Elizabeth to move to a more Puritan style of Protestantism. Elizabeth would not deviate from her own views and she forced some Puritan priests to resign after 1583.
- There were some Puritans who felt that there should be no bishops and that there were too many weak priests. They felt that Elizabeth should remove bishops and ensure that only enthusiastic priests were appointed.
- The Puritans were only a minority and Elizabeth had to consider the rest of the population, including the Catholics.
- Elizabeth felt safe in the knowledge that, although they might dislike the settlement, the Puritans would never plot with the Catholic powers of France and Spain to overthrow her.

**Key terms**

**Communion service** The service in which bread and wine are declared sacred and consumed as memorials of Jesus Christ's death

**Excommunication** Expulsion from the Roman Catholic Church

**House of Lords** The upper house of Parliament. It consisted of about 100 Lords, bishops and judges

**Papacy** The system of Roman Catholic Church government headed by the Pope

### 3.2 The Catholic challenge

- Many Catholics in the **House of Lords** spoke against the settlement but were unable to prevent the passing of the Acts of Supremacy and Uniformity. They did not want Elizabeth to be Head of the Church or accept Protestant religious ideas.
- Catholics were upset that the settlement did not permit the Latin Mass in services and some priests held the Mass secretly, often in the homes of Catholic nobles.
- Some Catholics did not attend church and Elizabeth decided not to enforce the recusancy fines too strictly.
- At first, the **papacy** did not challenge the settlement because it was felt that Elizabeth might change her mind, but Pope Pius V **excommunicated** Elizabeth in 1570. The excommunication encouraged Catholics not to obey Elizabeth and opened the way for plots to establish Mary, Queen of Scots as rightful ruler of England.
- The excommunication also gave justification for any rebellions against Elizabeth and for foreign intervention to help Mary, Queen of Scots.
- Spain did not wish to challenge Elizabeth in case Mary, Queen of Scots took the throne because this would strengthen France, Spain's enemy.
- France was experiencing religious turmoil and did not wish to challenge Elizabeth.

**Exam tip**

Ensure that you know both sides of the religious challenge to Elizabeth and how serious each one was.

## Spot the mistakes

Below is a paragraph which is part of an answer to the question below. However, the candidate has made a series of factual mistakes. Once you have identified the mistakes, rewrite the paragraph.

**Explain why there were challenges from the Catholics to Elizabeth's religious settlement.**

**You may use the following in your answer:**

- **Catholic features in church**
- **Catholic concerns over the acts of the settlement**

**You must also use information of your own.**

*Catholics were happy with the settlement. Puritans wanted to purify the Church but were ready to accept some Catholic features in church such as robes but were keen to get rid of others. Catholics were worried about the excommunication because they wanted Elizabeth to remain as queen. Catholics did not like services to be held in Latin and therefore held secret services at home. Vestment fines were levied on Catholics for holding services at home.*

## Memory map

Create a memory map to show the reasons why Puritans had mixed feelings about the religious settlement. Add some key words from the information on pages 8 and 10 and your own knowledge to the diagram below. Put positive feelings on the left side and negative feelings on the right side of the diagram.

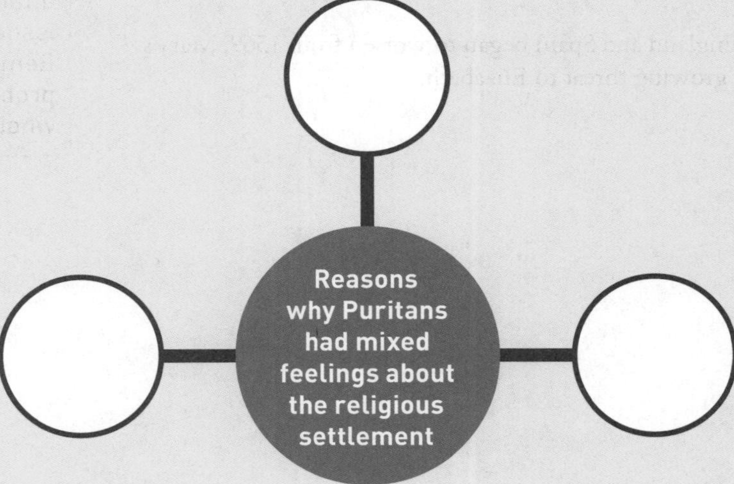

## 4 The problem of Mary, Queen of Scots

REVISED

Mary was Elizabeth's heir but the facts that she was Catholic, from a rival country and married to Francis, the King of France's son (he died in 1560), made her a challenger for the throne of England. She still continued to be a threat even after Francis's death.

### 4.1 Mary's arrival in England, 1568

- Mary was Elizabeth's cousin and heir but Elizabeth had not named her as successor. Mary and Elizabeth shared the same grandmother, Margaret Tudor, who was Henry VIII's sister. Unless Elizabeth married and had children, Mary could become ruler of England.
- Mary claimed that Elizabeth was not the rightful Queen of England because her mother's marriage to Henry VIII had been illegal.
- Mary had been forced to abdicate the Scottish throne in 1567 because it was thought she had been involved in the murder of her second husband. She was imprisoned but managed to escape and her forces were defeated in battle. She then fled to England in 1568.
- Elizabeth decided to keep Mary captive rather than allow her to have complete freedom because it was thought that Catholics might wish to place Mary on the throne.
- Elizabeth did not wish to execute a fellow monarch. Elizabeth held the view that a monarch was placed there by God.
- Mary's arrival increased Elizabeth's fears of plots and rebellions.

### 4.2 Relations between Elizabeth and Mary, 1568–69

- On arriving in England, Mary wanted help from Elizabeth to regain her throne in Scotland. Elizabeth would not help because she did not wish to antagonise the Protestant nobles who controlled Scotland.
- The Scots wanted to put her on trial; Elizabeth could have Mary executed but she did not wish to execute a fellow monarch, she feared Catholic reaction at home and abroad; she could accept her as her rightful heir but was concerned about Protestant reaction in England and Scotland.
- Elizabeth's fears seemed to be justified when the Revolt of the Northern Earls occurred in 1569, see page 66. This was a plot which sought to put Mary on the throne.
- As relations between England and Spain began to worsen from 1569, Mary's presence was seen as a growing threat to Elizabeth.

**Exam tip**

Remember that the problem of Mary cuts across religion, foreign affairs, domestic issues and Parliament. Remember that it is a problem that lasts the whole of this period.

## Identifying causation

Below is a list of statements about the problems caused for Elizabeth by Mary, Queen of Scots. Identify with a tick those which are statements of causation about these problems.

| | |
|---|---|
| Mary was Catholic and a focus for those who wanted to bring back Catholicism | |
| Mary had a large army in Scotland | |
| Foreign countries might offer Mary help | |
| Mary claimed she should be Queen of England | |
| Mary had close links with the Puritans | |
| Mary had close links with English nobles | |

## Causation

Below is an exam-style question.

**Explain why Elizabeth was unwilling to execute Mary, Queen of Scots.**

**You may use the following in your answer:**
- **Mary was a fellow monarch**
- **Fear of foreign intervention**

**You must also use information of your own.**

To answer the question above, you need to explain three causes. It is sensible to make use of the two given points. However, you will need to explain a third cause.

Write about the two suggested causes and then complete the writing frame below.

Cause:

Why I have chosen this cause:

Details to support this cause:

# Key topic 2 Challenges to Elizabeth at home and abroad, 1569–88

Mary's arrival in 1568 triggered various plots which culminated in her execution in 1587. During this period, relations with Spain deteriorated and there was fighting in the Netherlands and then naval action with the Armada.

## 1 Plots and revolts at home

REVISED

Several plots centred around Mary, Queen of Scots but Elizabeth's network of spies and informers was able to ensure that none was successful.

### 1.1 The Revolt of the Northern Earls, 1569

#### Reasons for the Revolt

- The **Duke of Norfolk**, a leading Catholic noble, planned to marry Mary.
- Norfolk objected to William Cecil's power. (Cecil was Elizabeth's chief minister throughout her reign.) Norfolk wanted to increase the influence of Catholics at court.
- Some northern nobles, like **Westmoreland** and **Northumberland**, wanted to have more power not only in the North but also at court.
- They wished to restore Catholicism.
- Even if Elizabeth was not removed, it was hoped that she would name Mary as her successor.

#### Significance of the Revolt

- Expected help from Spain and the Pope did not materialise.
- Most Catholics did not join the Revolt. Elizabeth was popular and there was no widespread desire to remove her.
- Elizabeth was able to raise a force of about 10,000, which was an indication of support for her.
- Her forces were larger than the rebels anticipated and caused them to retreat hastily.
- Elizabeth felt it necessary to confiscate land from some of the rebels and also execute about 600 of them.
- Northumberland was executed in 1572.

**Key individuals**

**Duke of Norfolk** Leading Catholic noble. He was imprisoned after the Revolt of the Northern Earls and after his release became involved in the Ridolfi Plot. He was then executed

**Duke of Northumberland** Leading northern Catholic noble. He was executed three years after the Revolt of the Northern Earls

**Duke of Westmoreland** Leading northern Catholic noble. He fled to the Netherlands after the Revolt of the Northern Earls failed

**Revision task**

What events changed Elizabeth's attitude to Mary, Queen of Scots in the years 1568–69?

## Eliminate irrelevance

1 Below are an exam-style question and part of an answer. Some parts of the answer are not relevant to the question. Identify these and draw a line through the information that is irrelevant, justifying your deletions in the margin.

**Describe two features of the Revolt of the Northern Earls.**

There was some opposition to Elizabeth because she was a woman. Some nobles did not like her because she brought back Catholicism and they did not like Protestant services. They wanted to have services like they had been before Elizabeth. The nobles in the North planned to replace Elizabeth with Mary.

Another feature was that the Catholic nobles wanted more power. They thought that if they had more power and gained help from Spain they could overthrow Elizabeth. They received no help from foreign countries.

2 Now have a go at the following question by using the writing frame below.

**Describe two features of Elizabeth's reaction to the Revolt of the Northern Earls.**

What is the first feature I will describe?

Details to support this feature:

What is the second feature I will describe?

Details to support this feature:

## How important

Copy and complete the table below:

- Briefly summarise why each factor was a threat to Elizabeth's position as queen in the Revolt of the Northern Earls.
- Make a decision about the importance of each factor in the Revolt. Give a brief explanation for each choice.

| Factor | Key features | Decisive | Important | Quite important |
|---|---|---|---|---|
| Fear of Mary | | | | |
| Involved areas of England away from London | | | | |
| Catholic nobles involved | | | | |
| Force raised against Elizabeth | | | | |
| Fear of foreign involvement | | | | |

# 1 Plots and revolts at home (cont.)

REVISED

After the Revolt of the Northern Earls, there followed three plots, each centred on Catholic dissatisfaction with Elizabeth and each seeking to enthrone Mary.

## 1.2 Plots and spies

### The Ridolfi Plot, 1571

- Mary used **Roberto Ridolfi** to carry messages to the Pope and Philip II of Spain, asking them to organise an invasion of England.
- The aim was to assassinate Elizabeth, place Mary on the throne and restore Catholicism.
- Elizabeth had been excommunicated in 1570 and many Catholics felt able to rebel against their queen.
- Spanish forces would invade England and help with removing resistance.
- Government spies and informers discovered the plot and the plot was foiled.
- From abroad, Ridolfi continued to write to Mary but after six months the plot evaporated.
- The Duke of Norfolk was arrested again and was executed in 1572.
- Elizabeth resisted Parliament's demands that Mary should be executed.

### The Throckmorton Plot, 1583

- Spanish and papal money was used to back a French invasion of England which would lead to the removal of Elizabeth and crowning of Mary.
- Mary used **Francis Throckmorton** as intermediary to contact the Spanish.
- Once again, Elizabeth's spies became aware of the plot and spied on Throckmorton.
- Throckmorton was eventually arrested. He was tortured until he confessed.
- Throckmorton was executed and the Spanish ambassador was expelled.
- There was insufficient evidence against Mary to execute her.

### The Babington Plot, 1586

- Plotters sought to kill Elizabeth, free Mary and restore Catholicism.
- Letters written by Mary were found by Elizabeth's spies which implicated Mary in the plot.
- **Anthony Babington**, one of the plotters, was arrested, tortured and executed.
- Mary was placed on trial.

### Spies

- After 1573, **Sir Francis Walsingham** used a network of spies and informers across England to protect Elizabeth from plotters.
- Letters to and from Mary were intercepted and the **ciphers** were decoded.
- Walsingham also used **double agents**.

## 1.3 The execution of Mary, Queen of Scots

- Mary was found guilty and executed in February 1587.
- Elizabeth was unwilling to sign the death warrant and her advisers and Parliament grew anxious with Elizabeth's reluctance.
- Parliament was concerned about the growing Catholic threat from Spain and France.

#### Key individuals

**Anthony Babington** A member of the Catholic gentry but his family professed to be Protestants. Became a jailer of Mary, Queen of Scots and became involved in the plot which bore his name. He was executed in 1586

**Francis Throckmorton** A devout Roman Catholic who plotted against Elizabeth. He met many of Mary's agents when he was living abroad

**Roberto Ridolfi** An Italian banker who had been involved in the Revolt of the Northern Earls. He had connections with senior Catholics in England and Europe

**Sir Francis Walsingham** Principal secretary to Elizabeth after 1573. He became known as her 'spymaster'

#### Key terms

**Cipher** A code used in writing in order to conceal its meaning

**Double agent** An agent who pretends to act as a spy for one country or organisation while in fact acting on behalf of an enemy

- Elizabeth experienced feelings of guilt after Mary's execution. She felt that she had overstepped the mark by killing a fellow monarch.
- There was no Catholic uprising in England following the execution.
- Scotland and France took no action but Spain continued to make plans to invade England.

## Support or challenge?

Below is an exam-style question that asks how far you agree with a specific statement. Below this is a series of general statements which are relevant to the question. Using your own knowledge and the information on the opposite page, decide whether these statements support or challenge the statement in the question and tick the appropriate box.

**You may use the following in your answer:**
- **Ridolfi Plot**
- **Throckmorton Plot**

**You must also use information of your own.**

**'Elizabeth's excommunication was the most serious threat to Elizabeth's rule in the years 1570–87.' How far do you agree?**

| Statement | Support | Challenge |
|---|---|---|
| Walsingham's spies and informers kept Elizabeth aware of opposition | | |
| The Throckmorton Plot involved Spain and the papacy and sought to involve France | | |
| Mary's involvement in the Babington Plot was clear for the first time and this forced Elizabeth to take action against her | | |
| Elizabeth's excommunication meant the Pope gave Catholics permission to rebel against her | | |
| The leading Catholic, the Duke of Norfolk, was executed after the Ridolfi Plot and this removed a major threat | | |
| Plots were similar because they wanted Catholicism and also to remove Elizabeth | | |
| The excommunication meant Catholics did not need to keep to their oath of allegiance | | |
| Mary's presence continued to encourage Catholic plotters | | |

## Understand the chronology

Place the events of Elizabeth's reign listed below in the correct chronological sequence in the timeline and include the dates.

| Year | Event |
|---|---|
| | |
| | |
| | |
| | |
| | |
| | |
| | |
| | |

A Mary Queen of Scots executed
B Walsingham began to use spies
C Duke of Northumberland executed
D The Babington Plot
E Revolt of the Northern Earls
F Elizabeth excommunicated
G The Throckmorton Plot
H The Ridolfi Plot

# 2 Relations with Spain

REVISED

Spain was a rival and enemy throughout Elizabeth's reign. It was a Catholic nation and its king had been married to Queen Mary. There was continued conflict and rivalry with England which culminated with the Armada in 1588.

## 2.1 Political and religious rivalry

- Elizabeth had refused to marry Philip of Spain when she became queen and he resented this.
- Philip of Spain detested Elizabeth's religious settlement and wanted to restore Catholicism to England.
- Spanish **ambassadors** became involved in several plots to remove Elizabeth.
- Elizabeth's support of the French Protestants angered Philip further.
- Measures against Catholics in England after 1570 angered Philip and convinced him that Elizabeth had to be removed at some time.

## 2.2 Commercial rivalry

- English traders began illegal **commerce** with Spanish settlers in the **New World** and also began to attack Spanish ports and treasure fleets.
- Men such as **John Hawkins** and other privateers also traded in slaves, challenging the Spanish **slave trade**.
- Hawkins, **Francis Drake** and other **privateers** attacked Spanish ships and stole bullion from them – key incidents were: San Juan de Ulúa (1568), Nombre de Dios (1572) and the seizure of the ship *Cacafuego* (1579) in Central and Southern America.
- Drake's activities angered the Spanish and his **circumnavigation** resulted in further conflict with that country. Philip resented attacks on his empire by Drake and other privateers.
- The Spanish feared Drake and nicknamed him 'El Draque' (The Dragon).

### Key terms

**Ambassador** A diplomatic official, sent by one ruler or state to another as its representative there

**Circumnavigation** Sailing all the way round the world

**Commerce** Trading goods or commodities between different countries

**New World** North and South America after the early voyages of European explorers

**Privateers** Sailors whose ships were authorised by a government during wartime to attack and capture enemy vessels

**Slave trade** The transporting and selling of human beings from Africa as slaves to the Americas by European countries

### Revision task

What part was played by the following in worsening relations between England and Spain?

- King Philip of Spain
- Spanish ambassadors to England
- privateers
- Drake's circumnavigation.

### Key individuals

**Francis Drake** A sea captain, privateer, navigator and slave trader. Drake was the first English sailor to circumnavigate the world, 1577–80. He attacked Spanish preparations for the Armada and played a vital role in fighting the Armada itself

**John Hawkins** A naval commander, privateer and slave trader. He was treasurer of the English navy after 1578 and one of the commanders against the Armada. He also helped to improve the design of English ships

### Exam tip

You will already be aware of Elizabeth's religious problems, but ensure that you know about political and commercial rivalry between England and Spain.

## Develop the detail

Below is an exam-style question. You are awarded 1 mark for identifying one feature up to a maximum of two features. The second mark is given for adding supporting information.

Describe two features of the rivalry between England and Spain.

*First feature – English privateers attacked Spanish ships.*

Now add supporting information to secure the second mark.

*Second feature – Philip of Spain did not like the restoration of the Protestant religion.*

Now add supporting information to secure the second mark.

## Concentric circles

In the concentric circles below, rank order the following reasons for increased rivalry between England and Spain, from the most important in the middle to the least important on the outside. Explain your decisions in the box below.

- trade
- privateers
- politics
- religion.

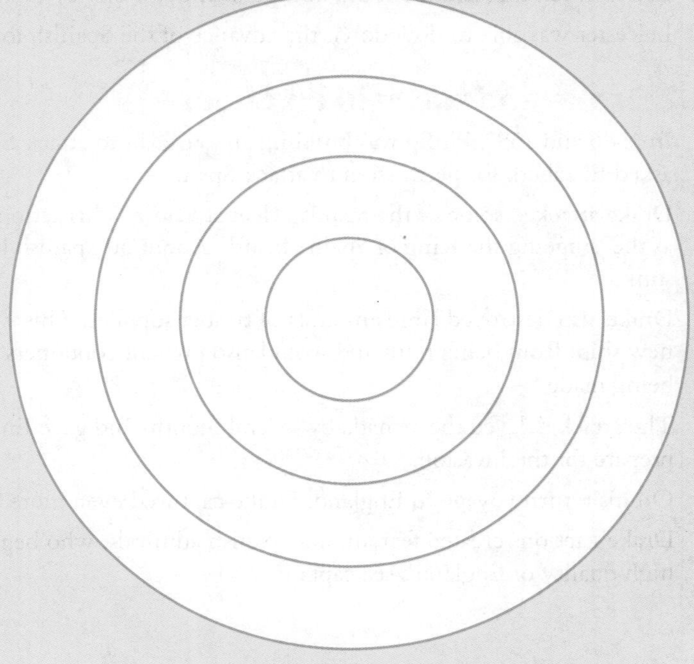

**EXPLANATION**

## 3 Outbreak of war with Spain, 1585–88

REVISED

Although there was hostility and rivalry between England and Spain throughout Elizabeth's reign, open war did not come until 1585 when England sent an army to protect Protestants in the Netherlands. In 1588, England faced invasion from a huge Spanish fleet and army.

### 3.1 English involvement in the Netherlands, 1585–88

- England needed to keep the Channel free from enemies and any challenge to its navy.
- Elizabeth disliked the way Protestants in the Spanish Netherlands were treated by Philip.
- Money and weapons were sent to help the Protestant rebels in the Netherlands and their ships were allowed to use English ports.
- After the **assassination of William of Orange**, the Dutch leader, Elizabeth feared that the Dutch would collapse and Spanish victory would lead to an invasion of England. Therefore, she needed to increase aid to the rebels.
- By the Treaty of Nonsuch (1585), Elizabeth agreed to send an army of 7000 to help the Dutch against the Spanish.
- The English army was commanded by the **Earl of Leicester** and he took the title of Governor of the Low Countries (Netherlands), much to the displeasure of Elizabeth. She thought it gave the impression that England wanted to take over Spanish territory permanently.
- Leicester felt that Elizabeth did not spend enough money on this campaign.
- Leicester was able to slow down the advance of the Spanish forces.

### 3.2 Drake and the raid on Cadiz

- In 1586 and 1587, Philip was building an **armada** to attack England. Drake asked Elizabeth for permission to attack Spain.
- Drake attacked some of the Spanish fleet at Cadiz. This action became known as the 'singeing the King of Spain's beard'. About 30 Spanish battleships were sunk.
- Drake also destroyed large amounts of timber supplies. This would prevent new ships from being built and would also prevent containers for food supplies being made.
- The attack delayed the armada by several months and gave England time to prepare for the invasion.
- On his return voyage to England, Drake captured even more Spanish treasure.
- Drake's actions created fear among Spanish admirals, who began to realise the high quality of England's sea captains.

#### Key terms

**Armada** Spanish word for a fleet of warships

**Assassination** The killing of a politically prominent person

#### Key individuals

**Earl of Leicester**
A leading English nobleman. He was a favourite of Elizabeth and many thought he would marry the Queen. He died in 1588

**William of Orange**
A leading nobleman of the Netherlands who began the revolt for independence against the Spanish. He was assassinated in 1584

#### Revision task

Draw a timeline of events from 1569 to 1588 showing the worsening relation between England and Spain.

#### Exam tip

Ensure that you understand that Elizabeth had to try to balance protecting England, helping Protestants in the Netherlands and at the same time trying not to antagonise Spain too much.

## How important

Copy and complete the table below.

- Briefly summarise why each factor worsened relations between England and Spain.
- Make a decision about the importance of each factor in worsening relations. Give a brief explanation for each choice.

| Factor | Key features | Decisive | Important | Quite important |
|---|---|---|---|---|
| The Treaty of Nonsuch | | | | |
| Drake's attack on Cadiz | | | | |
| The role of the Earl of Leicester | | | | |
| Elizabeth sending soldiers to the Netherlands | | | | |
| Elizabeth sending aid to the Netherlands | | | | |
| The death of William of Orange | | | | |
| Drake's activities after the attack on Cadiz | | | | |

## Spot the mistakes

Below is a paragraph which is part of an answer to the question below. However, it has factual mistakes. Identify the mistakes and rewrite the paragraph.

**Why did Francis Drake's activities against the Spanish increase after 1585?**

**You may use the following in your answer:**
- **Fear of invasion**
- **Involvement in the Netherlands**

**You must also use information of your own.**

One reason why Drake's activities increased was the fear of invasion. England traded with the Netherlands and did not wish to lose this trade. England was concerned that Spain might control the Channel and so Drake attacked Spanish ships in the Americas. Drake wanted to sail round the world and the Spanish might prevent this, so he had to attack the Spanish fleet in Cadiz and this was known as 'Singing the beard of the king'. Drake knew that if he traded in slaves the Spanish would react and he would be able to sink the Spanish fleet.

## 4 The Armada

REVISED

Philip's decision to invade England using an armada and forces from the Netherlands was well known and Elizabeth had time to prepare. Elizabeth arrested many Catholics to prevent potential leaders of uprisings and there were military preparations to try to counter the threat.

### 4.1 The Spanish invasion plans

- Because England was an island, Philip had no choice but to build a fleet which would be large enough to challenge England's navy and also carry sufficient soldiers to invade.
- Philip planned to sail the Armada to the Netherlands, collect additional Spanish forces and then invade England.
- The Spanish army would march on London.
- The invasion was to be a signal for English Catholics to rebel against Elizabeth. Philip called the invasion 'The Enterprise of England'.
- The Catholic Church would be restored following the removal of Elizabeth.

### 4.2 The English victory

- The Spanish had no deep harbours for their ships in the Netherlands.
- Building enough sturdy barges to transport troops from the Netherlands to England would be extremely difficult.
- Drake's attack on Cadiz in 1587 made Philip rush preparations.
- Philip appointed a new leader of the Armada, Medina Sidonia, who felt he was unsuitable for the position. In contrast, **Lord Howard**, the English admiral, provided excellent leadership for the English fleet.
- The Armada sailed into a storm just after its departure and repairs had to be made to several ships.
- The English had light, fast-moving battleships; the opposite of the Spanish. England's navy also converted over 100 merchant vessels to combat the Armada.
- When the Spanish fleet anchored at Calais, the English used fireships to disperse them and scattered the Armada.
- There followed a naval engagement at Gravelines that prevented the delayed Spanish forces in the Netherlands from joining up with the Armada.
- Following Gravelines, the Spanish fleet was driven north by strong winds and was unable to sail towards the Channel. The Armada then had to sail round Scotland and Ireland, and then returned to Spain.
- The Spanish lost about 50 ships and 20,000 men – the vast majority due to storms.

**Key individual**

**Lord Howard** English nobleman who became Lord High Admiral in 1585. He commanded all the naval forces against the Armada

#### Consequences of the English victory

- The war against Spain continued and the threat of invasion still existed. Philip built two further armadas but they each encountered storms and were driven back.
- Protestantism was maintained in England and anti-Catholic feeling in England grew.
- England continued to support the Protestants in the Netherlands.
- English sailors continued to attack Spanish treasure ships.
- Philip continued to stir up problems for Elizabeth by sending troops to Ireland in 1595 to help in a rebellion against her rule there.

## Relevance

Below are an exam-style question and a series of statements. Decide which statements are:

- relevant to the question (R)
- partially relevant to the question (PR)
- irrelevant to the question (I).

Tick the appropriate column.

**Explain why the Spanish Armada was defeated.**

**You may use the following in your answer:**
- **Superior English ships**
- **The weather**

**You must also use information of your own.**

| Factors | R | PR | I |
|---|---|---|---|
| Elizabeth had armies waiting ashore ready to fight the Spanish forces | | | |
| The English used fireships to create havoc | | | |
| Spanish supplies of food and water were insufficient | | | |
| Drake's circumnavigation had angered the Spanish | | | |
| The weather destroyed many Spanish ships | | | |
| Drake's attack on Cadiz damaged Spanish preparations | | | |
| The Spanish had insufficient barges for their armies, even if things had gone well | | | |
| The weather prevented Spanish ships from regrouping | | | |
| Medina Sidonia was not really a capable leader, in contrast to Admiral Howard | | | |
| The attacks on Spanish treasure ships helped the English | | | |
| The English ships were more manoeuvrable than the Spanish | | | |
| The English had converted some merchant ships | | | |

## Memory map

Use the information on page 22 to create a memory map to show the reasons why the Armada was defeated. Place the reasons in a clockwise manner, putting the most important reason first.

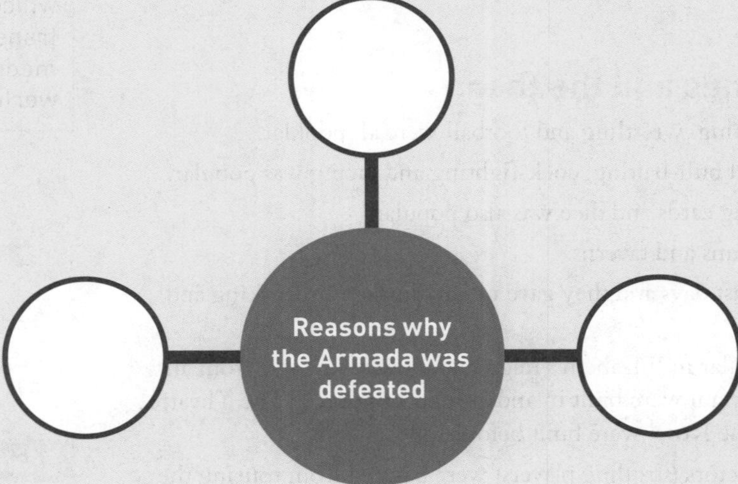

# Key topic 3 Elizabethan society in the Age of Exploration, 1558–88

Life in England changed a great deal during Elizabeth's reign for all classes of people. In addition, this era saw tremendous changes because of the voyages of exploration and discovery.

## 1 Education and leisure

REVISED

Education became an increasingly desirable asset during Elizabeth's reign. Changes brought by the **Renaissance**, the **Reformation** and the printing press meant that an educated class was more important than ever.

There was a host of leisure activities which had changed little over the years, but the growth of the theatre was one of the outstanding developments of Elizabeth's reign.

### 1.1 Education

- Elizabethans saw education as an important part of life and as a means to rise up the social ladder.
- Educational opportunities increased as the number of children attending schools in Elizabeth's reign increased, but the majority of the population was **illiterate**.
- Education was a luxury for most people and those who attended schools were mainly boys from the wealthier in society.
- Some children were taught in a local woman's house and the children of the nobility were taught at home by a private tutor. Great emphasis was placed on social **etiquette**.
- Grammar schools would be attended by children of the gentry, merchants and yeomen, although there would be some from the lower class. All children had to pay.
- Girls were taught at home.
- The sons of the very rich might attend a public school as boarders.
- A university degree was seen as a route to the **professions** for those who were not nobles. The two universities in England were Oxford and Cambridge. The Inns of Court, where lawyers trained in London, were known as England's third university.

### 1.2 Sport, pastimes and the theatre

- Hunting, archery, fishing, wrestling and football were all popular.
- Gambling on bear and bull-baiting, cock-fighting and racing was popular.
- Gambling with playing cards and dice was also popular.
- Many people visited inns and taverns.
- England had many feast days and they gave opportunities for drinking and dancing.
- Theatres became popular in Elizabeth's reign and attracted people from all sections of society. Several were built in and around London – 'The Theatre', 'The Curtain' and 'The Rose' were built before 1588.
- Wandering bands of actors (strolling players) were banned from touring the country by Act of Parliament in 1572. Elizabeth's advisers thought that rebellion and the spread of disease could be caused by the players.
- The theatre was cheap entertainment and there was some opposition to it because some thought it kept people away from church, enabled the plague to spread, encouraged thieves to congregate and caused people to miss work.

**Key individuals**

**Etiquette** The standard code of polite behaviour in society

**Illiterate** Unable to read and write

**Profession** A paid occupation, especially one that involves prolonged training and a formal qualification

**Reformation** The movement in the sixteenth century for the reform of abuses in the Roman Catholic Church that brought about the establishment of the Protestant Churches

**Renaissance** Time of the great revival of learning in Europe beginning in the fourteenth century and extending to the seventeenth century, which marked the transition from the medieval to the modern world

**Exam tip**

Remember to keep these two topics separate, unless they are **both** asked in the same question.

## Spot the mistakes

Below is an answer to the question below. However, it has factual mistakes. Identify the mistakes and rewrite the answer.

**Describe two features of Elizabethan education.**

*One feature was that a few people were illiterate. People would pay for boys and girls to go to school.*

*After attending school students would go to a university. The best two were Oxford and Cambridge.*

## Develop the detail

Below are an exam-style question and the first sentence of a paragraph which is part of the answer to the question. The sentence contains a limited amount of detail. Add extra detail to complete the answer fully. See pages 84–85 for tips on answering this type of question.

**Describe two features of the theatre in Elizabeth's reign.**

*There was a range of leisure activities for all people, from gambling to visiting the theatre.*

## 2 The problem of the poor

REVISED

There had always been poor people in society, but the number increased quickly in Elizabeth's reign. It has been estimated there were many hundreds of poor wandering the countryside in Elizabeth's reign. The wandering poor were called **vagabonds**. Response to the growth of the poor and vagabonds varied but there was a fear everywhere that the poor posed a threat to law and order in society.

### 2.1 Reasons for the increase in poverty and vagabondage

- Some farmers enclosed their land and switched to sheep farming. This meant fewer labourers were needed and they became unemployed and moved to the towns.
- Some farmers could not afford to pay increased rents and they moved into towns in search of work.
- Many spinners and weavers lost their jobs in the wool industry after England's exports fell dramatically after 1550.
- There was a rise in population but there were not enough jobs for everyone.
- Poor harvests and rising prices of food contributed towards poverty. Henry VIII had **debased the coinage** and people demanded higher prices as a result.
- **Inflation** increased after 1570. Although wages rose slowly the price of food and many goods rose more quickly.
- There was an increased number of poor because monasteries had helped them but following their **dissolution**, there was no system to help the poor.

### 2.2 Changing attitudes and policies towards the poor

- It was felt that some of the poor, especially the vagabonds, made no attempt to find work. Idleness was seen by some as a sin and punishments should be given to the idle.
- The poor and vagabonds were feared because not only might they spread the plague, they might cause a rebellion.
- Initially, Elizabeth thought that Justices of the Peace and local councillors were best suited to solve the problems of poverty, as was the case in Norwich. In London, specific hospitals were used for the poor, insane, sick and elderly.
- As poverty and the number of beggars increased, Elizabeth's government passed laws to deal with them. Government intervention was seen as necessary to overcome what was a national problem. Laws were passed in 1563, 1572 and 1576 which attempted to solve the problems.
- The 1563 Act for the Relief of the Poor said there was a class of people who were 'deserving poor' (the young, old and infirm); there were the 'deserving unemployed' (those who could work, but could not find employment) and there were the 'idle poor' (the beggars who turned to crime). The local parish could collect money to help the poor.
- The 1572 Vagabonds Act stated that if people were caught begging, they would be whipped and burned through the ear.
- The 1576 Act for the Relief of the Poor said that each county would build two houses of correction for beggars, where they would be forced to work. Justices of the peace in towns had to keep a stock of materials to ensure that those who were genuinely in need of work were given some work.

#### Key terms

**Debasement of the coinage** The reduction in the value of coins by extracting some of the pure metal (gold or silver) contained within so that more coins can be produced

**Dissolution** The abolition of monasteries in England and Wales by Henry VIII under two Acts (1536, 1539)

**Inflation** A general increase in prices and fall in the purchasing value of money

**Vagabond** A person who wanders from place to place without a home or job

#### Revision task

Why were the poor feared by many Elizabethan people?

#### Exam tip

Remember that you need to know the different types of poor and not to class them all as one group.

## Support or challenge?

Below is an exam-style question that asks how far you agree with a specific statement. Below this is a series of general statements which are relevant to the question. Using your own knowledge and the information on the opposite page and pages 6, 10, 12, 14 and 16, decide whether these statements support or challenge the statement in the question and tick the appropriate box.

**'The growth of poverty was the main domestic problem for Elizabeth in the years to 1588.' How far do you agree? Explain your answer.**

| Statement | Support | Challenge |
|---|---|---|
| The Northern Earls posed a great problem when they rebelled | | |
| The government passed three Acts to counter poverty | | |
| Mary, Queen of Scots was a major problem | | |
| Some people were unhappy with the religious settlement and challenged Elizabeth | | |
| Local councils devised methods to rid their areas of the poor because there was no overall plan to tackle the problem | | |
| Elizabeth did not name her heir and this created concerns about the future | | |
| The fact that the government became involved by passing Acts of Parliament showed that poverty caused anxiety for Elizabeth | | |
| The dissolution of the monasteries meant that there was no safety net for the poor | | |
| The population was rising and unemployment was rising too | | |
| There were three plots to remove Elizabeth and each sought to remove her and restore Catholicism | | |
| The Northern Earls gathered an army and marched south, reaching York. Elizabeth had to raise an army to oppose them | | |
| The poor were feared because they were to be found all over the country and were seen as potential rebels | | |

## Concentric circles

In the concentric circles below, rank order the following reasons for the growth in poverty in the reign of Elizabeth, from the most important in the middle to the least important on the outside. Explain your decisions.

- inflation
- poor harvests
- enclosure
- problems in the woollen industry
- little help from the remaining monasteries
- increased rents.

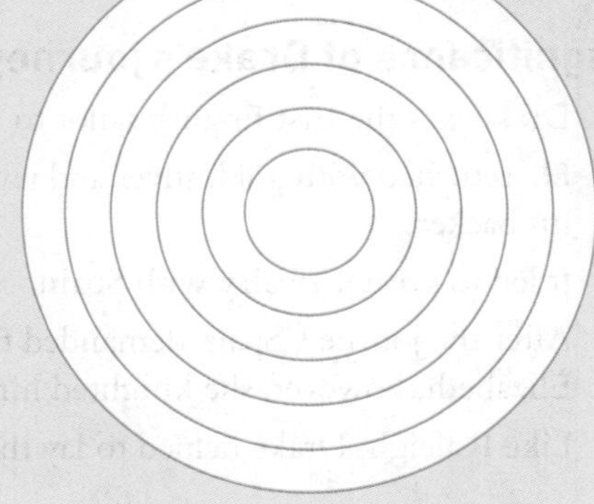

**EXPLANATION**

# 3 Exploration and voyages of discovery

REVISED

During Elizabeth's reign, English sailors became involved in exploration and voyages of discovery. New trade routes were sought and trading companies were founded including the Eastland Company in 1579 and the Levant Company in 1581.

## 3.1 Factors prompting exploration

- English sailors were able to capitalise on the experience of Portuguese and Spanish sailors.
- Development of charts showing longitude and latitude.
- New trading markets were needed following the collapse of the wool trade.
- Conversion of other lands to Protestantism; a wish to 'civilise' inhabitants of other lands.
- There was a need for new routes to India and China.

### Technology

New technology also had an impact on exploration and voyages of discovery:

- The printing press meant that maps and other geographical literature were more readily available to English sailors.
- More sophisticated **astrolabes** permitted sailors to determine positions with greater precision.
- Ship designs changed and this meant that stronger, bigger and faster ships could be built, which facilitated journeys across the Atlantic. The triangular lateen sail enabled ships to use the wind from all directions.
- English sailors used more rapid-firing guns, which gave them an advantage when facing the Spanish.

**Key term**

**Astrolabe** An instrument used by sailors to calculate their position by the stars

## 3.2 Reasons for Drake's circumnavigation

- Drake intended to attack Spanish ships and territories.
- Make a profit for himself and his backers (including Elizabeth).
- Gain revenge for the attack on John Hawkins' fleet.
- Weaken the power of Spain in Europe.
- Win new lands for Elizabeth.
- Establish new trade routes.

### Significance of Drake's journey

- Drake was the first English sailor to circumnavigate the world.
- He returned with gold, silver and jewels, and made a fortune for himself and his backers.
- It led to greater rivalry with Spain.
- After the journey, Spain demanded that Drake should be punished by Elizabeth; however, she knighted him.
- Like Raleigh, Drake helped to lay the foundations of England's future empire.

**Revision task**

What part did English sailors play in the relations between England and Spain?

## Develop the detail

Below is an exam-style question and the introduction to the answer. The sentence contains a limited amount of detail. Add extra detail to complete the answer fully. See pages 84–85 for tips on answering this type of question.

**Describe two features of technological development which enabled exploration.**

*The development of the astrolabe was very important.*

## You're the examiner

Below is an exam-style question.

**Explain why English sailors went on voyages of exploration and discovery in Elizabeth's reign.**

**You may use the following in your answer:**

- **Personal gain**
- **Rivalry with Spain**

**You must also use information of your own.**

1 Below are a mark scheme and a paragraph which is part of an answer to the question. Read the paragraph and the mark scheme. First decide which level you would award the paragraph (tip: it is not at level 4). Write the level below, along with a justification for your choice.

**Mark scheme**

| Level | Mark | |
|---|---|---|
| 1 | 1–3 | A simple or generalised answer is given, lacking development and organisation |
| 2 | 4–6 | An explanation is given, showing limited analysis and with only an implicit link to the question |
| 3 | 7–9 | An explanation is given, showing some analysis, which is mainly directed at the focus of the question |
| 4 | 10–12 | An analytical explanation is given which is directed consistently at the focus of the question |

Remember that for the higher levels students must:

- explain at least **three** reasons
- focus explicitly on the question
- support their reasons with precise details.

**STUDENT ANSWER**

*The wool trade collapsed and there was a need to find new markets and routes. So, English sailors attacked Spanish ships and sailed to the Spanish empire. Queen Elizabeth sometimes gave her support to sailors. Sailors knew they could make lots of money. Sailors did not like Catholics.*

Level ☐ Reason ______________________

______________________

2 Now suggest what the student has to do to achieve a higher level.

______________________

______________________

3 Try and rewrite this paragraph at a higher level.

4 Now try and write the rest of the answer to the question.

## 4 Raleigh and Virginia

REVISED

In the 1580s, Walter Raleigh promoted the idea of establishing a **colony** in the 'New World'. A colony would enable England to have an outlet for its growing population. Moreover, such a colony would have many resources such as gold and silver.

### 4.1 Significance of Raleigh

- Raleigh was important in creating the idea of setting up a colony in America.
- He was keen to show that a colony in North America would be crucial in attacking the Spanish **empire** and treasure ships.
- If Raleigh established colonies, the settlers would be able to prevent any French **colonisation**.
- There would the opportunity to acquire new resources and reduce England's dependency on Europe.
- Like Raleigh, Drake helped to lay the foundations of England's future empire.

### 4.2 Attempted colonisation of Virginia

- Elizabeth granted a patent to Raleigh to colonise Virginia in 1584.
- The first settlement of Virginia, in 1585, left over 100 men to colonise the land.
- Drake visited the colony on Roanoke Island in 1586 and the starving colonists returned to England with him.
- There was a second attempt at colonisation in 1587.

### 4.3 Reasons for the failure of Virginia

- The colonists were not able to produce enough food, and the Secotans, local Native Americans, had become hostile.
- The second group of colonists arrived too late in the year to plant crops.
- Relations with the local population were again poor.
- The harbour was poor.
- The leader of the settlers returned to England and arrived back at the colony in 1590 to find no trace of the colonists.

**Key terms**

**Colonisation** The action or process of settling among and establishing control over the indigenous people of an area

**Colony** An area under the full or partial political control of another country and occupied by settlers from that country

**Empire** A group of states or countries ruled over by a single monarch of another country

**Revision task**

Why did England wish to develop an empire?

**Exam tip**

The development of an empire was slow and relatively unsuccessful.

## Identifying causation

Below is a list of statements about England's first colonies. Identify with a tick those which are statements of causation about the beginnings of England's empire.

| | |
|---|---|
| It was known that there were extensive resources | |
| Raleigh wished to establish settlements | |
| The Native Americans were friendly towards Europeans | |
| France was about to establish colonies | |
| Settlements could be used as bases to attack the Spanish empire | |
| Queen Elizabeth wanted to establish settlements | |

## How important

Complete the table below.

- Briefly summarise why each factor contributed to the failure of England's colonies.
- Make a decision about the importance of each factor in the failure of the colonies. Give a brief explanation for each choice.

| Factor | Key features | Decisive | Important | Quite important |
|---|---|---|---|---|
| Settlers arrived at the wrong time of year | | | | |
| Poor harbour | | | | |
| Relations with the Native Americans were poor | | | | |
| Not enough seeds taken | | | | |
| Impact of the Armada | | | | |

## Revision timeline

Draw a timeline from 1558 to 1588 and place on it what you consider to be the ten most important events of Elizabeth's reign.

# Exam focus

Your History GCSE is made up of three exams:

- Paper 1 on a thematic study and historic environment.
- Paper 2 on a British depth study, in your case Early Elizabethan England, 1558–88, and a period study.
- Paper 3 on a modern depth study.

For the British depth study on Paper 2 you have to answer the following types of questions. Each requires you to demonstrate different historical skills:

- **Question 1** is a describe question. You have to describe two features of a given development or event.
- **Question 2** is an explain question. You have to write an explanation which analyses events or developments during in Elizabethan England and support your answer with precise detail. You can choose to write about the two stimuli, but you must also write about an event or development of your own.
- **Question 3** is a judgement question. You are asked to make a judgement on the importance of two different events/developments, supported by a precise and developed explanation.

The table below gives a summary of the question types for Paper 2 and what you need to do.

| Question number | Marks | Key words | You need to... |
|---|---|---|---|
| 1 | 4 | Describe **two** features of ... | • Ensure that you focus on a valid feature<br>• Fully describe each feature |
| 2 | 12 | Explain why ... You may use the following in your answer: [two given events/developments]<br>You **must** also use information of your own | • Analyse at least three events/developments<br>• Fully explain each with supporting detail |
| 3 | 16 | '... was the most important/ main/most ...' How far do you agree? Explain your answer | • Use the stimulus bullet points – failure to do so will prevent access to a higher level mark<br>• Ensure that you introduce aspects beyond the stimulus points<br>• Ensure that you focus on important/main/most<br>• Fully explain its importance using precise evidence |

## Question 1: Describe

Below is an example exam-style describe question. It is worth 4 marks.

**Describe two features of the Ridolfi Plot.**

### How to answer

- Underline key points in the question. This will ensure that you focus sharply on what is required.
- Identify two features of the Ridolfi Plot.
- Begin by stating the first feature: 'One feature of the Ridolfi Plot was … .'
- Then add some supporting information which amplifies the point you have just made.
- State the second feature. For example, 'A further consequence of the Ridolfi Plot was … .
- Then add some supporting information which amplifies the point you have just made.

Below is a sample answer to another exam-style describe question with comments around it.

**Describe two features of the Puritan challenge to Elizabeth's religious settlement.**

One feature of the challenge was that Puritans did not like Elizabeth using bishops. The Puritans felt that bishops should be removed and only zealous priests should be appointed.

A second feature was that Puritans preferred a plain church. They did not like Elizabeth continuing the Catholic practices of music, vestments or decorations.

The question is focused on by referring to the first feature.

Additional information is given about the first feature.

The question is focused on by referring to the second feature.

Additional information is given about the second feature.

## You're the examiner

Below is an exam-style describe question with two answers. Which is the better answer? Give three reasons why.

**Describe two features of the problems faced by Elizabeth when she became queen.**

### ANSWER 1

Elizabeth was not married and many people wanted an heir so there was pressure on her to marry. Elizabeth was unwilling to be pushed into marriage and she said she was married to England.

### ANSWER 2

One feature of her problems was that some people did not recognise her claim to the throne. She was the daughter of Henry VIII but many claimed his marriage to Anne Boleyn was not legal.

Secondly, Elizabeth was seen as weak because she was female. A husband would help her and hopefully a male heir would be produced.

Explain your reasons behind your choice.

1 ____________________

2 ____________________

3 ____________________

## Question 2: Explanation of causation

Below is an example of an exam-style explain question which is worth 12 marks.

**Explain why the Babington Plot was a threat to Queen Elizabeth.**

**You may use the following information in your answer:**
- **Involvement of Mary, Queen of Scots**
- **Spain**

**You must also use information of your own.**

### How to answer

- Look for the key points in the question and underline them.
- You can choose to write about the two points given in the question but you **must** include additional detail.
- If you write about the events in the question make sure you write about at least three events. Including three events is important because you **must** bring in detail of your own.
- Ensure that your events are in the correct chronological sequence.
- Ensure that you give detail about each of the events you write about.

Below is a sample answer to this exam-style explain question with comments around it.

The Babington Plot was a threat to Queen Elizabeth because it actually involved Mary, Queen of Scots. Previous rebellions and plots (Ridolfi and Throckmorton) had hoped to remove Elizabeth and place Mary on the throne. Elizabeth had always been unwilling to take action against her fellow monarch, but this plot actually threatened her life. On this occasion, Mary's involvement was quickly proved. A letter was discovered which plotted the assassination of Elizabeth and the letter showed that Mary consented to this action. This left Elizabeth with little choice – she had been unwilling to take strong measures against Mary, but if nothing was done now, then there would more than likely be further plots against her which could probably involve foreign powers.

> Using the words of the question gives immediate focus.

> There is a developed analysis of the first point, using precise details.

The plot was a threat because it eventually hoped that Philip of Spain would send his forces to England and they would help to remove Elizabeth and place Mary on the throne. Once again this was a clear threat to Elizabeth – Philip was beginning to make preparations to invade and the war in the Netherlands was making relations worse, so this new plot seemed to come at a crucial time for Elizabeth. She had already been helping the Protestants in the Netherlands and the plot once more showed the importance of religion.

> A link is made between the first and second points.

> There is a developed explanation of the second point.

The plot presented a threat because it also anticipated receiving help from Catholic forces from France and Elizabeth's position was heavily under threat and thus she had to take action. Moreover, if there were two countries attacking England and they combined with the supporters of Mary, the possibility of securing the Church of England as well as the throne was not very good. In the end, the plot proved to be the most problematic for Elizabeth, because she decided to put Mary on trial. Mary was eventually executed. The plot had led to an outcome Elizabeth never wanted.

> A link is made between the second and third points.

> There is a developed analysis of the point.

## 'Through the eyes' of the examiner

Below is an exam-style explain question with part of a sample answer. It would be useful to look at this an answer 'through the eyes' of an examiner. The examiner will look for the following:

- events in the correct sequence
- clear links between events
- an explanation of each event.

You need to:

- Highlight words or phrases which show that the answer has focused on the question.
- Underline where attempts are made to show links between one event and the next.
- In the margin write a word or phrase which sums up each specific explanation as it appears.

**Explain why Acts of Parliament were passed in Elizabeth's reign to help the poor.**

**You may use the following information in your answer.**

- **Inflation**
- **Enclosure**

**You must also use information of your own.**

*Poverty was a constant problem in Elizabeth's reign and the number of poor increased throughout her reign. There was no real system to help the poor and therefore any attempts which were made were done as a reaction to a worsening situation.*

*One of the key problems was inflation during Elizabeth's reign. Prices of many goods rose and did so quickly sometimes. Importantly, wages did not keep pace with price rises and so people found it difficult to maintain their standard of living. Not only did the cost of food rise (as the population rose, demand for food outstripped production and hence pressure on prices grew), ordinary people found that rents rose too and thus lives were made harder even in those areas where jobs had been plentiful. Added to this was the failure of harvests which further forced prices up.*

*Enclosure had been taking place in the reigns of Henry and Elizabeth. The main result of this was that labourers lost their land, as well as access to the common. The labourers could no longer provide for themselves and they not only lost land but also a place for their animals to graze. They were forced to move to the towns and look for jobs – but there were few. Hence the number of poor continued to grow.*

## Adding a third cause

The answer above does not include a third event. What would you choose as a third event and why? Try completing the answer, remembering to add details to support your chosen event.

## Question 3: Judgement

Below is an exam-style question.

**'The Revolt of the Northern Earls was Elizabeth's main domestic problem in the period 1569–86.' How far do you agree? Explain your answer.**

**You may use the following in your answer:**

- **Revolt of the Northern Earls**
- **The Poor**

**You must also use information of your own.**

### How to answer

- You are advised to use the two points offered in the question but above all, you **must** give some judgement on the demand of the question – it may be similarity, difference, change, continuity, causation or consequence – failure to do so will mean a low-level mark.
- Underline key points in the question. This will ensure that you focus sharply on what the question wants you to write about.
- Remember for each development that you choose, the focus of the question is **judgement** about the issue(s) mentioned in the first bullet point above.

Below is a part of a sample answer to this exam-style importance question with comments around it.

The Revolt of the Northern Earls was certainly very significant because it involved key members of the nobility. Moreover, the nobles were Catholics who owned large areas of land and could possibly raise large forces against the queen. These nobles – Northumberland, Westmoreland and Norfolk – also sought greater power at court and thus presented Elizabeth with another threat, especially as they did not like Cecil, her chief adviser. Elizabeth had to raise an army of about 10,000 to combat this revolt and such a force shows how significant this threat was. She dealt successfully with the Revolt but its seriousness can be seen further by the fact that she executed several hundred participants and confiscated their land as a warning to other would-be rebels.

There is an immediate focus on the key word of the question: importance.

A developed explanation is given using precise details.

The importance of the Revolt is focused on again.

## You're the examiner

Below are an answer to the exam-style judgement question above and a mark scheme. It has the paragraph from above and a second paragraph.

1 Read the answer and the mark scheme. Decide which level you would award the two paragraphs. Write the level below, along with a justification for your choice.

**Mark scheme**

| Level | Mark | |
|---|---|---|
| 1 | 1–4 | A simple or generalised answer is given, showing limited development, organisation of material and knowledge and understanding. There is no judgement or the judgement is asserted |
| 2 | 5–8 | An explanation is given is given showing some attempt to analyse importance. It shows some reasoning, but may lack organisation. Accurate and relevant information is added. Some weak judgement is offered. Top of Level 2 can only be reached if information beyond the two stimulus points is included |
| 3 | 9–12 | An explanation is given, showing analysis of importance, and is well structured. Accurate and relevant knowledge is included. It shows good knowledge and understanding of the required characteristics of the period. Judgement is offered with some justification. Top of Level 3 can only be reached if information beyond the two stimulus points is included |
| 4 | 13–16 | An explanation is given, showing analysis of importance, and is well structured. Accurate and relevant knowledge is included. It shows good knowledge and understanding of the required characteristics of the period. Judgement is clear and justified. Answers cannot reach Level 4 unless they add information beyond the two stimulus points |

*The Revolt of the Northern Earls was certainly very significant because it involved key members of the nobility. Moreover, the nobles were Catholics who owned large areas of land and could possibly raise large forces against the queen. These nobles – Northumberland, Westmoreland and Norfolk – also sought greater power at court and thus presented Elizabeth with another threat, especially as they did not like Cecil, her chief adviser. Elizabeth had to raise an army of about 10,000 to combat this revolt and such a force shows how significant this threat was. She dealt successfully with the Revolt but its seriousness can be seen further by the fact that she executed several hundred participants and confiscated their land as a warning to other would-be rebels.*

*The various plots against Elizabeth were just as important and because they happened every few years, they must be seen as the most important problem. The plots were very important because they aimed to get rid of Elizabeth and in some cases would have changed the religion of the country. They might also have led to wars and even invasion.*

Level ☐ Reason ______________________________

______________________________

2 Now suggest what the student has to do to achieve a higher level.

______________________________

______________________________

3 Try and rewrite the answer at a higher level.

Exam focus

# SUPERPOWER RELATIONS AND THE COLD WAR

1941–91

# Key topic 1 The origins of the Cold War, 1941–58

The **Cold War** began in 1945–46 following the Second World War. Ideological differences between the **superpowers** led to clashes over Berlin and the formation of rival military blocs. The Cold War intensified with the Soviet invasion of Hungary in 1956.

## 1 Early tension between East and West 1

REVISED

### 1.1 The ideological differences between the superpowers

Ideological differences caused mistrust between the superpowers, and meant they had different aims about post-war Europe. The USA feared the spread of communism; the Soviet Union wanted communist satellite states to prevent future invasions.

| | Communism (Soviet Union) | Capitalism (USA) |
|---|---|---|
| **Politics** | Only one political party – the Communist Party | Several parties – voters choose and change their governments |
| **Economy** | All industry and businesses owned by the state for the benefit of everyone<br>Everyone equal | Most industry and businesses privately owned<br>Some will be wealthier than others |
| **Influence** | Encourage communism in other countries | Encourage trade with other countries |

### 1.2 The Grand Alliance

The leaders of the **Grand Alliance** met in three conferences, where differences emerged.

#### The Tehran Conference, 1943

The first meeting of the Big Three – Stalin (leader of the Soviet Union), Roosevelt (US president) and Churchill (British prime minister). It was agreed:

- A second front would be opened in France in May 1944.
- The Soviet Union would enter the war against Japan after Germany's defeat.
- A **United Nations Organisation** would be set up after the war.
- Poland's post-war borders would be along the Oder and Neisse rivers; adding an area of eastern Poland to the Soviet Union.

#### The Yalta Conference, February 1945

| Agreements at the conference | Disagreements at the conference |
|---|---|
| The Declaration of Liberated Europe – to aid all peoples liberated from Nazi control<br>The Soviet Union would enter the war against Japan after Germany's defeat<br>To divide Germany and Berlin into four zones<br>To hunt down and try Nazi war criminals<br>To allow free elections in countries liberated from German occupation<br>Setting up a United Nations Organisation | Stalin wanted a higher figure of German **reparations** than Roosevelt or Churchill<br>Stalin wanted the Polish border to be further west and a 'friendly' Polish government. But he agreed to free elections |

**Key terms**

**Cold War** War waged against an enemy by every means short of fighting each other. Used to describe the relationship between the USA and Soviet Union 1945–91

**Grand Alliance** Alliance of the Soviet Union, USA and Britain during the Second World War

**Reparations** Compensation to be paid to other countries by Germany after the Second World War

**Superpower** A country or state that has great global power – in 1945, the USA and Soviet Union

**United Nations Organisation** International body set up in 1945 to promote peace and international cooperation and security

## The attitudes of Stalin, Truman and Churchill

- Roosevelt died in April 1945 and the new president, Truman, distrusted Stalin. He was convinced that the Soviet Union intended to take over Europe and he was determined to stand up to Stalin.
- Stalin suspected that the West did not want a strong Soviet Union. He wanted Soviet-controlled communist governments in Eastern Europe as a defence against future attacks. Before the Potsdam Conference the USA had successfully tested the atomic bomb. Stalin was furious that Truman hadn't consulted him. He thought that the USA was using the bomb as a warning.
- Churchill was suspicious of Stalin's motives. He thought that Soviet troops would remain in the Eastern European countries they had liberated from the Germans.

Clement Attlee replaced Churchill as British prime minister during the Potsdam Conference.

**Exam tip**

Students often confuse the key features of the Yalta and Potsdam conferences. Ensure you know who attended and what was agreed at each.

## The Potsdam Conference, July 1945

| Agreements at the conference | Disagreements at the conference |
|---|---|
| To divide Germany and Berlin into four zones<br>Germany to pay reparations in equipment and materials<br>De-Nazification: Nazi Party banned; Nazis removed from important positions; leading Nazis put on trial for war crimes<br>To move Poland's border west – along the Oder and Neisse rivers<br>Full participation in the United Nations Organisation | Stalin wanted massive compensation from Germany. Truman refused, seeing a revived Germany as a possible barrier to future Soviet expansion<br>Truman wanted free elections in Eastern European countries occupied by Soviet troops. Stalin did not |

## Memory map

Create a memory map to show the main ideological differences between the USA and the Soviet Union. Add some key words from the information on page 4 and your own knowledge to a copy of the diagram in this box. Highlight which differences you think were most important in causing the Cold War.

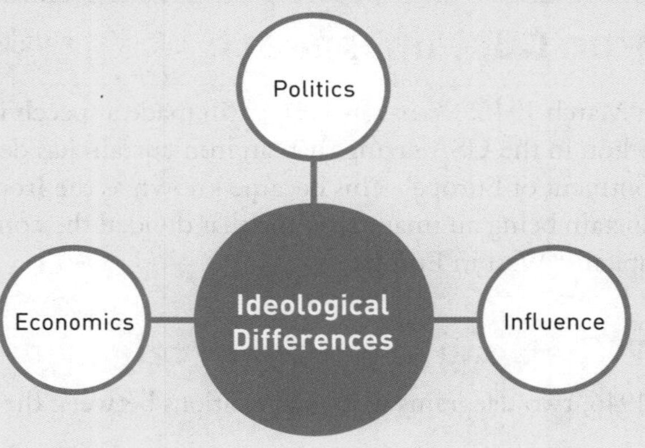

## Organising knowledge

Using the information on pages 4 and 5, copy and complete the table below to summarise the key features of the conferences held between the Grand Alliance during and after the Second World War and to make a judgement on how important they were in causing tensions between the superpowers.

| | Tehran | Yalta | Potsdam |
|---|---|---|---|
| Points agreed | | | |
| Areas of disagreement | | | |
| Importance in causing tensions | | | |

# 2 Early tension between East and West 2

REVISED

## 2.1 The creation of Soviet satellite states

In the years immediately following the end of the Second World War, the Soviet Union expanded its influence in Eastern Europe. This expansion was due to the Soviet desire for security. The Soviet Union had been invaded by Germany on two occasions – 1914 and 1941 – and had suffered huge casualties in the ensuing world wars. **Stalin** created Soviet-controlled states in Eastern Europe as a buffer against future invasions.

- Elections were held in each Eastern European country but were rigged to ensure that Soviet-controlled Communist parties took over.
- By 1948, Soviet **satellite states** with communist governments were established across Eastern Europe (see box).

### Soviet satellite states

Albania, Bulgaria, Czechoslovakia, East Germany (from 1949 the German Democratic Republic), Hungary, Poland, Romania.

### Consequences

- Security for the Soviet Union. Eastern Europe could now act as a buffer against a possible future invasion from the West.
- Increased rivalry. The USA, Britain and France believed that Stalin's motives were political – the expansion of the Soviet empire and communism throughout Europe, as shown in Long telegram.
- The Soviet Union now had control of Eastern Europe. This confirmed the divisions between East and West stated in Churchill's 'Iron Curtain' speech.

### 'Iron Curtain' speech

In March 1946, **Winston Churchill** made a speech in the small town of Fulton in the USA saying that 'an iron curtain has descended across the continent of Europe'. This became known as the Iron Curtain speech, the Iron Curtain being an imaginary line that divided the communist East from the capitalist West in Europe.

## 2.2 The Long and Novikov telegrams

In 1946, two telegrams worsened relations between the superpowers.

### The Long telegram

George Kennan was the USA's Deputy Chief of Mission at the US embassy in Moscow. He saw the Soviet Union as aggressive and suspicious and recommended firm action against Soviet expansion in Eastern Europe. His telegram, which became known as the Long telegram, greatly influenced **Truman**'s policies in the Cold War, especially his policy of **containment**.

### Novikov telegram

The Soviet Union knew about the Long Telegram. It retaliated with the Novikov telegram. This was written by Nikolai Novikov, the Soviet ambassador to the USA. He accused the USA of trying to achieve world dominance.

#### Key terms

**Containment** US policy to use its influence and military resources to prevent the spread of communism into non-communist countries

**Satellite state** A country under the influence or control of another state

#### Revision task

1. Using pages 4 and 6, create a timeline showing the key developments in relations between the superpowers in the years 1943–46.
2. Make a list of the consequences of the creation of Soviet-controlled satellite states in Eastern Europe.

#### Key individuals

**Winston Churchill** An experienced British politician who was appointed prime minister in 1940, and replaced by Clement Atlee in 1945. He was strongly opposed to communism

**Joseph Stalin** Succeeded Lenin as leader of the Soviet Union. He served as leader until his death in 1953. He was determined to prevent another invasion of the Soviet Union from the West

**Harry S. Truman** US president, April 1945 to January 1953. He was strongly opposed to the spread of communism

## Eliminate irrelevance

1 Below are an exam-style question and part of an answer. Some parts of the answer aren't relevant to the question. Identify these and draw a line through the information that is irrelevant, justifying your deletions in the margin.

**Explain two consequences of the creation of Soviet-controlled satellite states in Eastern Europe.**

> The Soviet Union took control of the countries in Eastern Europe by rigging elections to ensure that Soviet-controlled Communist parties took over. These countries included Bulgaria, Romania, Hungary, Poland and Czechoslovakia.
>
> One of the consequences of the creation of these states was security for the Soviet Union. The Soviet Union had been invaded from the west by Germany on two occasions, in 1914 and 1941, and had suffered huge casualties during the ensuing world wars. Stalin created Soviet-controlled states in Eastern Europe as a buffer against future invasions.
>
> The Novikov telegram was written by Nikolai Novikov, who was the Soviet ambassador to the USA at the time. He accused the USA of trying to achieve world dominance. Another consequence was increased rivalry. The USA, Britain and France believed that Stalin's motives were political – the expansion of the Soviet empire and communism throughout Europe.

2 Now have a go at the following question by using the writing frame below.

**Explain two consequences of the Potsdam Conference.**

What is the first consequence I will explain?

_______________

Details to support this consequence:

_______________

What is the second consequence I will explain?

_______________

Details to support this consequence:

_______________

## In the balance

1 Using the information on pages 4 and 6, copy and complete both sides of the scales to show who was most to blame for the early Cold War.

2 Overall, who was most to blame for the early Cold War? Explain your judgement.

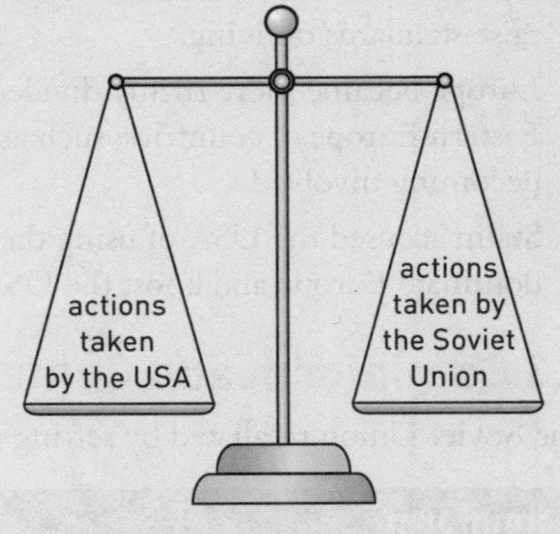

# 3 The development of the Cold War 1

REVISED

The rivalry between the superpowers intensified in the years 1947–49.

## 3.1 The Truman Doctrine, 1947

In 1947, Truman began a US policy of containment:

- This was because the USA, and especially Truman, believed that the Soviet Union was trying to spread communism, and also because Greece was being threatened with a communist takeover. By early 1947, Britain told the USA that it could no longer afford to support the Greek and Turkish governments.
- Truman announced US support for Greece in an important speech in March 1947 which became known as the Truman Doctrine.

### The consequences of the Truman Doctrine

- The Greek government was able to defeat the communists.
- The rivalry between the USA and the Soviet Union increased and the doctrine confirmed the division of the world into communist and non-communist.
- The USA became committed to the policy of containment and far more involved in European affairs.
- The USA decided on the Marshall Plan and Stalin set up Cominform.

## 3.2 The Marshall Plan, 1947

Truman backed up his policy of containment with economic aid to Europe. This was known as the Marshall Plan.

### Why was the Marshall Plan introduced?

- Truman believed that communism generally won support in countries where there were economic problems, unemployment and poverty. Many European countries had suffered badly as a result of the Second World War and were struggling to deal with the damage caused.
- If the USA could help these countries to recover economically and provide employment and reasonable prosperity, then there would be no need to turn to communism.

### Consequences of the Marshall Plan

- By 1953, the USA had provided $17 billion of aid to rebuild economies and raise standards of living.
- Europe became more firmly divided between East and West. Stalin prevented Eastern European countries, such as Czechoslovakia and Poland, from becoming involved.
- Stalin accused the USA of using the plan for its own selfish interests – to dominate Europe and boost the US economy.

## 3.3 Cominform and Comecon

The Soviet Union retaliated by setting up rival organisations.

| Cominform | Comecon |
|---|---|
| Cominform was the Communist Information Bureau and was set up in 1947 to enable the Soviet Union to co-ordinate Communist parties throughout Europe. It was the Soviet Union's response to the Truman Doctrine. It was introduced to ensure that the states in Eastern Europe followed Soviet aims in foreign policy | Comecon was the Soviet response to the Marshall Plan. The Council for Mutual Assistance (Comecon) was founded in 1949. It was supposed to be a means by which the Soviet Union could financially support countries in Eastern Europe. In reality, it was used by the Soviet Union to control the economies of these states |

**Key terms**

**Comecon** The Council for Mutual Assistance

**Cominform** The Communist Information Bureau

**Truman Doctrine** US President Truman's idea that it was the USA's duty to prevent the spread of communism to Eastern Europe and the rest of the world. To do this, he was prepared to engage the USA in military enterprises all over the world

**Revision task**

The Truman Doctrine and Marshall Plan were described as two sides of one coin. Sketch your own coin big enough to write on. On one side give a brief definition of the Truman Doctrine. On the other side give a brief definition of the Marshall Plan.

**Exam tip**

Students often confuse the Truman Doctrine and the Marshall Plan. Ensure you have a thorough knowledge of both. Remember that the Truman Doctrine is political aid to Western Europe to stop the spread of communism and the Marshall Plan is economic aid.

## RAG: Rate the timeline

Below are an exam-style question and a timeline. Read the question, study the timeline and, using three coloured pens, put a **red**, **amber** or **green** star next to the events to show:

**Red:** events and policies that have **no** relevance to the question
**Amber:** events and policies that have **some** relevance to the question
**Green:** events and policies that have **direct** relevance to the question

**Write a narrative account analysing the key ways in which the Cold War developed in the years 1945–47.**

**You may use the following information in your answer.**
- **The Potsdam Conference**
- **The Marshall Plan**

**You must also use information of your own.**

| | |
|---|---|
| 1941 | **1941** The formation of the Grand Alliance |
| 1942 | |
| 1943 | **1943** The Tehran Conference |
| 1944 | |
| 1945 | **1945** The Yalta Conference; **1945** The USA exploded the first atomic bombs; **1945** The Potsdam Conference |
| 1946 | **1946** Long and Novikov telegrams |
| 1947 | **1947** Truman Doctrine and Marshall Plan; **1947** The setting up of Cominform |
| 1948 | **1948** Beginning of Berlin blockade |
| 1949 | **1949** The setting up of NATO |
| 1950 | |
| 1951 | |
| 1952 | |
| 1953 | |
| 1954 | |
| 1955 | **1955** The setting up of the Warsaw Pact |
| 1956 | **1956** The Hungarian uprising |

## Adding a third factor

To answer the narrative account style question, you need to explain three developments. It is sensible to make use of the two given points. However, you need to explain a third development. In the space below, write down your choice for a third development in answer to the exam-style question in the 'Rate the timeline' activity above. Give reasons why you have chosen it.

Third development: ______________________________

______________________________

______________________________

______________________________

Why I have chosen this: ______________________________

______________________________

______________________________

______________________________

Details to support this point: ______________________________

______________________________

______________________________

______________________________

# 4 The development of the Cold War 2

REVISED

## 4.1 The Berlin Crisis, 1948–49

This was the first major crisis of the Cold War.

### The division of Germany into zones

- During the peace conferences of 1945 (see pages 92–93), the Allies had agreed to divide both Germany and Berlin into four zones of occupation. Berlin was in Soviet-controlled East Germany. The Western Allies were allowed access to their sectors by road, rail, canal and air.
- Stalin did not want the Allies inside Berlin.
- In 1947, the US and British zones in Berlin merged into one economic unit known as Bizonia.

### The Berlin blockade and airlift

- In June 1948, the Western powers announced plans to create a West German state and introduced a new currency, the western Deutschmark.
- On 24 June 1948, Stalin accused the West of interfering in the Soviet zone. He cut off road, rail and canal traffic in an attempt to starve West Berlin.
- Truman was determined to stand up to the Soviet Union and show that he was serious about containment. The only way into Berlin was by air. So the Allies decided to airlift supplies from their bases in West Germany.
- The airlift began on 28 June 1948 and lasted for ten months. It was the start of the biggest airlift in history.
- The airlift reached its peak on 16–17 April 1949 when 1398 flights landed nearly 13,000 tons of supplies in 24 hours.
- By May 1949, Stalin had lifted the **blockade**.

### Impact of the blockade and airlift

- It greatly increased East–West rivalry. Truman saw the crisis as a great victory. West Berlin had survived and stood up to the Soviet Union. For Stalin it was a defeat and a humiliation.
- It confirmed the divisions of Germany and Berlin. In May 1949, the Western Allies announced the Federal Republic of Germany (FRG). Stalin's response was rapid and in October 1949 the Soviet zone became the German Democratic Republic (GDR).
- It led to the creation of the North Atlantic Treaty Organization or **NATO**.

## 4.2 The formation of NATO, 1949

The Berlin Crisis had confirmed Truman's commitment to Western Europe. Western European states, even joined together, were no match for the Soviet Union and needed the formal support of the USA (see map on page 12). In April 1949, the North Atlantic Treaty was signed. NATO's main purpose was to prevent Soviet expansion.

### Consequences of the formation of NATO

- The USA was now committed to the defence of Western Europe.
- Stalin believed that NATO was aimed against the Soviet Union.
- Within six years, the Soviet Union set up the Warsaw **Pact** (see page 100).
- Europe was now divided in a state of permanent hostility between the superpowers.

**Key terms**

**Blockade**
The surrounding of a place with troops or ships to prevent the entry or exit of supplies

**NATO** A Western military alliance which was set up after the Berlin Crisis of 1948–49 to protect the freedom and security of its members

**Pact** A formal agreement between individuals or states

**Revision task**

Draw a flow chart to show the causes, events and results of the Berlin Crisis of 1948–49.

**Exam tips**

1. Students often confuse this crisis with the crisis over the Berlin Wall in 1961. An easy way to remember the difference is 'B' for blockade comes before 'W' for wall.
2. Questions on NATO are often not well answered as students fail to revise its features and importance. Ensure you revise these thoroughly.

## Develop the detail

Below are an exam-style question and a paragraph which is part of the answer to the question. The paragraph gives the importance of the Potsdam Conference but this is not supported with sufficient evidence. Complete the paragraph by adding more detail about the importance of the Potsdam Conference.

**Explain two of the following:**

- **The importance of the Potsdam Conference (1945) for relations between the USA and the Soviet Union.**
- **The importance of the Truman Doctrine (1947) for relations between the USA and the Soviet Union.**
- **The importance of the Berlin Crisis (1948–49) for the development of the Cold War.**

The Potsdam Conference was important because it led to differences between the Soviet Union and the USA over Germany. It also led to differences between the two superpowers over what should happen to countries in Eastern Europe.

## Spot the mistakes

Below is a paragraph written in answer to the question above. However, the student has made a series of mistakes, some factual and some in how the question is answered. Once you have identified the mistakes, rewrite the paragraph.

The Truman Doctrine of 1949 was important because it led to American support for the Italian government, which was now able to defeat communism. The USA became committed to a policy of containment and became far more involved in the affairs of Asia. It was also important because it led to the Long telegram, which provided economic aid to Europe.

Now have a go at the third option in the question: the importance of the Berlin Crisis (1948–49) for the development of the Cold War:

- jot down examples of its importance in relation to the given factor
- introduce the first example of its importance in relation to the given factor
- fully explain the example
- introduce the second example of its importance in relation to the given factor
- fully explain the example.

# 5 The Cold War intensifies 1

REVISED

The Cold War and East–West rivalry increased even more in the years after the Berlin Crisis.

## 5.1 The Warsaw Pact, 1955

In 1955, the Soviet Union set up the Warsaw Pact. It was a military alliance of eight nations and was designed to counter the threat of NATO.

**Key term**

**Arms race** A competition between nations for superiority in the development and accumulation of weapons

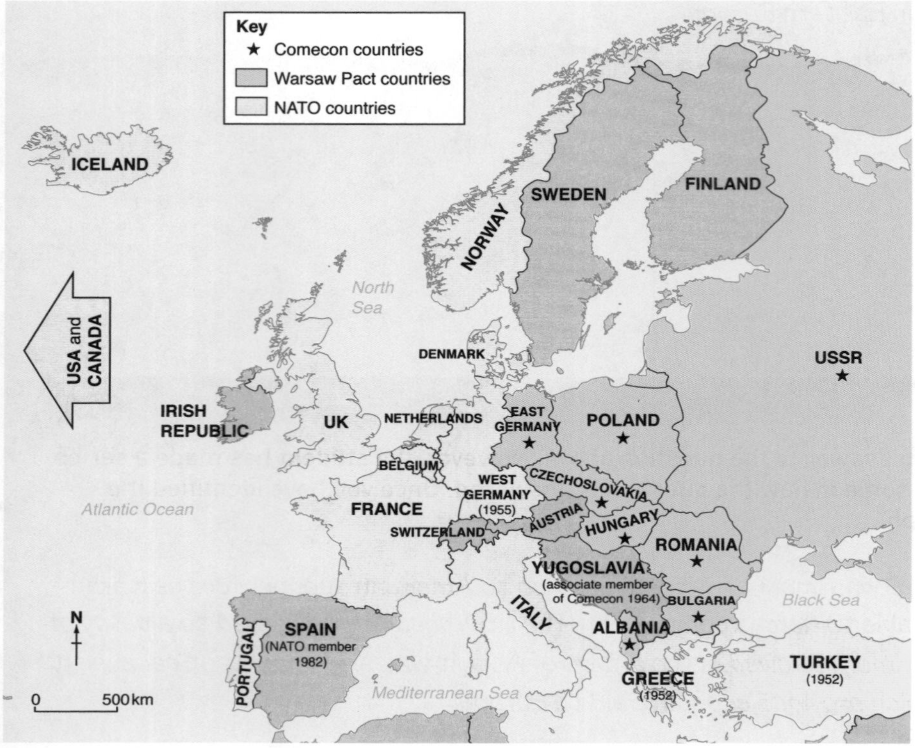

### Consequences

The existence of two rival alliance systems in the Cold War – in the west NATO and in the east the Warsaw Pact – increased rivalry between the USA and the Soviet Union and intensified the **arms race**.

Alliances, 1945–55.

## 5.2 The arms race

Both superpowers spent more and more money on arms development:

- By 1949, the Soviet Union had developed and tested its own atomic bomb. This was earlier than the USA had expected.
- Now that the USA and the Soviet Union had the atomic bomb, they both began to pour money into projects to build more and bigger bombs.
- Truman ordered a new powerful weapon to be built: the hydrogen or H-bomb.
- In 1953, the Soviet Union tested an H-bomb only a few months after the first US test.
- By 1953, both the USA and the Soviet Union possessed hydrogen bombs.
- Both countries continued to develop bigger and more powerful nuclear weapons.

**Revision task**

Try coming up with a mnemonic (a pattern of letters, ideas or associations) to help you remember which countries were part of the Warsaw Pact.

### The impact of *Sputnik*

- There was hope that the two superpowers would slow down their arms development.
- However, in 1957 the situation changed completely when a Soviet rocket launched *Sputnik*, a satellite which could orbit the earth in one and a half hours.
- The USA saw this launch as a military threat.
- The USA increased its spending on missiles and placed missile bases in some European countries.
- *Sputnik* therefore accelerated the arms programme due to US fears that the Soviet Union was overtaking them in arms development.

## Consequences and importance

Having read the information on pages 8, 10 and 12, make a copy of the table below. Explain the consequences and importance of each event for relations between the two superpowers.

| Event | Consequences | Importance |
|---|---|---|
| The Truman Doctrine | | |
| The Marshall Plan | | |
| Berlin Crisis | | |
| NATO | | |
| Arms race | | |
| Warsaw Pact | | |

## Matching dates and events

- Place the following events in the correct chronological order on the timeline below.
- Give one consequence of each event.

A Truman Doctrine
B Setting up of the Warsaw Pact
C Setting up of NATO
D Potsdam Conference
E Soviet Union tested the H-bomb
F Beginning of the blockade of Berlin
G Long telegram

| Year | Event | Consequence |
|---|---|---|
| 1945 | | |
| 1946 | | |
| 1947 | | |
| 1948 | | |
| 1949 | | |
| 1950 | | |
| 1951 | | |
| 1952 | | |
| 1953 | | |
| 1954 | | |
| 1955 | | |

# 6 The Cold War intensifies 2

REVISED

## 6.1 The Hungarian uprising, 1956

This further increased rivalry between the USA and the Soviet Union.

### Causes

The Soviet Union had established control of Hungary in the years after the Second World War (see page 94). Soviet influence was very unpopular as there was little freedom:

- The Hungarian economy was controlled by the Soviet Union through Comecon. This body prevented Hungary trading with Western Europe and receiving any Marshall Plan aid. Hungary was forced to trade on uneven terms with the Soviet Union. This meant that Hungary did not always receive a fair price for its exports there.
- Mátyás Rákosi from the Hungarian Communist Party led Hungary and used terror and brutality to keep control, killing an estimated 2000 people. The secret police (AVH) became a hated and dreaded part of Hungarian life.
- When Stalin died in 1953, the new leader of the Soviet Union, Malenkov, did not favour Rákosi and replaced him with Imre Nagy. This shows the control that the Soviet Union had in Hungary. However, in April 1955, Nagy was removed and Rákosi returned and resumed his unpopular dictatorship.

**Key individual**

**Nikita Khrushchev**
Leader of the Soviet Union from 1955 until 1964. In a 1956 'secret speech', he discussed Stalin's crimes for the first time, starting a process called de-Stalinisation, and later he presided over the Cuban Missile Crisis of 1962

### Events

In October 1956, demonstrations against Soviet control began. In response, Khrushchev sent troops and tanks to Budapest to try to restore peace.
On 26 October, Nagy was reinstated as prime minister. Nagy held talks with the Soviet Union and it was agreed that the tanks would be withdrawn.
On 30 October, Nagy released some political prisoners, the most famous of these being Cardinal Mindszenty.
On 31 October, Nagy's proposed reforms were published. His most controversial decision was his intention to withdraw Hungary from the Warsaw Pact.
On 4 November, Khrushchev decided that Nagy had gone too far, and 200,000 Soviet troops and 6000 tanks returned to Hungary.


### The Soviet invasion

- Khrushchev was anxious not to be seen as weak by other members of the Warsaw Pact.
- Khrushchev was afraid that events in Hungary could encourage similar revolts in other Soviet satellite states.
- Furthermore, Mao Zedong, the Chinese leader, was urging him to stand firm against any deviation from communism.
- Khrushchev was able to keep control, and a new Soviet-backed leader, Kádár, was installed. Nagy was arrested and shot in 1958.

## 6.2 International reaction

- There was very little that the West, especially the USA and Britain, could do to help the Hungarians.
- The West condemned the actions of the Soviet Union, but Hungary was too far away for military intervention.
- The Western powers were keen to avoid military confrontation with the Soviet Union.
- Britain, France and the USA were preoccupied with the Suez Crisis.

**Revision task**

Draw a timeline for the years 1945–56. On the timeline include the key events of the Cold War.

**Exam tip**

The events of 1956 in Hungary are complicated. Ensure you have a thorough understanding of the chronology of that year.

## Memory map

Use the information on the opposite page to create a memory map about the key features of the Hungarian uprising of 1956. Your diagram should include the reasons for the Soviet invasion, the events of the invasion, its importance and consequences.

## You're the examiner

Below is an exam-style question.

**Write a narrative account analysing the key events which increased rivalry between the two superpowers in the years 1949–56.**

**You may use the following information in your answer:**
- **NATO (1949)**
- **The Hungarian Crisis (1956)**

**You must also use information of your own.**

1 Below are a mark scheme and a paragraph which is part of an answer to the question. Read the paragraph and the mark scheme. Decide which level you would award the paragraph. Write the level below, along with a justification for your choice.

**Mark scheme**

| Level | Mark | |
|---|---|---|
| 1 | 1–2 | A simple or generalised narrative is provided, showing limited development, organisation of material and limited knowledge and understanding of the events included |
| 2 | 3–5 | A narrative is given showing some organisation of material into a sequence of events leading to an outcome. The account shows some analysis of the linkage between them but some of the passages may lack coherence and organisation<br><br>Accurate and relevant knowledge is added, showing some knowledge and understanding of the events.<br><br>*Maximum 4 marks for answers that do not go beyond aspects prompted by the stimulus points* |
| 3 | 6–8 | A narrative is given which organises material into a clear sequence of events leading to an outcome. The account of the events analyses the linkage between them and is coherent and logically structured<br><br>Accurate and relevant knowledge is included, showing good knowledge and understanding of the key features or characteristics of the events<br><br>*No access to Level 3 for answers that do not go beyond aspects prompted by the stimulus points* |

**STUDENT ANSWER**

In April 1949, the North Atlantic Treaty was signed. Although a defensive alliance, NATO's main purpose was to prevent Soviet expansion. The USA was now committed to the defence of Western Europe. Stalin did not believe it was a defensive alliance. He believed it was aimed against the Soviet Union. In 1956, the Soviet Union invaded Hungary. Khrushchev did not want to be seen as weak by other members of the Warsaw Pact. He was afraid that events in Hungary could encourage similar revolts in other Soviet satellite states. There was very little that the West, especially the USA and Britain, could do, apart from condemn the actions of the Soviet Union, to help the Hungarians.

Level ☐ Reason ______________________________

______________________________

2 Now suggest what the student has to do with this paragraph to achieve the next level.

______________________________

3 Try and rewrite this paragraph at a higher level.

# Key topic 2 Cold War crises, 1958–70

In the 1960s there were three major crises in the Cold War. Each one greatly increased tension between the superpowers. The first was in 1961 when the Soviet Union constructed the Berlin Wall separating East Berlin from West Berlin. The following year the two superpowers were on the brink of nuclear war due to the Cuban Missile Crisis. The third crisis was in 1968 and was due to developments in Czechoslovakia.

## 1 Increased tension over Berlin, 1958–61

REVISED

The Soviet Union's desire to remove the Western Allies from Berlin created a crisis in 1961.

### 1.1 Problems in East Germany

Even after 1949, Berlin continued to pose a problem for the USA and Soviet Union:

- Between 1949 and 1961, about 4 million East Germans fled to the West through Berlin. Khrushchev wanted the removal of the Allies because West Berlin was an area of capitalist prosperity and symbolised the success of Western Europe within communist territory.
- The Soviet Union also claimed that the USA and its Allies used West Berlin as a base for espionage.

#### The Berlin Ultimatum

In 1958, Khrushchev issued the Berlin **Ultimatum**. He accused the Allies of breaking the Potsdam Agreement, and told them that they should leave Berlin within six months. The US president, Eisenhower, seemed prepared to negotiate. He did not want to risk a war over Berlin.

#### Summit meetings, 1959–61

- In May 1959, the Geneva Summit of Foreign Ministers failed to reach agreement on the problem of Berlin.
- In September 1959, Khrushchev visited the USA to attend a summit meeting at Camp David. Disarmament was discussed and they agreed on a further summit meeting over Berlin.
- Khrushchev and Eisenhower were set to meet in Paris on 14 May 1960. Nine days before the **summit conference** was due to open, the Soviet Union announced that it had shot down an American U-2 spy plane near the city of Sverdlovsk. The pilot was captured and put on trial.
- Khrushchev demanded that all such flights stop and that the USA apologise for spying. Eisenhower would not and Khrushchev stormed out of the first session.
- At the Vienna summit of June 1961, Khrushchev again demanded that Western forces leave West Berlin. The new US president, **Kennedy**, refused.

### 1.2 The Berlin Wall, 1961

The differences over Berlin worsened in 1961 with the building of the Berlin Wall:

- On 13 August 1961, Khrushchev closed the border between East and West Berlin. East German troops and workers installed barbed-wire entanglements and fences.
- The USA and its Allies did nothing to stop the building of a wall.
- Over time, East German officials replaced the makeshift wall with one that was sturdier and more difficult to scale.

**Key terms**

**Summit conference** A meeting of heads of state or government, usually with considerable media exposure and tight security

**Ultimatum** A final demand or statement of terms, the rejection of which will result in retaliation or a breakdown in relations

**Key individual**

**John F. Kennedy** Won the US presidential election of 1960 and was the US leader during the Berlin Crisis of 1961 and the Cuban Missile Crisis of 1962. He was determined to get tough with communism but his presidency was short-lived as he was assassinated in 1963

**Revision task**

Prioritise the consequences of the events of the early 1960s in Berlin.

**Exam tip**

Ensure you do not confuse the events of 1961 with the Berlin Crisis of 1948–49.

## Consequences

- Peace was maintained, but at a price for the German people. Families were split, and travel restrictions made it very difficult for relatives to see one another.
- The construction of the Berlin Wall led to a serious stand-off between the two superpowers.
- President Kennedy worked behind the scenes to avoid conflict. He promised Khrushchev that if the Soviet Union removed its troops, the USA would do the same. This ended the stand-off.
- The flow of refugees was stopped.
- President Kennedy visited West Germany in 1963. He declared that the city was a symbol of the struggle between the forces of freedom and the communist world and coined the famous phrase '*Ich bin ein Berliner*' ('I am a Berliner').

### Identifying consequences

Below is an exam-style question.

**Explain two consequences of the Berlin Crisis of 1961.**

In answering this question, it is important that you focus on consequence. In the table below are statements about the Berlin Crisis. Identify (with a tick in the appropriate column) whether they are causes, events or consequences of the Berlin Crisis.

| Statement | Cause | Event | Consequence |
|---|---|---|---|
| The flow of refugees was stopped. It led to the Cuban Missile Crisis of 1962 | | | |
| On 13 August 1961, Khrushchev closed the border between East and West Berlin | | | |
| The construction of the Berlin Wall led to a serious stand-off between the two superpowers | | | |
| Between 1949 and 1961, about 4 million East Germans fled to the West through Berlin | | | |
| The East German officials replaced the makeshift wall with one that was sturdier and more difficult to scale | | | |
| It led to the Cuban Missile Crisis of 1962 | | | |
| East German troops and workers installed barbed-wire entanglements and fences | | | |
| The Soviet Union claimed that the USA and its Allies used West Berlin as a base for espionage | | | |

### How important

Here is an exam-style question:

**Explain the importance of the Berlin Crisis (1961) for the development of the Cold War.**

Below is a table showing the importance of the Berlin Crisis. Copy and complete the table by:

- making a decision about how important each factor was in the development of the Cold War
- briefly explaining each decision.

| Factor | Very important | Important | Quite important |
|---|---|---|---|
| Berlin Wall | | | |
| The Paris Summit, 1960 | | | |
| Kennedy's visit to Berlin | | | |

# 2 The Cuban Missile Crisis

REVISED

The Cuban Missile Crisis was the most serious crisis of the Cold War, with the two superpowers close to nuclear war.

## 2.1 Increased tension over Cuba

- The USA had strong economic interests in Cuba and controlled most of Cuba's industry, railways and electricity production.
- In 1959, Fidel Castro led a successful revolution against the unpopular and repressive military dictator of Cuba, General Batista, who had been under the influence of the USA.
- Castro wanted greater independence from the USA and took all American property that was located in Cuba. In response, the USA banned the import of Cuban sugar, which threatened to bankrupt the Cuban economy.
- The USA, aware that Castro had some connections to communism, refused to acknowledge his government. Castro removed US influence from Cuba and moved closer to the Soviet Union. The Soviet Union offered to buy Cuban sugar and to provide machinery and technological help.

### The Bay of Pigs incident

- In 1961, the USA organised an attempt to overthrow Castro, known as the Bay of Pigs invasion. This was a total failure for President Kennedy. The **CIA** had been convinced that the Cuban people would revolt against Castro. However, they underestimated his popularity and there was no uprising.
- As a result of this failure, Castro grew closer to the Soviet leader, Khrushchev, and, in May 1962, agreed to station Soviet nuclear weapons on Cuba. On 14 October, an American U-2 spy plane took photos revealing that missile sites were being built.

**Key term**

**CIA** Central Intelligence Agency: the arm of the US government tasked with espionage and intelligence activities

**Revision task**

Draw a table which includes the USA, the Soviet Union and Cuba. In the table, explain what each country gained from the Cuban Missile Crisis. Which country do you think gained the most from the crisis?

**Exam tip**

The Cuban Missile Crisis is a popular exam topic. Ensure you thoroughly revise the causes, events and results.

## 2.2 Events of the Cuban Missile Crisis

| Days in October 1962 | Events |
|---|---|
| 16 | Kennedy was told that Khrushchev intended to build missile sites in Cuba |
| 18–19 | Kennedy held talks with his closest advisers. The 'Hawks' wanted an aggressive policy, while the 'Doves' favoured a peaceful solution |
| 20 | Kennedy decided to impose a naval blockade around Cuba to prevent Soviet missiles and equipment reaching Cuba. The Americans searched any ship suspected of carrying arms or missiles |
| 21 | Kennedy made a broadcast to the American people, informing them of the potential threat and what he intended to do |
| 23 | Khrushchev sent a letter to Kennedy insisting that Soviet ships would force their way through the blockade |
| 24 | Khrushchev issued a statement insisting that the Soviet Union would use nuclear weapons in the event of a war |
| 25 | Kennedy wrote to Khrushchev asking him to withdraw missiles from Cuba |
| 26 | Khrushchev replied to Kennedy's letter. He said he would withdraw the missiles if the USA promised not to invade Cuba and to withdraw its missiles from Turkey |
| 27 | A US spy plane was shot down over Cuba. Attorney General Robert Kennedy (brother of the president) proposed a deal with the Soviet Union. The USA would withdraw missiles from Turkey as long as it was kept secret |
| 28 | Khrushchev accepted the deal |

## Consequences

The superpowers had almost gone to war: a war that would have destroyed much of the world. However, the crisis did lead to better relations:

- The 'hotline': to ensure that the two leaders could communicate more quickly and directly, a hotline telephone link was established between the White House and the Kremlin.
- The Limited Test Ban Treaty, 1963: both the USA and the Soviet Union agreed to stop testing nuclear weapons above ground and underwater.
- The Outer Space Treaty 1967: the two superpowers, together with Britain and several other countries promised to use outer space for peaceful purposes and not to place nuclear weapons in orbit.
- The Nuclear Non-proliferation Treaty, 1968: this was designed to stop the spread of nuclear weapons.
- Relations between the two superpowers also improved with the USA selling grain to the Soviet Union.

## You're the examiner

Below is an exam-style question.

**Write a narrative account analysing the key events of 1959–62 which led to the Cuban Missile Crisis (1962).**

> **You may use the following information in your answer.**
> ■ **Castro becomes leader** ■ **The Bay of Pigs invasion (1961)**
> **You must also use information of your own.**

1 Below is a paragraph which is part of an answer to the question. Read the paragraph and use the mark scheme on page 15. Decide which level you would award the paragraph. Write the level below, along with a justification for your choice.

**STUDENT ANSWER**

*Castro removed American influence from Cuba and moved closer to the Soviet Union. Khrushchev and the Soviet Union increased their influence in Cuba when they offered to buy Cuban sugar and to provide machinery and technological help. In 1959, Castro had led a successful revolution against the military dictator of Cuba, General Batista, who had been very much under the influence of America. The USA did not like Castro and the influence of the Soviet Union in Cuba. The USA organised an attempt to overthrow Castro, known as the Bay of Pigs invasion, to remove Castro. This failed because the CIA had been convinced that the Cuban people would revolt against Castro but they did not. The Cuban Missile Crisis then started.*

Level ☐ Reason ______________________________

______________________________

2 Now suggest what the student has to do to achieve a higher level.

______________________________

______________________________

3 Try and rewrite this paragraph at a higher level.

# 3 The Soviet invasion of Czechoslovakia, 1968

REVISED

This severely tested closer relations between the superpowers.

## 3.1 Increased tension over Czechoslovakia

In the 1960s there was growing opposition to Soviet control for several reasons:

- Antonín Novotný had been the Czech leader since 1957. He was unpopular because he was a hardline communist who refused to introduce reform.
- The Czech economy was in serious decline in the 1960s. This led to a fall in the standard of living. Novotný's attempts at economic reform were unsuccessful.
- Many Czechs began to demand greater democracy, including **Alexander Dubček**.

## 3.2 The Prague Spring

The 'Prague Spring' refers to a series of reforms introduced by Dubček in the spring of 1968. The reforms included:

- Greater political freedom including free speech and the abolition of press censorship.
- The powers of the secret police to arrest without trial were reduced.
- Travel restrictions were removed and fresh contact was made with the West, such as trade with West Germany.
- More power to regional governments and to the Czech parliament.
- The introduction of elements of capitalism in the economy.
- The production of new literature supporting the changes.
- The creation of works councils representing the workforce to improve working conditions in factories and increased rights for trade unions.
- A ten-year programme for political change which would bring about democratic elections, and create a new form of democratic socialism.

Dubček's reforms, however, encouraged the growth of opposition to communism and demands for even more radical reforms.

## 3.3 Re-establishing Soviet control

The Soviet Union was suspicious of the changes taking place in Czechoslovakia:

- **Brezhnev** was worried that Czechoslovakia might leave the Warsaw Pact and that NATO might move in.
- Brezhnev came under pressure from the East German leader, Walter Ulbricht, and the Polish leader, Gomułka, to stop reform in Czechoslovakia.

### Key features of invasion

- On 20–21 August 1968, thousands of Warsaw Pact troops entered Czechoslovakia.
- Czechs threw petrol bombs at the Soviet tanks as they moved through Prague. Buildings were set on fire and protesters assembled in Wenceslas Square.
- Dubček and the other leaders were arrested and taken to Moscow, and forced to accept the end of the Czech moves towards democracy.

### Key individuals

**Leonid Brezhnev**
Succeeded Khrushchev as leader of the Soviet Union in 1964. He remained as leader until his death in 1982. He supported the policy of *détente* and ordered the invasion of Afghanistan in 1979, which ended this policy and led to the Second Cold War

**Alexander Dubček**
A Slovak politician and, briefly, leader of Czechoslovakia. He attempted to reform the Communist regime during the Prague Spring of 1968 but he was forced to resign following the Warsaw Pact invasion of Czechoslovakia. In 1969 he was removed as leader. He was killed in a car accident in 1992

### Revision task

Place the following events in chronological order:

- Soviet invasion of Czechoslovakia
- Jan Palach set himself on fire
- Prague Spring
- Brezhnev Doctrine.

Give a brief explanation of the importance of each.

### Exam tip

You may well be asked to explain key developments in Czechoslovakia in 1968 or the consequences of the Soviet invasion. Ensure you thoroughly revise this crisis.

### Consequences of Soviet invasion

| States | Consequence |
|---|---|
| Czechoslovakia | Demonstrations against the Soviet invasion went on until April 1969. In January 1969, Jan Palach, a student, set fire to himself in Wenceslas Square to protest against the Soviet invasion |
| Soviet Union | It gave rise to the Brezhnev Doctrine. This redefined communism as a one-party state where all member countries had to remain part of the Warsaw Pact. It also sent out a message to the members of the Warsaw Pact that the Soviet Union would suppress any attempt to relax Communist control |
| Warsaw Pact states | Some Communist countries began to move away from Moscow. President Ceausescu of Romania refused to send troops to join the forces invading Czechoslovakia |

## 3.4 International reaction

The Soviet invasion temporarily worsened relations between East and West. The West, especially Britain and the USA, protested at Soviet actions. The USA did nothing else because they were preoccupied with the war in Vietnam.

Western European countries followed the USA's lead – they condemned the invasion but provided no military help. Western European Communist parties in Italy and France were outraged by the Soviet invasion.

### Relevance

Below are an exam-style question and a series of statements on the Soviet invasion of Czechoslovakia. Decide which statements are:

- relevant to the question (R)
- partially relevant to the question (PR)
- irrelevant to the question (I).

Tick the appropriate column.

**Explain two consequences of the Soviet invasion of Czechoslovakia (1968).**

| Statements | R | PR | I |
|---|---|---|---|
| The Soviet invasion temporarily worsened relations between East and West | | | |
| In the 1960s, there was growing opposition to Soviet control of Czechoslovakia | | | |
| Western European countries condemned the invasion but provided no military help | | | |
| Some Communists, including Ceausescu of Romania, began to move away from Moscow | | | |
| On 20–21 August 1968, hundreds and thousands of Warsaw Pact troops entered Czechoslovakia | | | |
| Czechs threw petrol bombs at the Soviet tanks as they moved through Prague | | | |
| Novotný had been the Czech leader since 1957 and was unpopular because he was a hardline Communist | | | |
| It gave rise to the Brezhnev Doctrine. This redefined communism as a one-party state | | | |
| Many Czechs began to demand greater democracy, including Dubček | | | |
| During the Soviet invasion, buildings were set on fire and protesters assembled in Wenceslas Square | | | |
| The 'Prague Spring' refers to a series of reforms introduced by Dubček in the spring of 1968 | | | |
| In January 1969, Jan Palach, a student, set fire to himself in Wenceslas Square to protest against the Soviet invasion | | | |

Now write an answer to this question.

# Key topic 3 The end of the Cold War, 1970–91

Cold War relations changed greatly during these years. During the 1970s, the policy of *détente* improved East–West relations. However, the Soviet Union's invasion of Afghanistan in 1979 brought about the Second Cold War. By 1989, the leaders of the USA and the Soviet Union had announced that the Cold War was over.

## 1 Attempts to reduce tension between East and West 1

REVISED

After the Cuban Missile Crisis there was a move to improve relations and relax tension between the USA and Soviet Union. This became known as *détente* or a policy of **thaw**.

### 1.1 *Détente* in the 1970s

*Détente* emerged due to developments in the late 1960s and early 1970s:

- The threat of a nuclear war during the Cuban Missile Crisis had had a sobering effect on all concerned.
- Both the USA and the Soviet Union were keen on arms limitation talks in order to reduce their ever-increasing defence spending.
- By 1968, the USA was seeking to end the war. After **Richard Nixon** became president, it was hoped that if the USA improved trade and technology links and made an offer of arms reduction, then Brezhnev might persuade his North Vietnamese ally to negotiate an end to the war. The idea of offering concessions was called 'linkage' by Nixon's advisers.
- Nixon had visited China three months earlier and Brezhnev did not want to see a Chinese–US alliance develop. The Soviet leader was keen to gain access to US technology and further grain sales.

### 1.2 SALT 1

The Strategic Arms Limitation Talks (**SALT** 1) began in 1969 and were completed in May 1972:

- The two superpowers agreed that there would be no further production of strategic **ballistic** missiles (short-range, lightweight missiles).
- Both powers agreed that submarines carrying nuclear weapons would only be introduced when existing stocks of intercontinental ballistic missiles (ICBMs) became obsolete.

SALT 1 was significant because it was the first agreement between the superpowers that successfully limited the number of nuclear weapons they held.

### 1.3 The Helsinki Agreements

These were signed in 1975. The USA and the USSR, along with 33 other nations, made declarations about three distinct international issues (called 'baskets' by the signatories).

| Security | Cooperation | Human rights |
|---|---|---|
| Recognition of Europe's frontiers<br>The Soviet Union accepted the existence of West Germany | There was a call for closer economic, scientific and cultural links – these would lead to even closer political agreement | Each signatory agreed to respect human rights and basic freedoms such as thought, speech, religion and freedom from unfair arrest |

**Key terms**

**Ballistic** The flight of an object through space, such as rockets that are fired from weapons. A ballistic missile is guided only when it is first launched

***Détente*** The relaxing of tension or hostility between nations

**SALT** Strategic Arms Limitation Talks: attempts by the USA and the Soviet Union to agree to limit the arms race

**Thaw** A period of improved relations between East and West

**Key individual**

**Richard Nixon** Served as US president from 1969 until his resignation in 1974. He was responsible for improved relations with both China and the Soviet Union

**Exam tip**

*Détente* is the least well-known period of the Cold War. Ensure you know what it means and its key features.

## 1.4 SALT 2

SALT 2 began in 1974 and the treaty was signed in June 1979. The terms were:

- A limit of 2400 strategic nuclear delivery vehicles for each side.
- A limit of 1320 multiple independently targetable re-entry vehicle (MIRV) systems for each side.
- A ban on the construction of new land-based ICBM launchers.
- The agreement would last until 1985.

However, the US Senate refused to ratify the SALT 2 agreements following the Soviet invasion of Afghanistan in December 1979 (see page 114).

### Revision task

How did the following improve relations between the superpowers?

- SALT 1
- the Helsinki Agreements
- SALT 2.

### Organising knowledge

Use the information on pages 22–23 to complete the table below to summarise the key features of *détente*.

| | |
|---|---|
| Meaning of *détente* | |
| SALT 1 | |
| Helsinki Agreements | |
| SALT 2 | |

### Linking events

Below are an exam-style question and a series of statements:

- Place the statements in the correct sequence.
- Show links between the events. You could use link phrases such as 'this led to', 'as a result of this'.

**You may use the following information in your answer:**

- **SALT 1 (1971)**
- **Helsinki Agreements (1975)**

**You must also use information of your own.**

**Write a narrative account analysing the key events of *détente* in the 1970s.**

| Statement | Order | Linking statements |
|---|---|---|
| The Helsinki Agreements were signed in 1975. The USA and the Soviet Union, along with 33 other nations, made declarations about three distinct international issues | | |
| The Strategic Arms Limitation Talks began in 1969 and were completed three years later | | |
| Each signatory at Helsinki agreed to respect human rights and basic freedoms such as thought, speech, religion and freedom from unfair arrest | | |
| SALT 2 was signed in June 1979. However, the US Senate refused to ratify the SALT 2 agreements following the Soviet invasion of Afghanistan in December 1979 | | |
| In 1975 there was a joint space mission in which an American Apollo spacecraft and a Soviet Soyuz spacecraft docked high above Earth. This marked the beginning of superpower cooperation in space | | |
| The two superpowers agreed that there would be no further production of strategic ballistic missiles and that submarines carrying nuclear weapons would only be introduced when existing stocks of intercontinental ballistic missiles became obsolete | | |
| At Helsinki there was a recognition of Europe's frontiers. The Soviet Union accepted the existence of West Germany | | |

# 2 Attempts to reduce tension between East and West 2

REVISED

## 2.1 Gorbachev's 'new thinking'

**Mikhail Gorbachev** was the last leader of the Soviet Union and was prepared to adopt drastic policies to improve superpower relations. He had to attempt to improve the relationship, as he knew that, without change, the Soviet Union would collapse.

Gorbachev's 'new thinking' involved three important strategies which greatly changed relationships with the West:

- he initiated sweeping reforms in the Communist Party and Soviet system in the USSR:
  - *perestroika* (restructuring) included economic reforms designed to make the Soviet economy more efficient
  - *glasnost* (openness) ensured censorship of the press was relaxed
- he ended the arms race with the USA and signed various arms reduction agreements
- he stopped Soviet interference in Eastern European satellite states such as Poland and Czechoslovakia.

## 2.2 The summit conferences

A series of summit meetings took place in the years 1985–90 to discuss arms limitations.

| Meeting | Result |
|---|---|
| Geneva, November 1985 | Although nothing was decided, the Geneva Accord was set out which committed the USA and Soviet Union to speed up arms talks. Both Gorbachev and US President **Ronald Reagan** promised to meet in the near future. It was clear to many observers that the two men had got on well |
| Reykjavík, 1986 | The leaders failed to reach agreement on arms limitation |
| Washington, December 1987 | This was more successful and the **Intermediate Nuclear Forces (INF) Treaty** was signed (see below) |
| Washington, 1990 | President Bush and Gorbachev agreed on the Treaty for the Reduction and Limitation of Strategic Arms (START) in which they agreed to reduce their strategic forces over seven years |

## 2.3 The INF Treaty, 1987

- The INF Treaty eliminated nuclear and conventional ground-launched ballistic and cruise missiles with ranges of 500–5500 kilometres (300–3400 miles). By the treaty's deadline, 1 June 1991, a total of 2692 of such weapons had been destroyed, 846 by the USA and 1846 by the Soviet Union.
- Also under the treaty, both nations were allowed to inspect each other's military installations.
- It was the first treaty to reduce the number of nuclear missiles that the superpowers possessed. It therefore went much further than SALT 1 (see page 110), which simply limited the growth of Soviet and US stockpiles.

### Key individuals

**Mikhail Gorbachev** Served as leader of the Soviet Union from 1985 until 1991. During this period he reformed the Soviet Union through his policies of *glasnost* and *perestroika*, improved relations with the USA and was mainly responsible for the ending of the Cold War

**Ronald Reagan** Served as US president from 1981 to 1989. At first he was determined to 'get tough' with the Soviet Union and communism but this approach softened in the later 1980s due to closer relations with Gorbachev

### Key term

**Intermediate-Range Nuclear Forces (INF) Treaty** A treaty between the USA and the Soviet Union for the elimination of their intermediate- and short-range missiles.

### Revision task

Put the following key developments in chronological order:

- Reykjavík summit
- INF
- Geneva summit.

Give a brief explanation of the importance of each for the Cold War.

### Exam tip

You will not need detailed knowledge of Gorbachev's policies in the Soviet Union but an understanding of how they affected relations with the USA

## Memory map

Use the information on page 24 to add details to the diagram below about the consequences and importance of Gorbachev's new thinking, the summit conferences and the INF.

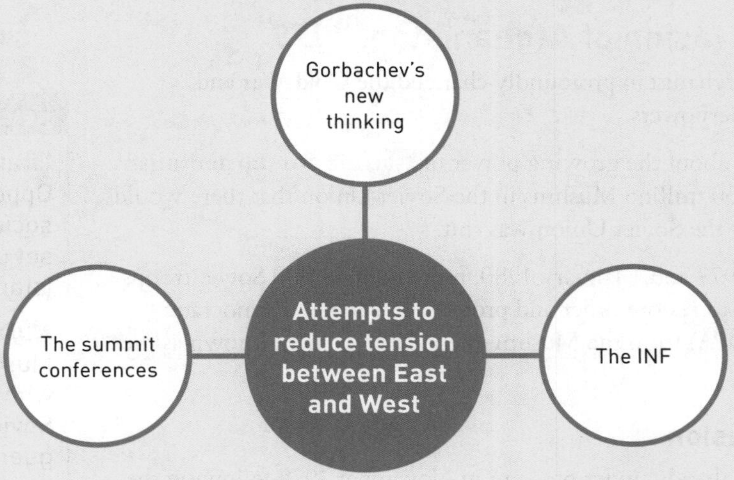

## Concentric circles

In the concentric circles below, rank order the importance of the summit conferences of the later 1980s and early 1990s for the Cold War, beginning with the most important in the middle to the least important on the outside. Explain your decisions.

- Geneva, 1985
- Reykjavík, 1986
- Washington, 1987
- Washington, 1990.

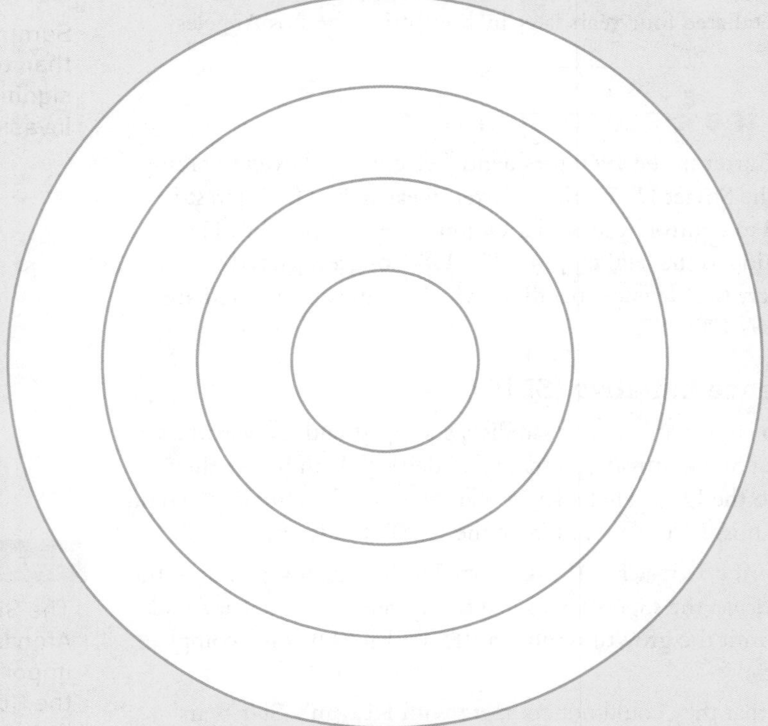

# 3 Flashpoints

REVISED

The attempts at *détente* in the 1970s had been quite serious, but there were a number of flashpoints in the world where the superpowers were at loggerheads.

## 3.1 The Soviet invasion of Afghanistan, 1979

The Soviet invasion of Afghanistan profoundly changed the Cold War and relations between the superpowers.

Brezhnev was concerned about the growing power of **Islamic fundamentalism** and wanted to show the 30 million Muslims in the Soviet Union that there would be no changes in the way the Soviet Union was run.

Between 25 December 1979 and 1 January 1980, more than 50,000 Soviet troops were sent to Afghanistan to restore order and protect the People's Democratic Party of Afghanistan (PDPA) from the Muslim guerrilla movement known as the ***mujahideen***.

### Significance of invasion

US President Carter was already under pressure in November 1979 following the seizure of US embassy staff as hostages in Iran. He had failed to solve that problem by the end of the year, and some in the USA were accusing him of being a weak leader. He therefore made a firm approach with the Soviet Union over the invasion:

- The Carter Doctrine stated that the USA would use military force if necessary to defend its national interests, especially oil interests, in the Persian Gulf region. It also promised US military aid to all the countries bordering Afghanistan.
- The tough line was continued when Carter asked the Senate not to ratify the SALT 2 treaty.
- Carter pressured the US Olympic Committee to boycott the Moscow Olympic Games of 1980. Sixty-one other countries followed the USA's example.
- The Soviet Union retaliated four years later by boycotting the Los Angeles Olympic Games.

## 3.2 Reagan and the 'Second Cold War'

Reagan, who defeated Carter in the 1980 presidential election, believed in taking a far tougher line with the Soviet Union than Carter. Reagan had no interest in *détente* and was prepared to confront the Soviet Union whenever possible. He described the Soviet Union as the 'evil empire'. The US Congress agreed to Reagan's demand for increased defence spending, which would cost more than a trillion dollars in the years 1981–87.

### The Strategic Defence Initiative (SDI)

- Reagan's plan was to launch an army of satellites equipped with powerful lasers which could intercept Soviet missiles in space and destroy them before they could do any harm to the USA. He believed that 'Star Wars' technology would make Soviet nuclear missiles useless and force the USSR to disarm.
- The **Strategic Defence Initiative (SDI)** proved to be a turning point in the arms race. During *détente*, the superpowers had been evenly matched and had worked together to limit the growth of nuclear stockpiles. SDI was a complete break from this policy.
- Soviet leaders knew that they could not compete with Reagan's 'Star Wars' plan. They were behind the USA in space and computer technology and the Soviet economy was not producing enough wealth to fund even more defence spending.

**Key terms**

**Islamic fundamentalism** Opposes secular Western society and seeks to set up a state based on Islamic law

***Mujahideen*** Afghan Muslim freedom fighters who fought against the Soviet occupation using guerrilla tactics

**Strategic Defence Initiative (SDI)** Also known as 'Star Wars', the plan was to develop a sophisticated anti-ballistic missile system in order to prevent missile attacks from other countries, specifically the Soviet Union

**Revision task**

Summarise in no more than ten words the significance of the Soviet invasion of Afghanistan.

**Exam tip**

The Soviet invasion of Afghanistan is a very important turning point in the Cold War. Ensure you have thorough knowledge of its features and significance.

## RAG: Rate the timeline

Below are an exam-style question and a timeline. Read the question, study the timeline and, using three coloured pens, put a **red**, **amber** or **green** star next to the events to show:

**Red:** events and policies that have **no** relevance to the question

**Amber:** events and policies that have **some** significance to the question

**Green:** events and policies that have **direct** relevance to the question

**Explain two of the following:**

- **The importance of the invasion of Afghanistan (1979) for relations between the USA and the Soviet Union.**
- **The importance of the SDI for relations between the USA and the Soviet Union.**
- **The importance of the Olympic Games of 1980 and 1984 for relations between the USA and the Soviet Union.**

| | |
|---|---|
| 1972 | **1972** SALT 1 signed |
| 1974 | **1974** Nixon visited Moscow |
| 1975 | **1975** The Helsinki Agreements |
| 1979 | **1979** SALT 2 signed; **1979** Soviet invasion of Afghanistan; **1979** Carter Doctrine; **1979** US Congress refused to ratify SALT 2 |
| 1980 | **1980** USA boycotted Moscow Olympics |
| 1981 | **1981** Reagan became US president and described the Soviet Union as the 'evil empire' |
| 1983 | **1983** Reagan announced the Strategic Defence Initiative |
| 1984 | **1984** USSR boycotted Los Angeles Olympics |
| 1985 | **1985** Reagan and Gorbachev met for the first time at the Geneva summit |
| 1986 | **1986** Reykjavík summit |
| 1987 | **1987** Intermediate Nuclear Forces Treaty |
| 1989 | **1989** Pulling down of the Berlin Wall |
| 1990 | **1990** START; **1990** Baltic states of Estonia, Latvia and Lithuania declared themselves independent; **1990** Collapse of the Soviet Union |
| 1991 | **1991** Gorbachev resigned; **1991** Warsaw Pact was formally ended |

## Develop the detail

Below is part of an answer to the first option in the question above. The paragraph contains a limited amount of detail. Annotate the paragraph to add additional detail to the answer.

The invasion of Afghanistan was important because it ended the period of *détente* and increased rivalry between the Soviet Union and the USA. It was important because it led to the Carter Doctrine. It was also important because it led to the USA boycotting the Moscow Olympics of 1980.

# 4 The collapse of Soviet control of Eastern Europe 1

REVISED

In the Soviet Union, Gorbachev's reforms (see page 112) encouraged criticism and eventually the downfall of Gorbachev, as well as the break-up of the Soviet Union and the end of the Warsaw Pact.

## 4.1 The impact of Gorbachev's 'new thinking' on Eastern Europe

The Soviet economy could no longer stand the strain of supporting forces in Eastern Europe.

In 1988, Gorbachev rejected the Brezhnev Doctrine and in 1989 he accepted that members of the Warsaw Pact could make changes to their own countries without expecting outside interference. This became known as the Sinatra Doctrine.

1988: strikes throughout the country

1989: free trade union – Solidarity – won elections. Mazowiecki became the first non-Communist prime minister in Eastern Europe

October 1989: Gorbachev visited East Germany and told them that Soviet troops would not put down East German demonstrations

23 October: 300,000 protested in Leipzig

4 November: 1 million protested in East Berlin

9 November: Berlin Wall pulled down

1991: Germany reunified as one country

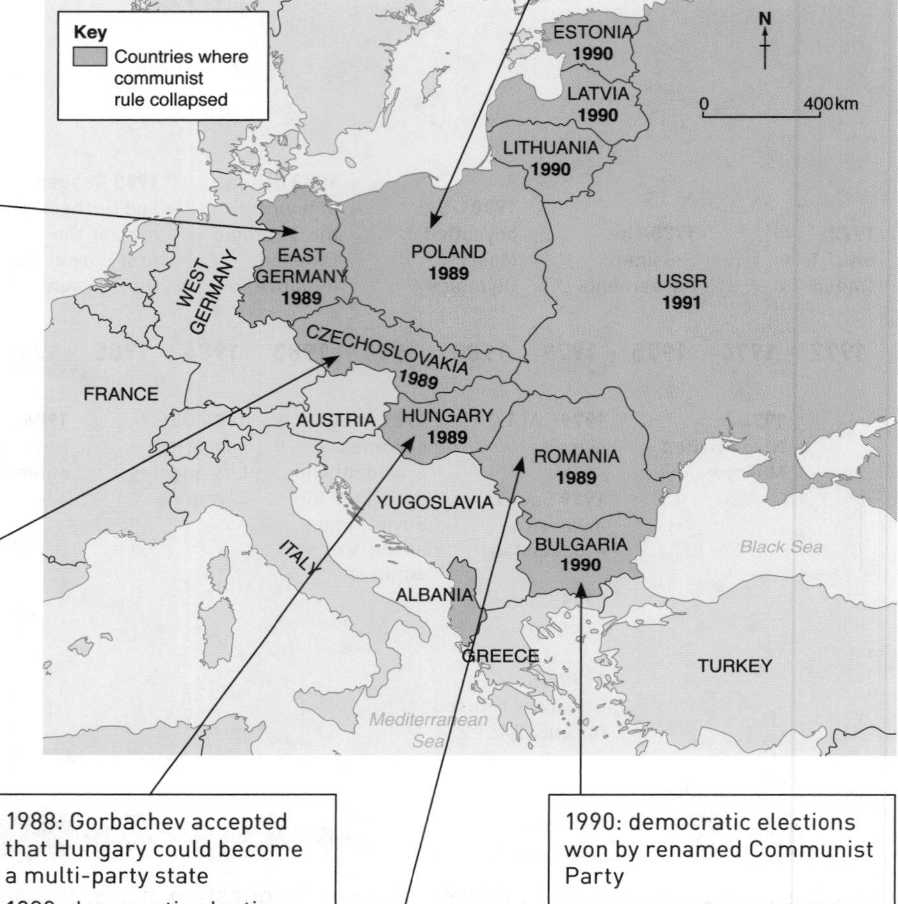


'The Velvet Revolution': a bloodless revolution that brought about the overthrow of the Communist government

17 November 1989: huge demonstrations against communism

24 November 1989: Communist government resigned

9 December 1989: Havel became the first non-Communist Czech president since 1948

1990: democratic elections won by Civic Forum – an alliance of non-Communist groups

1988: Gorbachev accepted that Hungary could become a multi-party state

1989: democratic elections won by Democratic Forum, an alliance of non-Communist groups

21 October 1989: the opening of Hungary's borders to East Germans and the West

1990: democratic elections won by renamed Communist Party

16 December 1989: secret police fired on demonstrators

21 December 1989: huge crowd in Bucharest booed President Ceausescu who fled but was later captured

1990: democratic elections won by National Salvation Front containing many non-Communists

## Organising knowledge

Use the information on page 28 to complete the table below to show developments in each country in the years 1988–91 as a result of Gorbachev's new thinking and their importance.

| State | Developments | Importance |
|---|---|---|
| Poland | | |
| Czechoslovakia | | |
| East Germany | | |
| Romania | | |
| Bulgaria | | |
| Hungary | | |

## Venn diagram

Complete the Venn diagram below showing the consequences of Gorbachev's policies for:

- the Soviet Union
- Eastern Europe
- the Cold War.

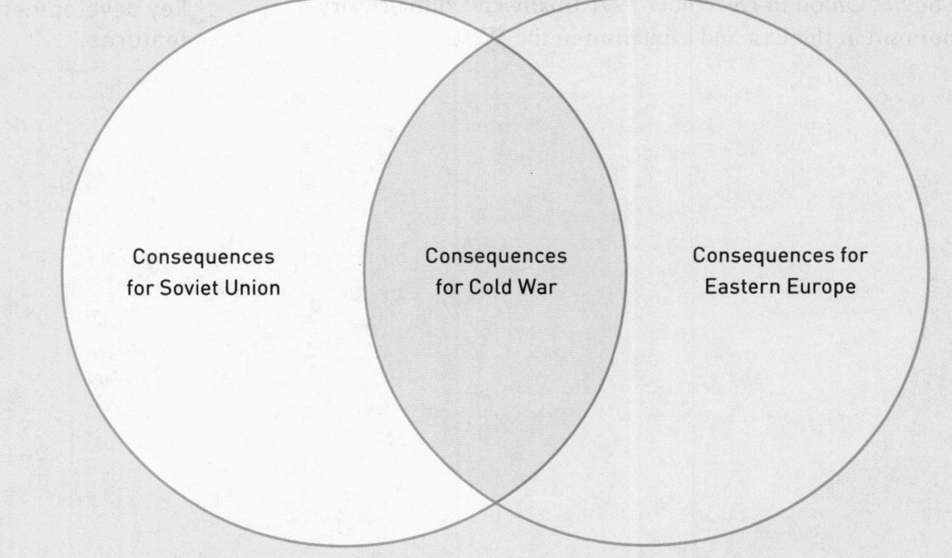

# 5 The collapse of Soviet control of Eastern Europe 2

REVISED

## 5.1 The fall of the Berlin Wall

- On 9 November 1989, the East German government announced the opening of the border crossings into West Germany. The people began to dismantle the Berlin Wall.
- Within a few days, over 1 million people had seized the chance to see relatives and experience life in West Germany. West and East Germany were formally reunited in October 1990.

## 5.2 The collapse of the Soviet Union

- Events in Eastern Europe had a catastrophic impact on the Soviet Union. The many nationalities and ethnic groups saw how the satellite states had been able to break away from Moscow.
- In 1990, the Baltic states of Estonia, Latvia and Lithuania declared themselves independent, which was accepted by Moscow in 1991. This led to other demands for independence within the Soviet Union.
- Gorbachev found that he was opposed by most sections of Soviet society. In August 1991, there was an attempted ***coup d'état*** which was defeated by Boris Yeltsin, who was president of the Russian Socialist Republic. Gorbachev was restored but he had lost his authority. Gorbachev resigned in December 1991 and the Soviet Union split into several independent states. Now there was only one superpower left – the USA.

## 5.3 The end of the Warsaw Pact and Cold War

In 1989, US President Bush had declared at the Malta Conference that the Cold War was over. However, communism was still undefeated and the Russian coup of August 1991 which overthrew Gorbachev could well have revived rivalry with the West.

- As Soviet control of Eastern Europe fell away, it became obvious that the Warsaw Pact could not survive.
- First Poland, then Hungary and finally East Germany all rejected communism and the Pact no longer served any purpose. Military cooperation stopped in early 1990 and the Warsaw Pact was formally ended in July 1991.
- The fall of the Soviet Union in December 1991 finally ended the rivalry between communism in the East and capitalism in the West.

**Key term**

***Coup d'état*** Armed rebellion or revolt against the existing government

### Revision task

Explain why Gorbachev was so liked and so hated at the same time.

**Exam tip**

Events in Eastern Europe and the Soviet Union, 1988–91, are complicated. Make sure you understand the key developments and features.

## Complete the paragraph

Below are an exam-style question and a paragraph which is part of an answer to this question. Complete the paragraph by providing a further explanation about each consequence.

**Explain two consequences of the collapse of the Soviet Union.**

*One consequence of the collapse of the Soviet Union was the ending of the Cold War. A second consequence was the break-up of the Soviet Union.*

## How important

Complete the table below.

- Briefly summarise the importance of each factor in bringing an end to the Cold War.
- Make a decision about the importance of each factor in bringing an end to the Cold War. Give a brief explanation for each choice.

| Factor | Key features | Decisive/Important/Quite important |
| --- | --- | --- |
| Gorbachev's 'new thinking' | | |
| Summit conferences | | |
| Fall of the Berlin Wall | | |
| INF | | |
| Collapse of the Soviet Union | | |

# Exam focus

Your History GCSE is made up of three exams:

- Paper 1 on a thematic study and historic environment.
- Paper 2 on a British depth study and a period study, in your case Superpower relations and the Cold War, 1941–91.
- Paper 3 on a modern depth study.

For the period study on Paper 2 you have to answer the following types of questions. Each requires you to demonstrate different historical skills:

- **Question 1** is a consequence question in which you have to explain two consequences of a given development or event.
- **Question 2** is a narrative question. You have to write an account which analyses events or developments during a given period in the Cold War and support each with detail. You can choose to write about the two given events, but you must also write about an event or development of your own.
- **Question 3** is an importance question. You are asked to make a judgement on the importance of two different events/developments, supported by a precise and developed explanation.

The table below gives a summary of the question types for Paper 2 and what you need to do.

| Question number | Marks | Key words | You need to ... |
|---|---|---|---|
| 1 | 8 | Explain **two** consequences of | • Ensure you focus on consequence<br>• Fully explain each consequence |
| 2 | 8 | Write a narrative account analysing ... You may use the following in your answer: [two given events/developments].<br>You **must** also use information of your own | • Analyse at least three events/ developments<br>• Fully explain each with supporting detail |
| 3 | 16 | Explain **two** of the following:<br>• The importance of ... for the ...<br>• The importance of ... for the ...<br>• The importance of ... for the ... | • Choose two of the three developments<br>• Ensure that you focus on importance<br>• Fully explain its importance using precise evidence |

## Question 1: Consequence

Below is an example exam-style consequence question. It is worth 8 marks.

**Explain two consequences of Gorbachev's 'new thinking'.**

### How to answer

- Underline key points in the question. This will ensure that you focus sharply on what is required.
- Identify two consequences of Gorbachev's 'new thinking'.
- Begin each paragraph by stating the consequence. For example, 'One consequence of Gorbachev's "new thinking" was … .'
- Give a fully developed explanation about the consequence including precise details.
- State the second consequence. For example, 'A further consequence of Gorbachev's "new thinking" was …'.
- Give a fully developed explanation about the second consequence including precise evidence.

Below is a sample answer to another exam-style consequence question with comments around it.

**Explain two consequences of the Berlin Crisis of 1948–49.**

One consequence of the Berlin Crisis of 1948–49 was that it greatly increased East–West rivalry. This was because Truman saw the crisis as a great victory. The Berlin airlift had been very effective in ensuring that supplies reached West Berlin. This reached its peak on 16–17 April 1949 when 1398 flights landed nearly 13,000 tons of supplies in 24 hours. West Berlin had survived and stood up to the Soviet Union. However, for Stalin it was a defeat and a humiliation as he had not been able to prevent the airlift from supplying West Berlin and had been forced to back down and reopen road and rail routes.

Another consequence of the Berlin Crisis of 1948–49 was the creation, in 1949, of the North Atlantic Treaty Organization. This was because the Berlin Crisis had confirmed Truman's commitment to Western Europe and convinced him that Western European states, even joined together, were no match for the Soviet Union and needed the formal support of the USA. NATO was signed by the USA, Canada, Britain and nine other countries of Western Europe and, although a defensive alliance, its main purpose was to prevent Soviet expansion.

The question is focused on through referring to the first consequence.

A detailed explanation of this consequence is given.

Precise evidence is given in this explanation.

The question is focused on through referring to the second consequence.

A detailed explanation of the second consequence is given.

Precise evidence is given in this explanation.

## The better answer

Below is an exam-style consequence question with two answers. Which is the better answer? Give three reasons why.

**Explain two consequences of the creation of the Soviet invasion of Afghanistan.**

### ANSWER 1

In 1979, the Soviet Union invaded Afghanistan. The Soviets wanted to keep their influence in Afghanistan. President Carter was furious and criticised the invasion. Afghan rebels opposed the invasion. The USA supported these rebels. One consequence was that the USA refused to attend the Moscow Olympics of 1980.

### ANSWER 2

One consequence of the Soviet invasion of Afghanistan was the Carter Doctrine. President Carter was furious with the invasion and introduced this doctrine which stated that the USA would use military force if necessary to defend its national interests in the Persian Gulf region. It also promised US military aid to all the countries bordering Afghanistan. In subsequent years, the USA gave military support to the *mujahideen*, Afghan rebels who fought against the Soviet occupation.

Another consequence of the Soviet invasion of Afghanistan was to end the period of *détente* between the superpowers. One feature of *détente* was the SALT talks. SALT 2 talks had begun in 1974 but, in 1969, the US Senate refused to ratify this agreement. *Détente* gave way to increased rivalry between the USA and the Soviet Union and the beginning of the Second Cold War. In retaliation to the Soviet invasion, the USA boycotted the Moscow Olympics of 1980.

1 ______________________________

2 ______________________________

3 ______________________________

## Question 2: Narrative account

Below is an example of an exam-style narrative question which is worth 8 marks.

**Write a narrative account analysing the ways in which relations between the USA and the Soviet Union worsened in the years 1979–85.**

**You may use the following information in your answer:**

- **Soviet invasion of Afghanistan (1979)**
- **Strategic Defence Initiative**

**You must also use information of your own.**

### How to answer

- Look for the key points in the question and underline them.
- You can choose to write about the two events given in the question and an event of your own, or write entirely about events of your own.
- If you write about the events in the question make sure you write about at least three events. Including three events is important because you *must bring in an event of your own*.
- Ensure that your events are in the correct chronological sequence.
- Ensure that you give detail about each of the events you write about.
- Use linking words between each event and the next. Try to use phrases such as 'this led to', 'as a result of this'.

Below is a sample answer to this exam-style narrative question with comments around it.

In 1979, relations between the USA and the Soviet Union worsened because of the Soviet invasion of Afghanistan. Between 25 December 1979 and 1 January 1980, more than 50,000 Soviet troops were sent to Afghanistan to restore order and protect the People's Democratic Party of Afghanistan (PDPA) from the Muslim guerrilla movement known as the *mujahideen*. The US president was furious with the Soviet Union and took a tough line. He introduced the Carter Doctrine stated that the USA would use military force if necessary to defend its national interests in the Persian Gulf region. It also promised US military aid to all the countries bordering Afghanistan.

> Using the words of the question gives immediate focus.

> There is a developed analysis of the first event, using precise details.

As a result of Carter's get tough policy, relations continued to worsen and there was a Second Cold War. The Senate delayed passing the SALT 2 treaty and the USA cancelled all shipments of grain to the Soviet Union and US companies were forbidden to sell high-technology equipment there, such as computers and oil-drilling tools. Moreover, Carter pressured the US Olympic Committee to boycott the Moscow Olympic Games of 1980. Sixty-one other countries followed Carter's example. Superpower politics had now intruded into the Olympics. Indeed, the Soviet Union retaliated by boycotting the Los Angeles Olympics of 1984.

> A link is made between the first and second events. An event not given in the question is introduced.

> There is a developed analysis of the second event.

Superpower relations during this Second Cold War were further worsened by Reagan and the Strategic Defence Initiative. Reagan believed in taking a far tougher line with the Soviet Union than Carter. He made it clear that he had no interest in *détente* and was prepared to confront the Soviet Union whenever possible. Reagan's plan was to launch an army of satellites equipped with powerful lasers, which would intercept Soviet missiles in space and destroy them before they could do any harm to the USA. The Soviet Union was furious. Soviet leaders knew that they could not compete with Reagan's 'Star Wars' plan. They were behind the USA in space and computer technology whilst the Soviet economy was not producing enough wealth to fund even more defence spending.

> A link is made between the second and third events.

> There is a developed analysis of the third event.

## 'Through the eyes' of the examiner

Below is an exam-style narrative question with part of a sample answer. It would be useful to look at this answer 'through the eyes' of an examiner. The examiner will look for the following:

- events in the correct sequence
- clear links between events
- an explanation of each event.

You need to:

- highlight words or phrases which show that the answer has focused on the question
- underline where attempts are made to show links between one event and the next
- in the margin, write a word or phrase which sums up each specific explanation as it appears.

**Write a narrative account analysing the main events in rivalry between the USA and the Soviet Union in the years 1948–56.**

**You may use the following information in your answer:**

- **Berlin Crisis (1948–49)**
- **Warsaw Pact (1955)**

**You must also use information of your own.**

The first event which increased rivalry between the superpowers was the Berlin Crisis of 1948–49. On 24 June 1948, Stalin accused the West of interfering in the Soviet zone. He cut off road, rail and canal traffic in the attempt to starve West Berlin. Truman was determined to stand up to the Soviet Union and show that he was serious about containment. The only way into Berlin was by air. So the Allies decided to airlift supplies from their bases in West Germany. The airlift began on 28 June 1948 and lasted for ten months and was the start of the biggest airlift in history. The airlift continued into the spring and reached its peak on 16–17 April 1949 when 1398 flights landed nearly 13,000 tons of supplies in 24 hours. In May 1949, Stalin lifted the blockade. It greatly increased East–West rivalry. Truman saw the crisis as a great victory. West Berlin had survived and stood up to the Soviet Union. For Stalin it was a defeat and a humiliation. It led to the creation of the North Atlantic Treaty Organisation or NATO, which Stalin saw as an alliance aimed against the Soviet Union.

In retaliation to the establishment of NATO, in 1955 the Soviet Union set up the Warsaw Pact, which further increased rivalry between the two superpowers. It was a military alliance of eight nations headed by the Soviet Union and was designed to counter the threat of NATO. Members were to support each other if attacked. A joint command structure was set up under the Soviet Supreme Commander. This meant that there were now two major alliance systems – NATO and the Warsaw Pact – with each determined to be stronger than the other, which, in turn, intensified the arms race with the development of even more powerful weapons of mass destruction.

## Adding a third event

The answer above does not include a third event. What would you choose as a third event and why? Try completing the answer, remembering to add details to support your chosen event.

## Question 3: Importance

Below is an exam-style question.

**Explain two of the following:**

- **The importance of the Hungarian uprising (1956) for the development of the Cold War.**
- **The importance of the Cuban Missile Crisis (1962) for relations between the USA and the Soviet Union.**
- **The importance of the Soviet invasion of Czechoslovakia (1968) for the development of the Cold War.**

### How to answer

- You must choose **two** of these three developments. Your choice should be based on the two you feel provide greater opportunity for you to focus on *importance*.
- For the two you have chosen underline key points in the question. This will ensure that you focus sharply on what the question wants you to write about.
- Remember for each development that you choose that the focus of the question is its *importance* for a further factor and/or event.

Below is a part of a sample answer to this exam-style importance question with comments around it.

The Hungarian uprising was important for the development of the Cold War because it demonstrated Soviet determination to maintain control in Eastern Europe and worsened relations between the two superpowers. In October 1956, demonstrations against Soviet control began, Khrushchev sent troops and tanks to Budapest to try to restore peace and, on 26 October, Nagy was reinstated as prime minister. Nagy held talks with the Soviet Union and it was agreed that the tanks would be withdrawn. On 31 October, Nagy's proposed reforms were published. His most controversial decision was his intention to withdraw Hungary from the Warsaw Pact. On 4 November, Khrushchev decided that Nagy had gone too far, and 200,000 Soviet troops and 6000 tanks returned to Hungary. Khrushchev was able to keep control, and a new Soviet-backed leader, Kádár, was installed. Nagy was arrested and shot in 1958.

There is an immediate focus on the key word of the question: importance.

A developed explanation is given using precise details.

There was very little that the West, especially the USA and Britain, could do, apart from condemn the actions of the Soviet Union, to help the Hungarians. Hungary was too far away for military intervention. Britain, France and the USA were preoccupied with the Suez Crisis. The crisis was important because it highlighted the determination of the Soviet Union to maintain its control of Eastern Europe and prevent any further attacks on Communist control. It was also important because it intensified superpower rivalry. The USA was furious with the brutal suppression of the uprising by the Soviet Union. American criticism infuriated the Soviet Union who regarded Eastern Europe as their sphere of influence.

The importance of the Hungarian uprising is focused on again.

## You're the examiner

Below is the second part of the answer to the exam-style importance question and a mark scheme.

1 Read the answer and the mark scheme. Decide which level you would award the paragraph. Write the level below, along with a justification for your choice.

**Mark scheme**

| Level | Mark | |
|---|---|---|
| 1 | 1–2 | A simple or generalised answer is given, showing limited development, organisation of material and limited knowledge and understanding |
| 2 | 3–5 | An explanation is given is given showing some attempt to analyse importance. It shows some reasoning, but may lack organisation. Accurate and relevant information is added |
| 3 | 6–8 | An explanation is given, showing analysis of importance, and is well structured. Accurate and relevant knowledge is included. It shows good knowledge and understanding of the required characteristics of the period |

The Soviet invasion of Czechoslovakia increased East–West rivalry during the Cold War. The 'Prague Spring' refers to a series of reforms introduced by Dubček. The reforms included greater political freedom including free speech and the abolition of press censorship. Soon after, hundreds and thousands of Soviet troops entered Czechoslovakia. Czechs threw petrol bombs at the Soviet tanks as they moved through Prague. Buildings were set on fire and protesters assembled in Wenceslas Square. The Soviet invasion gave rise to the Brezhnev Doctrine which said that all member countries had to remain part of the Warsaw Pact. Britain and the USA protested at Soviet actions. The USA did nothing else because they were fighting in Vietnam. The Soviet invasion was important because it worsened relations.

Level ☐ Reason ______________________________

______________________________

2 Now suggest what the student has to do to achieve a higher level.

______________________________

______________________________

______________________________

______________________________

3 Try and rewrite this part of the answer at a higher level.

4 Now try and write an answer for the second bullet in the exam-style importance question.

[illegible]

Level: ______ Reason: ______

# WEIMAR AND NAZI GERMANY

## 1918–39

# Key topic 1 The Weimar Republic, 1918–29

The **Weimar Republic** faced challenges to its authority in its early years from 1919 to 1924. It experienced a period of recovery in the years 1924–29, during which there were important changes in society.

## 1 The origins of the Republic, 1918–19

REVISED

The Weimar Republic was set up due to the legacy of the First World War.

### 1.1 The legacy of the First World War

Defeat in the First World War in 1918 led to revolution in Germany.

#### The Revolution of October/November 1918–19

- The First World War started in 1914 and the USA joined the Allies in the war against Germany in April 1917. By the early autumn of 1918, the German army was being pushed back in France. The British naval blockade had resulted in shortages of food for the German people. German defeat was imminent.
- In early October 1918, a new government was formed led by Prince Max of Baden. He approached US President Wilson about ending the war. Wilson said that he would not discuss peace terms with Germany while **Kaiser Wilhelm** and his military advisers were in control.
- At the end of October 1918, the German navy mutinied. Sailors at Kiel refused to put to sea and fight the British. Unrest began to spread across Germany.
- On 9 November, Kaiser Wilhelm's abdication was announced.
- On 10 November, a new republic was set up under Chancellor Ebert. The following day, Ebert signed the **armistice** with the Allies.

### 1.2 The setting up of the Weimar Republic

In January 1919, a new democratic **constitution** for Germany was drawn up. It was finalised in August 1919 and had both strengths and weaknesses.

#### Strengths of the new constitution

- It established the most advanced democracy in Europe – men and women had the vote at the age of 20 at a time when in Britain the age was 21 for men and 30 for women.
- The President was elected every seven years and had the power to appoint the Chancellor (head of the government).
- The Reichstag (parliament) had the power to pass or reject changes in the law. Members of the Reichstag were elected by **proportional representation** every four years.
- It established the right of free speech and freedom of religious belief.

#### Weaknesses of the new constitution

- Article 48 said that in an emergency the President could make laws without going to the Reichstag. This gave the President too much power.
- Proportional representation often led to many small parties gaining seats, including extremist groups such as the Nazis. No one party was large enough to secure a majority. **Coalition governments** were often weak and short lived.
- The army generals and judges were the same men who had served the Kaiser. Many of them opposed the Weimar Republic.

**Key terms**

**Armistice** The agreement to end hostilities in war

**Coalition government** Two or more political parties joining to form a government when no single political party gets a majority of the seats, in order to have sufficient support to pass laws

**Constitution** The basic principles according to which a country is governed

**Proportional representation** The number of votes won by a party determines the number of seats they get in parliament

**Weimar Republic** The republic that existed in Germany, 1919–33

**Key individual**

**Kaiser Wilhelm** The last German Emperor, ruling from 1888 to 1918

**Revision task**

Create a timeline showing the main developments in Germany, 1918–19, adding in dates and events.

**Exam tip**

You need to know the weaknesses of the German constitution, especially the effects of proportional representation and Article 48.

## Strengths and weaknesses

1 Using the information on page 4, copy and complete both sides of the scales to show the strengths and weaknesses of the Weimar constitution.

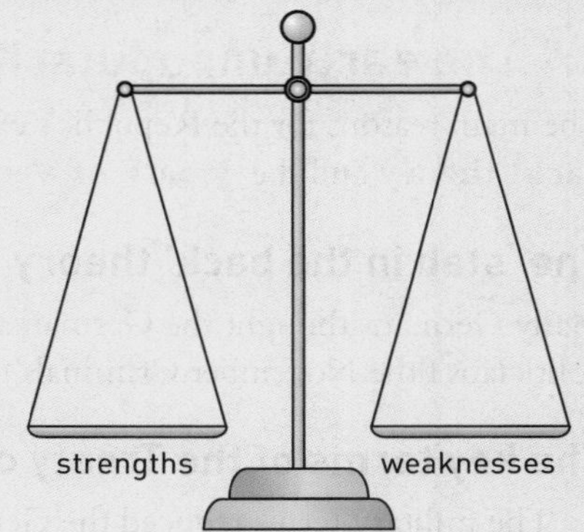


2 Do you think the strengths outweigh the weaknesses? Give reasons for your answer.

## You're the examiner

1 Below are an exam-style question, a mark scheme and a paragraph written in answer to the question. Read the paragraph and the mark scheme and decide what mark you would give the answer.

**Give two things you can infer from Source A about German reactions to the Versailles peace treaty. (4 marks)**

### SOURCE A

*From a speech by Count Brockdorff-Rantzau, head of the German Versailles delegation to the Allied powers, 7 May 1919.*

We shall be made to pay and, as the guilty, we shall be punished. We are required to admit that we alone are to blame for the war. Such an admission on my lips would be a lie. We emphatically deny that Germany, whose people were convinced that they were waging a war of defence, should be burdened with the sole responsibility for the war.

| Mark scheme | |
|---|---|
| 2 marks | 1 mark for each valid inference up to a maximum of two inferences |
| 2 marks | The second mark for each inference is for supporting detail selected from the source |

### STUDENT ANSWER

The source suggests that many Germans strongly opposed the War Guilt clause. The source also suggests that the War Guilt clause was unfair.

Mark ☐ Reason ____________________

2 Now write an answer which could gain 4 marks.

# 2 The early challenges to the Weimar Republic, 1919–23

REVISED

## 2.1 The early unpopularity of the Republic

The main reasons for the Republic's early unpopularity were the **'stab in the back' theory** and the **Treaty of Versailles**.

### The 'stab in the back' theory

Many Germans thought the German army had been 'stabbed in the back' by the politicians ('the November Criminals') who signed the armistice in November 1918.

### The key terms of the Treaty of Versailles

- The military terms reduced the German army to 100,000 and demilitarised the Rhineland. Germany was not allowed tanks, military aircraft or submarines.
- The territorial terms robbed Germany of key industrial areas, such as the iron of Alsace-Lorraine and the coalfields of the Saar. Germany lost thirteen per cent of its land.
- The financial terms seemed too harsh – with **reparations** set at £6.6 billion.
- Germany had to accept the blame for starting the war (the War Guilt clause).

Opponents of the Treaty described it as a *diktat* or dictated peace.

## 2.2 Challenges to the Republic from the left and right

The Republic faced threats from the left and right; there were several uprisings.

### Opposition from the left – the Spartacists

- The **Spartacists**, led by Rosa Luxemburg and Karl Liebknecht, demonstrated against the government in December 1918. Sixteen people died in clashes with the army.
- They formed the German Communist Party and on 5 January 1919 staged an uprising in Berlin to overthrow the government and create a Communist state.
- The rising was crushed and Liebknecht and Luxemburg were killed.

### Opposition from the right – the Kapp Putsch

- The ***Freikorps*** were furious about the Treaty of Versailles. In March 1920, they attempted to take power in Berlin, through a **putsch** led by Dr Wolfgang Kapp.
- Kapp set up a new right-wing government in Berlin. The army would not put the putsch down, showing its lack of support for the Weimar Republic.
- Berlin workers supported Weimar and went on strike; the putsch collapsed.

## 2.3 The challenges of 1923

The German government could not pay its first reparations payment. In January 1923, the French marched into the Ruhr industrial area, determined to get payment in kind by taking goods. The workers chose passive resistance to the occupation and went on strike. This meant that fewer goods were being produced. The German government printed more money to pay the strikers which, alongside fewer goods, turned inflation into **hyperinflation**. By November 1923, the German mark was worthless: $1 was worth 4,200,000,000 marks.

| Hyperinflation losers | Hyperinflation winners |
|---|---|
| Old-age pensions became worthless | Businesses were able to pay off debts |
| People's savings lost all value | The rise in food prices helped farmers |
| Wages could not keep up with inflation and many people could not afford everyday necessities such as bread | |

### Key terms

***Freikorps*** Private armies set up by German army officers at the end of the First World War; mainly consisted of ex-soldiers

**Hyperinflation** Extremely high inflation, where the value of the money plummets and it becomes almost worthless

**Putsch** An attempt to seize power by force

**Reparations** War damages (money) to be paid by Germany to countries it had fought against

**Spartacists** A Communist group who wanted to create a Communist state

**'Stab in the back' theory** The belief that Germany could have won the war and that politicians had stabbed the army in the back at the end of the war

**Treaty of Versailles** The peace treaty ending the First World War, signed on 28 June 1919

### Revision task

Make a table to show the reasons for German discontent with the Treaty of Versailles, using these headings:

- military terms
- War Guilt
- Rhineland
- reparations
- loss of land.

### Exam tip

Be aware of the terms of the Treaty of Versailles, how they affected Germany and why they brought widespread opposition.

## RAG: Rate the timeline

Below are an exam-style question and a timeline. Read the question, study the timeline and, using three coloured pens, put a **red**, **amber** or **green** star next to the events to show:

**Red:** events and policies that have **no** relevance to the question
**Amber:** events and policies that have **some** relevance to the question
**Green:** events and policies that have **direct** relevance to the question.

**Explain why there were challenges to the Weimar Republic in the years 1919–23.**

> You may use the following in your answer:
> - The Spartacists
> - Hyperinflation
>
> You **must** also use information of your own.

| | |
|---|---|
| 1918 | **1918 November** Kaiser Wilhelm II abdicated; **1918 November** Germany signed the armistice; **1918 November** The 'stab in the back' theory |
| 1919 | **1919 January** Spartacist uprising; **1919 June** Signing of the Treaty of Versailles; **1919 August** Weimar constitution finalised |
| 1920 | **1920** Kapp Putsch |
| 1921 | |
| 1922 | |
| 1923 | **1923** French occupation of the Ruhr; **1923** Hyperinflation; **1923** Stresemann became foreign secretary |
| 1924 | **1924** Dawes Plan |
| 1925 | **1925** Locarno Treaties |
| 1926 | **1926** Germany joined League of Nations |
| 1927 | |
| 1928 | **1928** Kellogg–Briand Pact |
| 1929 | **1929** Young Plan |

## Spot the mistakes

Below is a paragraph which is part of an answer to the question in the timeline activity above. However, it has factual mistakes. Identify the mistakes and on a separate piece of paper rewrite the paragraph.

*One reason why there were challenges to the Weimar Republic in the years 1919–23 was the presence of groups who wanted to form a Communist state. One of these groups was the Spartacist League, which was led by Karl Liebknecht and Gustav Stresemann. In December 1920, there were Spartacists' demonstrations against the government which led to clashes with the army and resulted in the deaths of sixteen Spartacists. At the end of the month, the Spartacists formed the Nazi Party. In January 1921, the Spartacists began their attempt to overthrow the Weimar government in order to create a Communist state. Ebert used the SS to put down the uprising.*

# 3 The recovery of the Republic, 1924–29

REVISED

The German economy recovered from the disasters of 1923 while relations with other countries, especially Britain and France, improved.

## 3.1 Reasons for economic recovery

There were several reasons for the economic recovery of the Republic, including:

- the role of Stresemann
- the Rentenmark
- the Dawes Plan
- American loans
- the Young Plan.

### The role of Stresemann

In August 1923, **Gustav Stresemann** was appointed Chancellor to deal with the problems of hyperinflation. It was his decision to call off passive resistance in the Ruhr and to negotiate the **Dawes Plan**.

### The Rentenmark

In November 1923, Stresemann introduced the **Rentenmark** to replace the German mark. This was a temporary measure in order to stabilise the currency and restore confidence. The Rentenmark's value was based on property values rather than on gold reserves. It was converted into the Reichsmark the following year, backed by gold reserves.

### The Dawes Plan

The Dawes Plan of 1924 reorganised Germany's reparation payments:

- Payments were staged to match Germany's capacity to pay.
- Payments began at 1 billion marks for the first year and increased over a period of four years to 2.5 billion marks a year.
- In return, the French withdrew their troops from the Ruhr.

### American loans

- The Dawes Plan also aimed to boost the German economy through US loans.
- Over the next six years, US companies and banks gave loans of nearly $3 billion.

### The Young Plan

In 1929, Germany negotiated a further change to reparations known as the **Young Plan**:

- A timescale for payment was set, with Germany making payments until 1988.
- The reparation figure was reduced from £6 billion to £1.85 billion.

## 3.2 Stresemann's achievements abroad

Stresemann was responsible for several successes abroad that greatly assisted German recovery.

- Stresemann greatly improved relations with Britain and France by ending passive resistance in the Ruhr. The **Locarno Pact** of 1925 followed, signed by Germany, Britain, France, Italy and Belgium. By this agreement, Germany agreed to keep its existing borders.
- Germany had to become a member of the **League of Nations** for the Pact to come into operation. It was given a permanent seat in September 1926, which recognised its return to a Great Power.
- In 1928, Germany signed the **Kellogg–Briand Pact** along with 64 other nations. It was agreed that these nations would keep their armies for self-defence but would solve all future disputes by 'peaceful means'.

#### Key terms

**Dawes Plan** Introduced in 1924 to restructure Germany's annual reparations payments

**Kellogg–Briand Pact** International agreement to solve all disputes peacefully

**League of Nations** International body established after the First World War to maintain peace

**Locarno Pact** Series of agreements guaranteeing Germany's frontiers with neighbouring countries

**Rentenmark** New currency brought in by Stresemann to restore the value of the mark

**Young Plan** Introduced in 1929 to reduce German reparation payments

#### Key individual

**Gustav Stresemann** In 1919, he became leader of the German People's Party. From August to November 1923, he served as Chancellor of Germany and, later in the same year, he was appointed foreign secretary, a position he held until his death in 1929

#### Exam tips

1. Make sure you are aware of Stresemann's policies both at home and abroad.
2. You should have precise knowledge about the terms of both the Dawes Plan and the Young Plan. This will impress an examiner.

## Eliminate irrelevance

Below is an exam-style question:

**Explain why the Weimar Republic recovered in the years 1924–29.**

**You may use the following in your answer:**
- **The Dawes Plan**
- **The Locarno Pact**

**You must also use information of your own.**

Below is part of an answer to the question above. Some parts of the answer are not relevant to the question. Identify these and draw a line through the information that is irrelevant, justifying your deletions in the margin.

*The Weimar government experienced hyperinflation in 1923. By November 1923 the German mark was worthless. Many people suffered due to the effects of hyperinflation, including pensioners who found that their pensions became worthless and people with savings who found that they lost all value.*

*German recovery in the years 1924–29 was partly due to the work of Stresemann who introduced the Dawes Plan which aimed to boost the German economy through US loans, beginning with a loan of 800 million marks. Reparations were sensibly staged to match Germany's capacity to pay. Reparation payments would begin at 1 billion marks for the first year and would increase over a period of four years to 2.5 billion a year. In return, France withdrew its troops from the Ruhr.*

*A further reason for German recovery was the Locarno Pact. Stresemann was determined to improve Germany's relations with Britain and France and restore German prestige abroad. The Locarno Pact of 1925, which also included Italy and Belgium, achieved all of these aims and guaranteed Germany's frontiers with France, Belgium and Italy. This, in turn, led to Germany being invited to join the League of Nations.*

*German recovery ended in 1929 with the Wall Street Crash in the USA. Many German businesses were forced to close. They were heavily dependent on loans from the USA.*

*German farmers also suffered as prices fell even more in the years after 1929.*

## Choosing a third cause

To answer the exam-style question in the eliminate irrelevance activity above, you need to explain three causes. It is sensible to make use of the two given points. However, you will need to add one of your own. In the spaces below, write down your choice for a third point and the reasons behind it.

Reason: ______________________

Why I have chosen this reason: ______________________

Details to support this reason: ______________________

# 4 Changes in society, 1924–29

REVISED

The period 1924–29 is often described as the 'golden age' of the Weimar Republic.

## 4.1 Changes in the standard of living

For many Germans, these years saw an improvement in their standard of living.

### Wages

- The real value of wages increased each year after 1924 – benefiting German workers. By 1928, Germany had some of the best paid workers in Europe.
- While unemployment fell generally, it remained high in the professions such as lawyers, civil servants and teachers.

### Housing

Weimar governments also attempted to deal with a shortage of housing. Between1924 and 1931 more than 2 million new homes were built and by 1928, homelessness had been reduced by more than 60 per cent.

### Architecture

A new group of architects and designers emerged, called the ***Bauhaus*** who used bold designs and unusual materials, and basic shapes and colours.

### Unemployment insurance

The Unemployment Insurance Law (1927) required workers and employees to make contributions to a national scheme for **unemployment welfare**.

**Key terms**

***Bauhaus*** An architectural and design movement – means 'School of Building'

**Unemployment welfare** Payments made to the unemployed by the state

## 4.2 Changes in the position of women

Debate about the status of women was an important feature of Weimar Germany.

### Politics

- In 1919, women over 20 were given the vote.
- The Weimar constitution introduced equality in education, equal opportunity in civil service appointments and equal pay in the professions.
- By 1926, there were 32 women deputies in the Reichstag.

### Leisure

Women enjoyed much more freedom, socially. They:

- went out unescorted and drank and smoked in public
- were fashion conscious, often wearing shorter skirts
- had their hair cut short and wore makeup.

### Employment

- There was a growing number of women in new areas of employment, most noticeably in public employment such as the civil service and teaching, but also in shops and on the assembly line.
- Those women who worked in the civil service earned the same as men.
- By 1933, there were 100,000 women teachers and 3000 women doctors.

**Revision task**

Summarise in no more than ten words the changes to women in Germany in the years 1924–29.

**Exam tip**

Cultural changes are generally not as well revised as the recovery of the Republic under Stresemann. Ensure you have precise knowledge of these changes.

## 4.3 Cultural changes

Some of the most exciting art and culture in Europe emerged during this period.

### Art

*Neue Sachlichkeit* (new objectivity) was a new approach to art which portrayed society in an objective way. It was associated with painters such as George Grosz and Otto Dix.

### Cinema

This was a golden age for the German cinema. Fritz Lang was its best known director. He produced *Metropolis* (1927), the most technically advanced films of the decade. German actress Marlene Dietrich became one of the most popular films stars in the world, often playing strong and glamorous women.

### Inference

Below are an exam-style question and part of an answer.

**Give two things you can infer from Source A about women in Weimar Germany.**

*Women had greater freedom socially. The details from the source which support this are the women who are shown in a bar drinking alcohol with men.*

Now make a second inference and use details from the source to support it.

### Utility

Use the questions and statements in the white boxes around the photo to make notes in answer to the following question:

How useful is Source A for an enquiry into the position of women in the Weimar Republic in the 1920s? Explain your answer, using Source A and your knowledge of the historical context.

**SOURCE A**

*A photograph showing women in a famous Berlin bar in the 1920s.*

What is useful about the contents of the source?

What is useful about the nature, origins or purpose of the source?

Contextual knowledge to support your answer

# Key topic 2 Hitler's rise to power, 1919–33

In 1919–20, the **Nazi Party** was set up and, in the Munich Putsch of 1923, Hitler unsuccessfully tried to seize power by force. There was limited backing for the Nazis during 1924–28 but the Depression in 1929 brought increased support. Political developments in 1932 led to Hitler becoming Chancellor in 1933.

## 1 Early development of the Nazi Party, 1920–22

REVISED

The Nazi Party, led by Adolf Hitler, emerged in the early 1920s and was able to take advantage of the problems experienced by the Weimar Republic.

### 1.1 Hitler's early career

Hitler was born in Austria in 1889. When he was sixteen, he went to Vienna to become an artist. This did not work out. From 1908 to 1913 he was virtually a 'down-and-out' on the streets of Vienna. It was during these years that Hitler developed his hatred of Jews:

- **Anti-Semitism** was widespread in Vienna.
- He was envious of the wealthy Jews and blamed them for his own problems.

In 1914, Hitler joined the German army and served with distinction, winning the Iron Cross. He found it hard to accept the armistice, believing that Germany was on the verge of winning the war when it was betrayed by the politicians.

Hitler stayed in the army after the war, working for the intelligence services. He came across the **German Workers' Party (DAP)**, led by Anton Drexler, and joined it in 1919.

In 1920, the party was renamed the National Socialist German Workers' Party (NSDAP or Nazi Party).

### 1.2 The early growth and features of the Nazi Party

Hitler was good at public speaking and in February 1920 he was put in charge of recruitment and propaganda, attracting new members to the party. By 1921, he was strong enough to challenge Drexler and take over the leadership of the party himself.

- The political meetings generated much violence. In order to protect Nazi speakers, protection squads were used. These developed into the *Sturmabteilung* (**SA**) in 1921. It attracted many ex-soldiers, especially from the *Freikorps*. The SA would disrupt the meetings of Hitler's opponents, especially the Communists, and often beat up opposition supporters.
- By 1922, the Nazi Party had 6000 members, rising to 50,000 two years later.
- The Nazi Party drew up a **Twenty-Five Point Programme** (see box below). This was their political manifesto. It was vague and deliberately designed to appeal to as many groups as possible.

#### Key terms

**Anti-Semitism** Hatred of Jews

**German Workers' Party (DAP)** An anti-Weimar government party set up by Anton Drexler

**Nationalise** To change from private ownership to state ownership

**Nazi Party** The National Socialist German Workers' Party set up by Hitler in 1920

**SA** Hitler's private army set up to protect Nazi meetings and disrupt those of his opponents

**Twenty-Five Point Programme** The main aims and principles of the Nazi Party

#### Exam tip

You need to be aware of the impact of the DAP and the early Nazi Party on Hitler's career, including the Twenty-Five Point Programme and the setting up of the SA.

### Key features of the Twenty-Five Point Programme

- The union of all Germans to form a Greater Germany.
- Getting rid of the Treaty of Versailles.
- Citizenship of the state to be granted only to people of German blood. Therefore no Jew was to be a citizen of the nation.
- The government to **nationalise** all businesses that had been formed into corporations.
- All newspaper editors and contributors to be German, and non-German papers to appear only with the permission of the government.

## Inference

An inference is a message that you can get from a source by reading between the lines. Below are an exam-style inference question and a series of statements. Decide which of the statements:

- make(s) inferences from the source (I)
- paraphrase(s) the source (P)
- summarise(s) the source (S)
- cannot be justified from the source (X).

**Give two things you can infer from Source A about Hitler's speeches.**

### SOURCE A

*A member of the Nazi Party describing one of Hitler's speeches in 1922.*

My critical faculty was swept away. Leaning forward as if he were trying to force his inner self into the consciousness of all these thousands, he was holding the masses, and me with them, under a hypnotic spell by the sheer force of his belief ... I forgot everything but the man; then glancing around, I saw that his magnetism was holding these thousands as one.

| Statements | I | P | S | X |
|---|---|---|---|---|
| Hitler was holding the masses under a hypnotic spell | | | | |
| Hitler attacked the Jews and the Weimar Republic in his speeches | | | | |
| Hitler was a very effective speaker | | | | |
| Hitler's speeches attracted many supporters to the Nazi Party | | | | |
| Hitler's critical faculty was swept away and there were thousands of supporters | | | | |
| Hitler made promises in his speeches | | | | |
| He forgot everything but Hitler | | | | |
| Hitler was able to impress people with the sheer force of his belief | | | | |

## Identifying causation

Below is a list of statements about the early years of the Nazi Party. Identify with a tick which are statements of causation about the growth of the Nazi Party.

| | |
|---|---|
| Hitler's qualities as a speaker brought increased membership of the Nazi Party | |
| The Twenty-Five Point Programme included destroying the Treaty of Versailles | |
| The establishment of the SA attracted more members to the Nazi Party | |
| The Twenty-Five Point Programme increased the appeal of the Nazi Party | |
| The DAP was renamed the Nazi Party | |
| The SA was used to protect Nazi meetings and attack the meetings of rival parties | |

# 2 The Munich Putsch and the lean years, 1923–29

REVISED

## 2.1 The Munich Putsch, 1923

In 1923, Hitler, supported by **General Ludendorff**, made his first attempt to seize power.

**Key individual**

**General Ludendorff**
One of the German army leaders during the First World War. After the war, he criticised the new republic and accused it of having 'stabbed the army in the back'

### Background to the Putsch

- The Weimar Republic was more unpopular than ever due to the effects of hyperinflation.
- Hitler wanted to overthrow the Republic by organising a putsch in Bavaria and then march on Berlin.
- In 1922, the Italian leader, Mussolini, had successfully marched on Rome and taken over the Italian government with the support of the regular army. Hitler knew that he would have to win over the German army to be successful.
- Hitler thought the Bavarian leaders would support him, including Gustav von Kahr, Otto von Lossow and Hans Seisser.

### Events of the Putsch

- On 8 November 1923, Hitler and the SA burst into a beer hall, disrupting a political meeting attended by Kahr, Seisser and Lossow.
- The three leaders were held at gunpoint until they offered their support for the Putsch. They were then released.
- The following day, Hitler and Ludendorff, with about 3000 supporters, including members of the SA, marched through Munich hoping to win mass public support. Seisser and Lossow had changed their minds and organised troops and police to resist them. Sixteen marchers were killed. Hitler fled.
- On 11 November, Hitler was arrested and the Nazi Party was banned.

**Revision task**

List the main changes to the Nazi Party in the years 1920–29. Put an arrow beside each to indicate whether it meant the party's fortunes were up, down or not altered by the change.

### Consequences of the Putsch

- In February 1924, Hitler was put on trial. The charge was high treason.
- Hitler turned his trial into a propaganda success, using it to attack the Weimar Republic. It provided him with nationwide publicity.
- The court was sympathetic to Hitler and gave him the minimum sentence for the offence – five years.
- Hitler was imprisoned in Landsberg Prison for only nine months. He wrote *Mein Kampf*, which contained his political views.
- Hitler realised that he needed complete control over the party and that in future he would try to gain power by legal methods – winning elections.

**Exam tip**

Remember to give a balanced evaluation of the Munich Putsch. Although it failed and Hitler was imprisoned, it did bring some benefits to Hitler and the Nazi Party.

## 2.2 The lean years, 1924–29

The Nazi Party survived in secret until the ban was lifted in 1924. The period 1924–29 was a time of mixed fortunes for the Nazi Party.

| The party did not do well | The party made progress |
|---|---|
| • There were quarrels and disagreements during Hitler's period in prison<br>• Economic recovery meant there was little support for extremist parties<br>• It only won twelve seats in the 1928 election | • It won 32 seats in the 1924 elections<br>• *Mein Kampf* provided key ideas for the development of the Nazi Party with its focus on the importance of propaganda and anti-Semitism<br>• Hitler reorganised the party to make it more efficient, with party branches run by *Gauleiters*<br>• At the 1926 Bamberg party conference, Hitler continued to strengthen his position. Possible rivals to Hitler's leadership were won over or removed<br>• Membership increased to 100,000 members by 1928 |

## You're the examiner

Below is an exam-style question.

**Explain why the Nazi Party lost support in the years 1923–29.**

**You may use the following in your answer:**
- **The Munich Putsch**
- **Stresemann**

**You must also use information of your own.**

1 Opposite is a mark scheme and below is a paragraph which is part of an answer to the question. Read the paragraph and the mark scheme. Decide which level you would award the paragraph. Write the level below, along with a justification for your choice.

Remember that for the higher levels, students must:
- explain at least three reasons
- focus explicitly on the question
- support their reasons with precise details.

**Mark scheme**

| Level | Mark | |
|---|---|---|
| 1 | 1–3 | A simple or generalised answer is given, lacking development and organisation |
| 2 | 4–6 | An explanation is given, showing limited analysis and with implicit links to the question |
| 3 | 7–9 | An explanation is given, showing some analysis, which is mainly directed at the focus of the question |
| 4 | 10–12 | An analytical explanation is given which is directed consistently at the focus of the question |

**STUDENT ANSWER**

*On the second day of the Munich Putsch, Hitler and Ludendorff, with about 3000 supporters, some of whom were members of the SA, decided to march through Munich hoping to win mass public support. Armed police blocked their way and sixteen of the marchers were killed when the police opened fire. Hitler stayed in the background and then fled the battle. On 11 November Hitler was arrested for his part in the uprising.*

*Hitler was in prison for nine months.*

Level ☐ Reason ______________________________

______________________________

2 Now suggest what the student has to do to achieve a higher level.

______________________________

______________________________

______________________________

3 Try and rewrite this paragraph at a higher level.

4 Now try and write the rest of the answer to the question.

# The Munich Putsch: Interpretation questions

REVISED

Look at Sources A and B and Interpretations 1 and 2 below and then carry out the activities on page 17.

## SOURCE A

*A painting of the Munich Putsch of 1923 made later by one of its participants, showing the police opening fire on the Nazis. Hitler is standing with his arm raised and Erich von Ludendorff is on his right.*

## SOURCE B

*From Hitler's recollections of the Munich Putsch, given in 1933.*

It was the greatest good fortune for us Nazis that the Putsch collapsed because:

1 Co-operation with General Ludendorff would have been absolutely impossible.
2 The sudden takeover of power in the whole of Germany would have led to the greatest difficulties in 1923 because the essential preparations had not been made by the National Socialist Party.
3 The events of 9 November 1923, with their bloody sacrifice, have proven the most effective propaganda for National Socialism.

## INTERPRETATION 1

*From* Germany 1858–1990: Hope, Terror and Revival *by A. Kitson, published in 2001.*

Kahr was forced to promise Hitler his support, but this support was short-lived. The next day it became clear to Hitler that neither Kahr nor the army were going to support his march. The Bavarian police were sent to stop the few thousand supporters that had gathered and opened fire, killing 16 Nazis. Hitler was driven away. Two days later he and other Nazi leaders were arrested and accused of high treason. The Nazi Party was banned and Hitler was Hitler was given the minimum sentence of five years' imprisonment.

## INTERPRETATION 2

*From* Encyclopedia of the Third Reich *by Louis L. Snyder, published in 1998.*

On the surface the Beer-Hall Putsch seemed to be a failure, but actually it was a brilliant achievement for a political nobody. In a few hours Hitler catapulted his scarcely known, unimportant movement into headlines throughout Germany and the world. Moreover, he learned an important lesson: direct action was not the way to political power. It was necessary that he seek political victory by winning the masses to his side and also by attracting the support of wealthy industrialists. Then he could ease his way to political supremacy by legal means.

## Develop the detail

Below are an exam-style question and a paragraph which is part of an answer to the question. The paragraph contains a limited amount of detail. Annotate the paragraph to add additional detail to the answer.

**Study Interpretations 1 and 2. They give different views on the consequences of the Munich Putsch of 1923. What is the main difference between the views? Explain your answer, using details from both interpretations.**

A main difference is that Interpretation 1 emphasises failures of the Munich Putsch. Interpretation 2 does not.

## Complete the paragraph

Below are an exam-style question and a paragraph which is part of an answer to this question. The paragraph gives a reason why the interpretations differ but does not give details from one of the sources to support this difference. Complete the paragraph adding the support from Sources A and B.

**Suggest one reason Interpretations 1 and 2 give different views about the consequences of the Munich Putsch of 1923. You may use Sources A and B to help explain your answer.**

The interpretations may differ because they give different weight to different sources. For example, Source A provides some support for Interpretation 1, which stresses the defeat of Hitler's attempt to seize power and the failure of the Munich Putsch.

## Support or challenge?

Below is an exam-style question and below that are a series of general statements which are relevant to the question. Using your own knowledge and the information on page 42, write a C next to the statements that challenge the view given in Interpretation 2 about the Munich Putsch and write an S next to the statements that support the view in the interpretation.

**How far do you agree with Interpretation 2 about the consequences of the 1923 Munich Putsch? Explain your answer, using both interpretations and your knowledge of the historical context.**

| Statement |
|---|
| Interpretation 2 suggests that the Munich Putsch was a brilliant success for Hitler |
| Hitler was a laughing stock because he had fled the gunfight in the street |
| Interpretation 1 stresses the failures of the Munich Putsch, especially when the Nazis were stopped by the Bavarian police |
| Hitler turned his trial into a propaganda success, using it to attack the Weimar Republic whom he accused of treason because of the armistice and signing the Treaty of Versailles |
| Interpretation 2 suggests that the Munich Putsch encouraged Hitler to change his tactics for achieving power |

| Statement |
|---|
| The Nazi Party was weak after the Putsch because Hitler was in prison and there were arguments and differences between the leading members |
| Interpretation 1 suggests that the aftermath of the Putsch was a failure, with the Nazi Party banned and Hitler arrested |
| The court was sympathetic to Hitler. Instead of sentencing him to death as it might have done, it gave him the minimum sentence for the offence – five years |
| Hitler and the Nazis had failed to get the support of the leaders of Bavaria |
| Hitler spent most of his time in prison writing *Mein Kampf* (*My Struggle*) |

# 3 The growth in support for the Nazis, 1929–32

REVISED

## 3.1 The growth of unemployment – causes and impact

In October 1929, the **Wall Street Crash** led to US loans being recalled and, as a result, many German businesses sacked workers and were forced to close. German farmers also suffered as prices fell further. By 1932, over 6 million people were unemployed. The Weimar Republic failed to deal with unemployment and lost support. There was a growth in support for right- and left-wing parties, such as the Nazi Party and Communist Party.

- The Weimar Republic was blamed for allowing the economy to become too dependent on US loans.
- There was disagreement in government about the level of unemployment contributions. Chancellor Müller resigned in March 1930.
- Brüning became Chancellor after Müller. Brüning's reduction of government spending, pay cuts, cuts to unemployment benefit and increase in taxes lost him support. In May 1932, he resigned.
- Elections were called in July and November 1932. The Communist Party gained 100 seats (16.9%) in the November 1932 elections.

**Key term**

**Wall Street Crash** Collapse of the US stock market on 29 October 1929 leading to the Depression and world economic crisis

## 3.2 Reasons for growth in support for the Nazi Party

In the September 1930 elections, the Nazi Party won 107 seats and, by July 1932, it was the largest party, with 230 seats. This increased support was due to several reasons. Three of the main ones are outlined below.

### Hitler

- Posters and rallies built Hitler up as a superman. The campaigns focused around his personality and his skills, especially as a speaker.
- Unemployment had hit everyone; thus Hitler tried to appeal to all sections of society. The Nazi message was that the Weimar Republic had caused the economic crisis and that weak coalition governments had no real solutions to offer. The Nazis alone could unite Germany in a time of economic crisis.
- Hitler provided the German people with a scapegoat – blaming the Jews for Germany's problems.
- Hitler won support from business and industrialists who donated funds to the Nazi Party. They were especially concerned at increased support for the Communist Party.

### The SA

- By 1932, the SA numbered 600,000. It organised parades through towns and cities, impressing many Germans who saw order and discipline in a time of chaos.
- It was used to intimidate any opposition, especially the Communists.

### Goebbels

**Josef Goebbels** was a master of propaganda and used every possible method to get across the Nazi message:

- Posters targeted different audiences and were timed to have maximum impact. Their message was generally simple but clear.
- He chartered planes to fly Hitler all over Germany to speak at four or five rallies per day.

**Key individual**

**Josef Goebbels** Joined the Nazi Party in 1922 and, in 1928, was elected to the Reichstag. Appointed head of propaganda of the Nazi Party in 1929. In 1933 he was appointed Minister of Public Propaganda and Enlightenment

**Revision task**

Using pages 12–18, produce a list of factors that changed the fortunes of the Nazis between the beginning of the 1920s and the early 1930s.

**Exam tip**

Remember that Germany was affected by hyperinflation in 1923, not during the Depression of 1929–32.

## Concentric circles

In the concentric circles, rank order the following reasons for increased support for the Nazis in the years 1929–32, beginning with the most important in the middle to the least important on the outside. Explain your decisions.

- the Depression
- Hitler's appeal
- Nazi propaganda
- the SA.

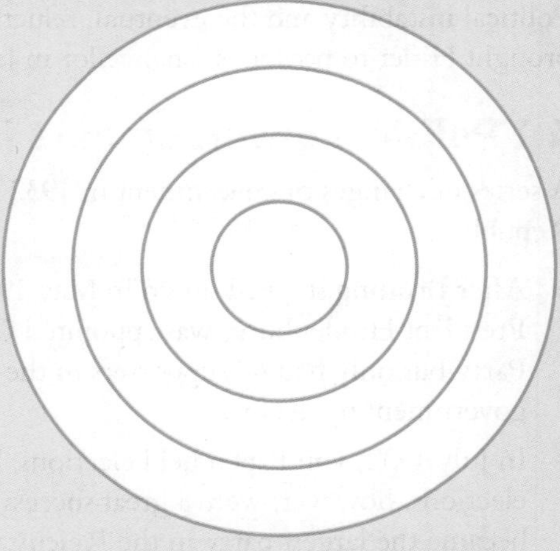

## Focusing on the question

Below is an exam-style question.

**Explain why there was increased support for the Nazis in the years 1929–32.**

**You may use the following in your answer:**
- **The Depression**
- **Hitler**

**You must also use information of your own.**

It is important that you make it clear in your answer that you are focusing on the question. Look at the paragraph below, which is part of an answer to the question.

The wording of the question is used.

One important reason for increased Nazi support in the years 1929–32 was the Depression. This was because the Depression brought about great hardship for many German people and increased the level of unemployment to over 6 million by 1932. The Nazi Party was able to appeal to a significant number of these unemployed people.

The information about the Depression focuses on increased support for the Nazis.

Now write another paragraph in answer to the question.

# 4 How Hitler became Chancellor, 1932–33

REVISED

Political instability and the eventual, reluctant, support of President **Hindenburg** brought Hitler to power as Chancellor in January 1933.

## 4.1 Political developments in 1932

A series of changes of government in 1932 further weakened the Weimar Republic:

- After Brüning stepped down in May 1932, **Franz von Papen**, a friend of President Hindenburg, was appointed Chancellor. He was leader of the Centre Party but only had 68 supporters in the Reichstag and was dependent on government by decree.
- In July 1932, von Papen held elections, hoping to gain more support. The elections, however, were a great success for the Nazis, who won 230 seats and became the largest party in the Reichstag. Hitler demanded the post of Chancellor. Hindenburg, who disliked Hitler, refused to appoint him.
- In November, von Papen arranged another election for the Reichstag, hoping to win more support. This time he won even fewer seats. The Nazi Party's seats fell to 196.
- Von Papen suggested abolishing the Weimar constitution. Von Schleicher, an army leader, persuaded Hindenburg that this would result in civil war. Hindenburg lost confidence in von Papen, who resigned.
- In the following month, Hindenburg appointed von Schleicher as Chancellor, who lasted less than two months.

## 4.2 The part played by Hindenburg and von Papen

- Von Papen was determined to regain power. To this end he met Hitler in early January 1933 when they agreed that Hitler should lead a government with von Papen as the Vice-Chancellor.
- They had the support of the army, major landowners and leaders of industry who disliked von Schleicher's plans to bring together different strands from the left and right parties and were worried about a Communist takeover.
- Von Papen convinced President Hindenburg that a coalition government with Hitler as Chancellor would save Germany and bring stability. Von Papen said that he would be able to control Hitler – he would 'make Hitler squeak'.
- On 31 January 1933, Hindenburg invited Hitler to become Chancellor.

### Key individuals

**Paul von Hindenburg**
A leading general in the First World War, becoming chief of the general staff in 1916. He retired from the army in 1918 and supported the 'stab in the back' theory. President of Germany 1925–34

**Franz von Papen** Entered politics in 1918 as a member of the Catholic Centre Party and four years later was elected to the Reichstag. He eventually became a favourite of Hindenburg. When Hitler became Chancellor, in January 1933, von Papen was his Vice-Chancellor

### Revision task

Summarise the part played by the following in Hitler's rise to power:

- Hindenburg
- von Schleicher
- von Papen.

### Exam tip

The events of 1932 are very complex. However, you will need a thorough knowledge of what took place, especially the role of Hindenburg and von Papen.

## Understand the chronology

Place the events between March 1932 and January 1933 listed below in the correct chronological sequence in the timeline.

| Date | Event |
|---|---|
| March 1932 | |
| April | |
| May | |
| June | |
| July | |
| August | |
| September | |
| October | |
| November | |
| December | |
| January 1933 | |

### EVENTS

- **A** Hitler demanded the post of Chancellor. Hindenburg refused to appoint him
- **B** Von Papen arranged for another election for the Reichstag, hoping to win more support
- **C** Hindenburg appointed von Schleicher, an army leader, as Chancellor
- **D** Von Papen became Chancellor
- **E** The Nazis' seats fell to 196
- **F** The Nazis won 230 seats, becoming the largest party in the Reichstag
- **G** Hitler became Chancellor of Germany
- **H** Chancellor Brüning was forced to resign
- **I** Hindenburg invited Hitler to become Chancellor
- **J** Von Papen and Hitler agreed that Hitler should become Chancellor and von Papen Vice-Chancellor

## Utility

Below are a utility question and an answer focusing on the utility of the contents of the source. On a separate piece of paper complete the answer by explaining the utility of the nature, origins and purpose of the source. You could look at page 42 for guidance on how to answer the utility question to help you.

**How useful is Source A for an enquiry into the political developments in Germany, 1932–33, which led to Hitler being appointed Chancellor? Explain your answer, using Source A and your knowledge of the historical context.**

### SOURCE A

*A cartoon from the British magazine* Punch, *January 1933.*

*'The Temporary Triangle.*
*Von Hindenburg and Von Papen (together):*
*"For He's a Jolly Good Fellow,*
*For He's a Jolly Good Fellow,*
*For He's a Jolly Good Fellow,"*
*(aside: "Confound him!")*
*"And So Say Both of Us".'*

*Source A is useful because it suggests that Hitler became Chancellor because of the actions of Hindenburg and von Papen. This is shown in the cartoon with Hitler being carried by the two men who are singing 'for he's a jolly good fellow'. This is supported by my knowledge of the events which brought Hitler to power. Von Papen and Hindenburg did work together to make Hitler Chancellor. Von Papen met Hitler in early January 1933 where they agreed that Hitler should lead a government with von Papen as the Vice-Chancellor. Von Papen then convinced President Hindenburg that a coalition government with Hitler as Chancellor would save Germany and bring stability. Von Papen said that he would be able to control Hitler – he would 'make Hitler squeak'.*

# Key topic 3 Nazi control and dictatorship, 1933–39

From January 1933 to August 1934, the Nazis secured control of all aspects of the German state. Hitler then consolidated his dictatorship through setting up a police state and using propaganda and censorship.

## 1 The creation of a dictatorship, 1933–34

REVISED

### 1.1 Setting up the dictatorship

From January 1933 to August 1934, Hitler secured control of the German state, removing all opposition.

#### The Reichstag Fire, February 1933

- On 27 February 1933, the **Reichstag** building was burned down. A Dutch Communist, Marius van der Lubbe, was put on trial and found guilty of starting the fire. Hitler blamed the Communist Party for the fire.
- Hitler persuaded Hindenburg to pass an emergency decree – the 'Decree for the Protection of the People and the State' – giving the police powers to detain people without trial.

#### The Enabling Act, March 1933

The 'Enabling Act' gave Hitler the power to make laws without the Reichstag's consent. Using these powers, Hitler:

- Removed further opposition to the Nazi government, including banning all **trade unions**. The unions were merged into a 'German Labour Front'.
- Banned all other political parties. By July 1933, Germany was a one-party state.

### 1.2 The Night of the Long Knives, 30 June 1934

The SA (see page 142) led by Röhm was a threat to Hitler's power. He removed this threat by purging the SA in the **Night of the Long Knives**.

#### Reasons for the purge

- The SA were increasingly out of control at a time when Hitler was trying to establish a dictatorship through legal methods.
- Röhm wanted a social revolution: to bring about greater equality in society.
- Leading Nazis such as Himmler were concerned about Röhm's growing influence. Himmler wanted to replace the SA with his own **SS**.

#### Events of the Night of the Long Knives

- Hitler arranged a meeting with Röhm and 100 other SA leaders. They were arrested by the SS, taken to Munich and shot.
- About 400 people were murdered in the purge.

#### *Results*

- Hitler got rid of would-be opponents.
- The SA now had a minor role.
- After Hindenburg died in August 1934, the army leaders swore an **oath of allegiance** to Hitler, giving him unconditional obedience.

### 1.3 Hitler becomes Führer

After Hindenburg's death, Hitler declared himself '**Führer**', combining the post of Chancellor and President. He called a referendum and more than 90 per cent of the voters (38 million) agreed with his action.

**Key terms**

**Führer** German title meaning leader

**Night of the Long Knives** 30 June 1934, when Hitler purged Röhm and the SA

**Oath of allegiance** A promise made by the German armed forces to be loyal to Hitler

**Reichstag** German state parliament

**SS** *Schultzstaffel* or 'protection squad'. Originally Hitler's bodyguards, they became the most powerful troops in the Third Reich, and wore distinctive black uniforms

**Trade unions** Organisations set up to protect and improve the rights of workers

**Revision task**

Draw a timeline for the creation of a dictatorship from January 1933 to August 1934. On the timeline include the key events which helped Hitler to create a Nazi dictatorship.

**Exam tip**

Ensure you thoroughly revise the sequence of events in 1933, beginning with when Hitler became Chancellor until the death of Hindenburg.

## Identify the view

Read the interpretation and identify the view that is offered about the Reichstag fire of February 1933.

**INTERPRETATION 1**

*From* Germany 1866–1945 *by S. Eddy and T. Lancaster, published in 2002.*

The popular view, especially among foreign journalists, was that since the Nazis had most to gain that they set fire to the Reichstag. It has been argued, for example, that the fire was too big to have been the work of one man, van der Lubbe, and that the timing of the fire, six days before the election, was simply too convenient for the Nazis.

1 What view is offered by the interpretation about the Reichstag fire?

______________________________

______________________________

2 a) Now use your knowledge to agree with or contradict the view given in the interpretation. To plan an answer to this question, make a copy of and complete the following table.

| View given in interpretation | |
|---|---|
| Knowledge which supports this view | |
| Knowledge which contradicts this view | |

b) Write a paragraph supporting and challenging this view.

## RAG: Rate the timeline

Below are an exam-style question and a timeline. Read the question, study the timeline and, using three coloured pens, put a **red**, **amber** or **green** star next to the events to show:

**Red:** events and policies that have **no** relevance to the question

**Amber:** events and policies that have **some** relevance to the question

**Green:** events and policies that have **direct** relevance to the question.

**You may use the following in your answer:**
- **The Reichstag fire (1933)**
- **The Night of the Long Knives (1934)**

**You must also use information of your own.**

**Explain why Hitler was able to establish a dictatorship of the Nazi Party in the years 1933–34.**

**1932**
- **1932 May** Von Papen became Chancellor
- **1932 July** The Nazis became the largest party in the Reichstag
- **1932 November** Von Schleicher became Chancellor

**1933**
- **1933 January** Hitler appointed Chancellor
- **1933 February** The Reichstag fire
- **1933 March** The Enabling Act
- **1933 April** The boycott of Jewish shops
- **1933 May** Trade unions banned
- **1933 July** The Nazis became the only legal party in Germany

**1934**
- **1934 June** The Night of the Long Knives
- **1934 August** Hindenburg died
- **1934 August** Hitler combined the posts of Chancellor and Führer
- **1934** Local councils banned Jews from public places

**1935**
- **1935** The Nuremberg Laws were passed, denying the Jews citizenship of Germany

# 2 The police state

REVISED

## 2.1 The Gestapo, SS, SD and concentration camps

The Nazis created a police state through the use of these different agencies – establishing a climate of fear.

### The SS (protection squad)

- Led by Himmler, the SS were responsible for the removal of all opposition and became the main means of intimidating Germans into obedience.
- By 1934, the SS had more than 50,000 members, growing to 250,000 by 1939.

### The Gestapo (secret police)

- Set up in 1933 by Goering, in 1936 the **Gestapo** came under the control of Himmler and the SS.
- It could arrest and imprison without trial those suspected of opposing the state.
- Only it had the power to send political opponents to **concentration camps**.

### The SD

- Set up in 1931, the **SD** was the intelligence agency of the Nazi Party under the command of Himmler, and organised by Heydrich.
- Its main aim was to find actual and potential enemies of the Nazi Party and ensure that they were removed.

### Concentration camps

- In 1933, the Nazis established concentration camps to detain political prisoners. These were run by the SS and SD.
- Prisoners were classified into different categories, each denoted by wearing a different coloured triangle. For example, black triangles were for vagrants and red triangles were for political prisoners.
- By 1939, there were more than 150,000 people under arrest for political offences.

**Key terms**

**Concentration camps** Prisons for political prisoners and enemies of the state

**Concordat** An agreement between the Pope and a government concerning the legal status of the Catholic Church

**Gestapo** *Geheimestaatspolizei*: the secret police of the Nazi regime

**Reich Church** Official Protestant Church of the Nazi regime

**SD** *Sicherheitsdienst*: the intelligence agency of the Nazis

**Revision task**

What part was played by the following in the establishment of the Nazi police state?

- the Gestapo
- the SS
- concentration camps
- the legal system.

## 2.2 Nazi control of the legal system

Hitler wanted to ensure that all laws were interpreted in a Nazi fashion:

- All judges had to become members of the National Socialist League for the Maintenance of Law. This meant Nazi views were upheld in the courts.
- In 1934, the People's Court was established to try cases of treason. The judges were loyal Nazis.
- In October 1933, the German Lawyers Front was established. Lawyers had to swear that they would 'follow the course of the Führer'. There were more than 10,000 members by the end of the year.

## 2.3 Nazi policies towards the Churches

In Germany, about two-thirds of the people were Protestant and one-third was Roman Catholic.

### The Catholic Church

Hitler was determined to reduce the influence of the Catholic Church:

- Catholics owed their first allegiance to the Pope, not Hitler. They had divided loyalties. Hitler said a person was either a Christian or a German but not both.
- There were Catholic schools and youth organisations whose message to the young was at odds with that of the Nazi Party.

**Exam tip**

Make sure you know the precise details about the various organisations used by the Nazis.

In 1933, Hitler signed a **Concordat** agreeing not to interfere with the Catholic Church. In return, the Catholic Church agreed to stay out of politics. Within a year, Hitler began to break the agreement and attack the Catholic Church:

- Catholic schools were made to remove Christian symbols and were eventually abolished.
- Priests were harassed and arrested. Many criticised the Nazis and ended up in concentration camps.
- Catholic youth movements were closed down.

### The Protestant Church

In 1933, Protestant groups which supported the Nazis united to form the '**Reich Church**'. Its leader, Ludwig Müller, became the first Reich Bishop in September 1933.

Many Protestants opposed Nazism, which they believed conflicted with their Christian beliefs. They were led by Pastor Niemöller (see page 152). In December 1933, they set up the Pastors' Emergency League for those who opposed Hitler.

## Inference

An inference is a message that you can get from a source by reading between the lines. Below are an exam-style inference question, the source and a series of statements. Decide which of the statements:

- make(s) inferences from the source (I)
- summarise(s) the source (S)
- cannot be justified from the source (X).

**Give two things you can infer from Source A about the Nazi police state.**

**SOURCE A**

*An incident reported in the Rhineland, July 1938.*

In a café, a 64-year-old woman remarked to her companion at the table: 'Mussolini [the leader of Italy] has more political sense in one of his boots than Hitler has in his brain.' The remark was overheard and five minutes later the woman was arrested by the Gestapo who had been alerted by telephone.

| Statements | I | S | X |
|---|---|---|---|
| People were frightened of the Gestapo | | | |
| A woman suggested that Mussolini had more sense than Hitler | | | |
| The Nazis made use of informers and spies | | | |
| Many people were arrested by the Gestapo | | | |
| You were not allowed to criticise Hitler and the Nazis | | | |
| A woman was arrested because she criticised Hitler | | | |

## Spot the mistakes

Below is a paragraph about the Churches in the police state. However, it has factual mistakes. Identify the mistakes and rewrite the paragraph.

*In Germany, most of the population was Roman Catholic. At first Hitler decided to cooperate with the Catholic Church. In 1935, he signed an agreement known as a Concordat. In 1933, those Protestant groups that supported the Nazis agreed to unite to form the 'Reich Church'. Their leader, Pastor Niemöller, became the first Reich Bishop in September 1933. Many Protestants opposed Nazism, which they believed conflicted greatly with their own Christian beliefs. They were led by Ludwig Müller and, in December 1934, they set up the Reich League for those who opposed Hitler.*

# 3 Controlling and influencing attitudes

REVISED

## 3.1 Goebbels and the Ministry of Propaganda

**Censorship** and propaganda were used to ensure that people accepted and conformed to Nazi thinking. In 1933, Goebbels was appointed as Minister of Public Propaganda and Enlightenment.

### Censorship

- No book could be published without Goebbels' permission.
- Newspapers that opposed Nazi views were closed down. Editors were told what could be printed.
- The radio was controlled.

### Propaganda

- Posters were used to put across the Nazi message.
- Goebbels ordered the mass production of cheap radios. By 1939, 70 per cent of German homes had a radio. It was important that the Nazi message was heard.
- Mass rallies and marches projected the image of power and terror. Every year a party rally was held at Nuremberg.
- Success in sport was important to promote the Nazi regime.

### The Berlin Olympics of 1936

- A major sporting showcase, the Olympics was designed to impress the outside world and was a public relations success.
- Hitler's plans to highlight the superiority of the **Aryan** race were sabotaged by the success of the black athletes in the US Olympic team, especially Jesse Owens, who won the 100 metres, 200 metres, long jump and 4 × 100 metres relay.

**Key terms**

**Aryan** Nazi term for someone of supposedly 'pure' German stock

**Censorship** Controlling what is produced and suppressing anything considered against the state

**Third Reich** Nazi name for Germany. Means 'Third Empire'

**Revision task**

How were the following used by the Nazis to maintain their dictatorship?

- the radio
- cinema
- sport.

## 3.2 Nazi control of culture and the arts

The Nazis used culture and arts to promote their ideals. Artists were encouraged to use 'Aryan themes' such as the family, national community and heroism.

### Music

Hitler hated modern music. Jazz, which was 'black' music, was seen as racially inferior and was banned. Instead, the Nazis promoted traditional German folk music and the classical music of Brahms, Beethoven and especially Richard Wagner.

### Films

The Nazis also controlled the cinema. All films were accompanied by a 45-minute official newsreel which glorified Hitler and Germany.

### Art

Hitler hated modern art, which he believed was backward, unpatriotic and Jewish. Such art was called 'degenerate', and banned. Art highlighting Germany's past greatness and the strength and power of the **Third Reich** was encouraged.

### Theatre

Theatre concentrated on German history and political drama. Cheap theatre tickets were available to encourage people to see plays which often had a Nazi political or racial theme.

**Exam tips**

1. Do not confuse Goebbels' propaganda methods before and after Hitler came to power.
2. Remember that Nazi control was based on fear, through the police state, and persuasion, through censorship and propaganda.

## Architecture

Hitler encouraged the 'monumental style' for public buildings. These large stone buildings were often copies from ancient Greece or Rome and showed the power of the Third Reich. Hitler admired the Greek and Roman style of building because he said the Jews had not 'contaminated' it.

## Literature

All books, plays and poems were carefully censored and controlled to put across the Nazi message. Encouraged by Goebbels, students in Berlin burned 20,000 books written by Jews, Communists and anti-Nazi university professors in a massive bonfire in Berlin in May 1933.

### How important

Complete the table below.

- Briefly summarise why each factor enabled Hitler to establish his dictatorship in the years 1933–39.
- Make a decision about the importance of each factor in achieving and maintaining Hitler's dictatorship. Give a brief explanation for each choice.

| Factor | Key features | Decisive/important/quite important |
|---|---|---|
| Reichstag fire | | |
| The Enabling Act | | |
| The SA | | |
| The Night of the Long Knives | | |
| Law courts | | |
| SS and Gestapo | | |
| Concentration camps | | |
| Churches | | |
| Censorship | | |
| Propaganda | | |

### Causation

Below is an exam-style question.

**Explain why the Nazi Party was able to establish a dictatorship in Germany in the years 1933–39.**

**You may use the following in your answer:**
- **The SS**
- **Censorship**

**You must also use information of your own.**

To answer the question above, you need to explain three causes. It is sensible to make use of the two given points. However, you will need to explain a third cause. You could select one of these from the table in the 'How important' activity above. Write down your choice and the reasons behind it.

Cause: ______________________________

______________________________

Why I have chosen this cause: ______________________________

______________________________

Details to support this cause: ______________________________

______________________________

# 4 Opposition, resistance and conformity

REVISED

Between 1933 and 1939, about 1.3 million people were sent to concentration camps, seeming to indicate quite widespread opposition to the regime. It has also been estimated that about 300,000 people left Germany. However, although there was some opposition it was never co-ordinated or enough to threaten the regime in the years 1933–39.

## 4.1 The extent of support for the Nazi regime

Many Germans gained much from Hitler's successes after 1933 and consequently supported him:

- There were economic successes which began to erase the Depression (see page 18).
- Germany's international standing grew, seeming to remove the shame of the Treaty of Versailles. The Saar was returned in 1935, the army was built up after 1935 and in 1936 the Rhineland was remilitarised.
- Some Germans were happy to see the Communists, Socialists and SA leaders removed.

## 4.2 Opposition from the Churches

- Many Catholic priests opposed Nazi policies and were arrested. At least 400 were sent to Dachau concentration camp. In many respects this had the opposite effect to what the Nazis wanted. Priests who were sent to concentration camps were seen as **martyrs**. Catholic Churches were packed every Sunday.
- Many Protestant pastors opposed Hitler and the Reich Church. They were led by Pastor Niemöller, who set up the '**Confessional Church**'. **Niemöller** and many other pastors were arrested and sent to concentration camps. Nazi repression did not destroy Protestant opposition. Instead it created martyrs.

## 4.3 Opposition from the young

Although many young people joined the **Hitler Youth**, it was not popular with some of its members. Not all young people accepted the Nazi ideas and some set up other groups.

### The Edelweiss Pirates

The **Edelweiss Pirates** were not a unified group but a loose band across many cities, first emerging in 1934. In Cologne they were called the Navajos, and Essen had the Roving Dudes.

- They listened to forbidden swing music and daubed walls with anti-Nazi graffiti.
- They could be recognised by their badges, for example the *edelweiss* or skull and crossbones.
- They wore clothes which were considered outlandish by the Nazis – checked shirts, dark short trousers and white socks.
- By 1939 they had a membership of 2000.
- They created no-go areas for Hitler Youth in their cities.

### The Swing Youth

**Swing Youth** tended to come from the middle classes. They loved swing music, which was hated by the Nazis who classed it as non-German, developed by 'Negros' and Jews. They rebelled against the order and discipline of the Nazis and took part in activities which were frowned upon.

**Key terms**

**Confessional Church** Protestant Church set up by Pastor Niemöller in opposition to the Reich Church

**Edelweiss Pirates** A loosely organised youth group who rebelled against Nazi ideas

**Hitler Youth** Organisation set up for the young to convert them to Nazi ideals

**Martyr** A person who is persecuted and/or killed because of their religious or other beliefs

**Swing Youth** Young people who loved swing music and challenged Nazi views about the young

**Key individual**

**Martin Niemöller** Served in the German navy as a U-boat commander during the First World War. In 1929 became a pastor in the Protestant Church and a supporter of Hitler. Began to criticise Hitler when, from 1937, members of the Protestant Church were arrested. Survived seven years in a concentration camp before being released in 1945

**Revision task**

Give two reasons why there was little opposition to the Nazi regime.

## Eliminate irrelevance

Below is an exam-style question and part of an answer. Some parts of the answer are not relevant to the question. Identify these and draw a line through the information that is irrelevant, justifying your deletions in the margin.

**Explain why there was opposition to the Nazi regime in the years 1933–39.**

**You may use the following in your answer:**

- **The Catholic Church**
- **The Edelweiss Pirates**

**You must also use information of your own.**

One reason for opposition to the Nazi policies was the Catholic Church. Hitler decided to cooperate with the Catholic Church. In 1933, Hitler signed an agreement known as a Concordat. Hitler promised not to interfere with the Catholic Church. In return, the Catholic Church agreed to stay out of politics. Many Catholic priests criticised Nazi policies and were arrested and sent to Dachau concentration camp. In many respects this had the opposite effect to what the Nazis wanted. Priests who were sent to concentration camps were seen as martyrs and encouraged even more opposition to the Nazis.

There was also opposition to the Nazi regime from young people. The Nazis set up the Hitler Youth. There were four separate organisations that were developed which recruited girls and boys from the ages of 10–18 under the control of Baldur von Shirach, Youth Leader of the Reich. One group that opposed the Nazis was the Edelweiss Pirates. Its members rebelled against Nazi ideas by listening to forbidden swing music and daubed walls with anti-Nazi graffiti. They could be recognised by their badges, for example the *edelweiss* or skull and crossbones. They wore clothes which were considered outlandish by the Nazis – check shirts, dark short trousers and white socks.

## Memory map

Use the information on page 28 to add details to the diagram below about opposition, resistance and conformity.

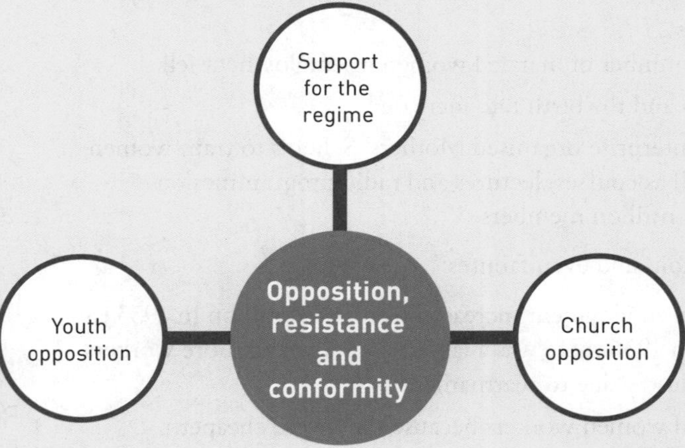

# Key topic 4 Life in Nazi Germany, 1933–39

This topic examines how the lives of German citizens were changed by Nazi policies. It considers the Nazis' racial policies and their persecution of Jews and other minority groups.

## 1 Nazi policies towards women

REVISED

The Nazis had a traditional view of the role of women. Their policies reflected this.

### 1.1 Nazi views on women and the family

The Nazis wanted to reverse the developments of the 1920s (see page 134). They thought women should be homemakers and childbearers, and not go out to work. Their slogan '*Kinder, Kirche, Küche*' summed up their view:

- They wanted to increase the birth rate and strengthen the Third Reich.
- Women had a central role in producing the genetically pure Aryan race, ensuring the future of a strong Nazi state.

**Key term**

***Kinder, Kirche, Küche*** Nazi slogan meaning Children, Church and Cooking

### 1.2 Nazi policies towards women

Nazi policies brought about changes in women's employment, domestic roles and appearance.

- *Employment*: women were encouraged to give up their jobs, get married and have large families. Women doctors, civil servants and teachers were forced to leave their professions. Girls were discouraged from higher education and gaining the qualifications needed for professional careers.
- *Marriage and family*: in 1933, the Law for the Encouragement of Marriage provided loans to help young couples marry, as long as the wife left her job. Couples kept one-quarter of the loan for each child born, up to four children. Maternity benefits were also increased. On Hitler's mother's birthday (12 August) medals were awarded to women with large families.
- *Appearance*: the ideal Nazi woman was blonde, blue-eyed and sturdily built with broad hips for childbearing. She wore traditional clothes and did not smoke or drink. Women were discouraged from wearing trousers, high heels and makeup. Dyeing or styling hair was frowned on, as was slimming, which was seen as bad for childbearing.

**Revision task**

How do you explain the following? The Nazis believed that a woman's place was in the home and yet more women were in employment by 1939.

### 1.3 Successes and failures of Nazi policies

There were successes:

- In the first few years the number of married women in employment fell.
- The number of marriages and the birth rate increased.
- The German Women's Enterprise organised Mothers' Schools to train women in household skills, as well as courses, lectures and radio programmes on household topics. It had 6 million members.

However, there were limitations and even failures:

- The number of women in employment increased from 4.85 million in 1933 to 7.14 million in 1939. From 1936 there was a labour shortage and more workers were needed in heavy industry due to rearmament.
- Many employers preferred women workers because they were cheaper. Women's wages remained only two-thirds of men's.
- Some women resented the loss of more professional jobs such as doctors, lawyers and schoolteachers.

**Exam tip**

Remember that women had an important family and childbearing role in Nazi Germany.

## You're the examiner



Below is an exam-style question.

**Explain why the position of women changed in Nazi Germany in the years 1933–39.**

**You may use the following in your answer:**
- **Employment**
- **Appearance**

**You must also use information of your own.**

1 Below are a mark scheme and a paragraph which is part of an answer to the question. Read the paragraph and the mark scheme. Decide which level you would award the paragraph. Write the level below, along with a justification for your choice.

**Mark scheme**

| Level | Mark | |
|---|---|---|
| 1 | 1–3 | A simple or generalised answer is given, lacking development and organisation |
| 2 | 4–6 | An explanation is given, showing limited analysis and with only an implicit link to the question |
| 3 | 7–9 | An explanation is given, showing some analysis, which is mainly directed at the focus of the question |
| 4 | 10–12 | An analytical explanation is given which is directed consistently at the focus of the question |

Remember that for the higher levels, students must
- explain at least three reasons
- focus explicitly on the question
- support their reasons with precise details.

### STUDENT ANSWER

The ideal Nazi woman was blonde, blue-eyed and sturdily built. She was expected to have broad hips for childbearing and to wear traditional, not fashionable clothes. She did not wear makeup nor did she smoke or drink. Losing weight was frowned on because it could be bad for childbearing.

The Nazis believed that a woman's place was in the home and were determined to get women to give up their jobs. Instead, they wanted them to get married and have large families. Women in the professions such as doctors and civil servants had to give up their jobs. Labour exchanges and employers were encouraged to give first choice of jobs to men. Women had a much more domestic role.

Level ☐ Reason ____________________

____________________

2 Now suggest what the student has to do to achieve a higher level.

____________________

____________________

3 Try and rewrite this paragraph at a higher level.

4 Now try and write the rest of the answer to the question.

# 2 Nazi policies towards the young

REVISED

The Nazis tried to make young people into loyal Nazis through controlling education and youth movements.

## 2.1 Nazi control of the young through education

Teachers had to accept and put across Nazi ideals or be sacked. Nearly all joined the Nazi Teachers' Association.

The curriculum changed to put across key Nazi ideals and prepare students for their future roles. Textbooks were rewritten to fit the Nazi view of history and racial purity and had to be approved by the Ministry of Education. *Mein Kampf* became a standard text.

With boys, the emphasis was on preparation for the military. Girls learned needlework and cookery to become good homemakers and mothers.

- History: this was rewritten to glorify Germany's past and the Nazi Party.
- Physical education: took fifteen per cent of curriculum time to ensure that girls were fit to be mothers and boys were prepared for military service.
- Eugenics: a new subject about selective breeding, more especially the creation of a master race. Children were taught that they should not marry so-called inferior races, such as Jews.
- Race studies: a new subject to put forward Nazi ideas on race, in particular the superiority of the Aryan race.
- Geography: pupils were taught about lands which were once part of Germany and the need for more living space (*lebensraum*) for Germans.

## 2.2 Hitler Youth and the League of German Maidens

The Nazis wanted to control the leisure time of the young. They closed down all youth movements belonging to other political parties and the Churches. There were four separate youth organisations for 10–18-year-olds, under the control of Baldur von Shirach, Youth Leader of the Reich:

- German Young People for boys aged 10–13
- Young Girls for girls aged 10–14
- **Hitler Youth** for boys aged 14–18
- **League of German Maidens** for girls aged 14–18.

From 1936 membership was compulsory, although many did not join.

For the boys, the focus was on military training, sport, hiking and camping. The girls were kept separate from the boys. The main emphasis was on physical fitness and preparing them for motherhood through domestic skills. They were taught how to make beds and cook.

## 2.3 Successes and failures of Nazi policies

There were some successes:

- Membership of the Hitler Youth expanded from 5.4 million in 1936 to 7 million in 1939.
- Many young people enjoyed the exciting and interesting activities such as camping.
- Others enjoyed the great sense of comradeship and belonging to something that seemed powerful.

On other hand, there were failures:

- At least 3 million youngsters had not joined the Hitler Youth by the end of 1938.
- Some members found the activities boring, especially military drilling.

**Key terms**

**Hitler Youth** Organisation set up for boys in Germany to convert them to Nazi ideals

**League of German Maidens** Youth organisation for girls aged between 14 and 18 to prepare them for motherhood

**Revision task**

Summarise the differences in the experiences of girls and boys in Nazi Germany in education and youth movements.

**Exam tip**

Remember to focus on the different Nazi aims in their policies towards the young: for boys it was preparation for the military and for girls it was preparation for motherhood.

## Utility

Look at the two sources, the exam-style question and the two answers below. Which answer is the better answer to the question and why? You could look at page 42 for guidance on how to answer the utility question to help you make your judgement.

**How useful are Sources B and C for an enquiry into the Hitler Youth movement? Explain your answer, using Sources B and C and your own knowledge of the historical context.**

### SOURCE B

*From a British magazine, 1938.*

There seems little enthusiasm for the Hitler Youth, with membership falling. Many no longer want to be commanded, but wish to do as they like. Usually only a third of a group appears for roll-call. At evening meetings it is a great event if 20 turn up out of 80, but usually there are only about 10 or 12.

### SOURCE C

*A Nazi poster of 1936 for the League of German Maidens.*

### ANSWER 1

Source B is useful because it suggests that the Hitler Youth movement was not popular. At least 3 million youngsters had not joined the Hitler Youth by the end of 1938. It is also useful because it was from a British magazine which may well try to give a more objective and balanced view of life in the Hitler Youth.

Source C is useful because it provides an example of the propaganda used by the Nazis to encourage support for the Hitler Youth and more young people, in this case girls, to join. It is also useful because it provides evidence of the popularity of the movement as the girl looks happy and enthusiastic. Membership of the Hitler Youth certainly expanded from 5.4 million in 1936 to 7 million in 1939.

### ANSWER 2

Source B is useful because it was written at the time. Source B is also useful because it tells me that there seems little enthusiasm for the Hitler Youth. It also says that only ten or twelve turn up for evening meetings.

Source C is useful because it is from the time of the Nazis. Source C is useful because it shows me a member of the League of German Maidens holding a Nazi flag. She has blonde hair. She is wearing a uniform.

# 3 Employment and living standards

REVISED

Nazi policies reduced unemployment; however, there is debate about the standard of living during this period.

## 3.1 Nazi policies to reduce unemployment

Hitler was determined to reduce unemployment. This stood at 6 million in 1932 and had more or less been removed by 1938.

### Job-creation schemes

In 1933, 18.4 billion marks were spent on job-creation schemes, rising to 37.1 million by 1938. One scheme was a massive road-building programme to create **autobahns**. This improved the efficiency of German industry by allowing goods to cross the country more quickly and enabled the swift transportation of German troops.

### The Reich Labour Service (RAD)

The **Reich Labour Service** provided young men with manual labour jobs. From 1935, it was compulsory for men aged 18–25 to serve for six months. Workers lived in camps, wore uniforms, received very low pay and carried out military drill as well as work.

### Invisible unemployment

Some unemployed people were 'invisible' and not counted in official unemployment figures:

- Jews dismissed from their jobs. From 1933, many Jews were forced out of their jobs, especially in the professions such as lawyers and doctors.
- Women doctors, civil servants and teachers dismissed from their jobs.
- Women who had given up work to get married.
- Unmarried men under 25 who were pushed into RAD schemes.
- Opponents of the regime held in concentration camps.

### Rearmament

**Rearmament**, especially after 1936, created more jobs:

- More money was spent on manufacturing weapons, and other heavy industry grew, such as the iron industry. By 1939, 26 billion marks were spent on rearmament.
- From 1935, all men aged 18–35 had to do two years' military service. The army expanded from 100,000 in 1933 to 1,400,000 by 1939.

## 3.2 Changes in the standard of living

There is a debate about whether Germans were better or worse off during the period 1933–39.

| Better off | Worse off |
|---|---|
| • There was more or less full employment.<br>• The '**Strength Through Joy**' (KdF) tried to improve the leisure time of German workers through leisure and cultural trips. These included concerts, theatre visits, sporting events, weekend trips, holidays and cruises.<br>• '**Beauty of Labour**' tried to improve working conditions. It organised the building of canteens, swimming pools and sports facilities. It installed better workplace lighting and improved noise levels. | • Lack of freedom. German workers lost their rights under the Nazis. In 1933, trade unions were banned (replaced by the **German Labour Front**). The Labour Front did not permit workers to negotiate for better pay or reduced hours of work. Strikes were banned.<br>• Volkswagen swindle. This idea to encourage people to put aside money every week to buy a Volkswagen was a con trick. By 1939 not a single customer had taken delivery of a car. None of the money was refunded.<br>• **Invisible unemployment**. |

**Key terms**

**Autobahns** German motorways

**Beauty of Labour** A department of the KdF that tried to improve working conditions

**German Labour Front** An organisation of employers and workers which replaced trade unions

**Invisible unemployment** Unemployed people not included in the official unemployment statistics

**Rearmament** Building up the German armed forces

**Reich Labour Service** A scheme to provide young men with manual labour jobs

**Strength Through Joy** An organisation set up by the German Labour Front to try to improve the leisure time of German workers

**Revision task**

Rank order the various methods used by the Nazis to reduce unemployment beginning with the most effective and ending with the least effective.

## Relevance

Below are an exam-style question and a series of statements. Decide which statements are:

- relevant to the question (R)
- partially relevant to the question (PR)
- irrelevant to the question (I).

Tick the appropriate column.

**Explain why the Nazis were able to reduce unemployment in Germany in the years 1933–39.**

> **You may use the following in your answer:**
> - **The National Labour Front**
> - **Job-creation schemes**
>
> **You must also use information of your own.**

| Nazi policies | R | PR | I |
|---|---|---|---|
| In 1933, 18.4 billion marks were spent on job-creation schemes, rising to 37.1 million by 1938 | | | |
| From 1933, more and more Jews were forced out of their jobs | | | |
| The Strength Through Joy movement organised leisure activities and provided the public with cheap holidays | | | |
| The Labour Front replaced trade unions. Workers were not allowed to leave their jobs without permission | | | |
| Germany had built a network of motorways, known as autobahns | | | |
| Beauty of Labour tried to improve working conditions by organising the building of canteens and sports facilities for workers | | | |
| The Reich Labour Service was made compulsory in July 1935 for all men aged 18–25, who had to serve six months | | | |
| The Depression brought unemployment which had reached 6 million by 1932 | | | |
| Many women were dismissed from their jobs, especially in the professions. Others were tempted by marriage loans to give up their jobs and marry | | | |
| The RAD was not popular. Men were paid very low wages and had to put up with uncomfortable tented camps, long hours of work and boring jobs | | | |
| The drive for rearmament created more jobs as more money was spent on manufacturing weapons | | | |
| Billions were spent producing tanks, ships and aircraft. Heavy industry especially benefited | | | |

## Better or worse?

1. Using the information on page 34, copy and complete both sides of the scales to show whether workers were better or worse off.
2. Do you think workers were better or worse off overall? Give reasons for your answer.

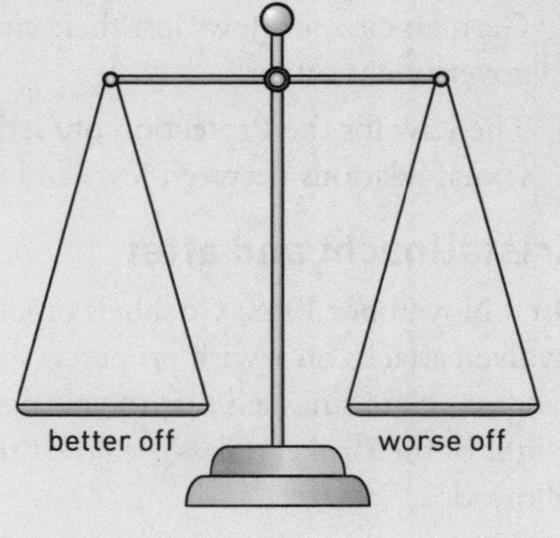

# 4 The persecution of minorities

REVISED

Hitler used the Jews as scapegoats for many of Germany's problems. The Nazis also persecuted **Slavs**, **Gypsies**, homosexuals and those with disabilities.

## 4.1 Nazi racial belief and policies

Central to the Nazis' policy was the aim to create a pure Aryan racial state. They thought this could be achieved by **selective breeding** and destroying the Jews. Jews and Slavs were seen as inferior *Untermenschen* or subhumans.

## 4.2 The treatment of minorities

Germans with disabilities were seen as a 'burden on the community'. There were also socially undesirable groups such as homosexuals and Gypsies.

### People with disabilities

The 1933 Sterilisation Law allowed the sterilisation of those suffering from physical deformity, mental illness, epilepsy, learning disabilities, blindness and deafness.

### Homosexuals

Homosexuality remained illegal. Nazi views about the importance of family life meant that same-sex relationships could not be tolerated. Gay men were arrested and sent to concentration camps.

### Gypsies

The Nazis wanted to remove Germany's 30,000 Gypsies because they were non-Aryan and threatened racial purity. In 1935, the Nazis banned all marriages between Gypsies and Germans.

## 4.3 The persecution of the Jews

The persecution of the Jews gradually increased in the years 1933–39.

### Early policies, 1933–34

- In 1933, the SA organised a boycott of Jewish shops and businesses.
- Jews were excluded from government jobs.
- In 1934, local councils banned Jews from public spaces such as parks.

### The Nuremberg Laws, 1935

The Nuremberg Laws were a series of measures aimed against the Jews, including:

- The Reich Citizenship Law stated that only those of German blood could be German citizens. Jews lost their citizenship, and the right to vote and hold government office.
- The Law for the Protection of German Blood and Honour forbade marriage or sexual relations between Jews and German citizens.

### Kristallnacht and after

On 8 November 1938, Goebbels organised anti-Jewish demonstrations which involved attacks on Jewish property, shops, homes and synagogues. So many windows were smashed that the events of 9 November 1938 became known as the 'Night of the Broken Glass' or **Kristallnacht**. Worse persecution of the Jews followed.

In January 1939, the SS was given the responsibility for eliminating Jews from Germany. This would be achieved by forced **emigration**:

- On 30 April, Jews were forced into **ghettos**.
- By the summer of 1939, about 250,000 Jews had left Germany.

#### Key terms

**Emigration** The act of leaving one's country to settle in another country

**Ghettos** Densely populated areas of a city inhabited by a particular ethnic group, such as Jews

**Gypsy** A race of people found across Europe who generally travel across the continent rather than living in one place

**Kristallnacht** The 'night of the broken glass'. The name given to a night of violence against Jews due to the amount of shattered glass which littered the streets

**Nuremberg Laws** Laws passed in 1935 which denied German citizenship to Jewish people

**Selective breeding** Nazi policy designed to create a master race

**Slavs** Eastern Europeans including Poles and Russians

#### Revision task

What were the following?

- The master race
- The Sterilisation Law of 1933
- The Nuremberg Laws
- Kristallnacht.

#### Exam tip

Remember that other minority groups apart from the Jews were persecuted by the Nazis.

You could get a question about how life for Jews changed in Nazi Germany 1933–39. It was a gradual build-up of Nazi policies against the Jews.

## Making an inference from a visual source

An inference is a message that you can get from a source. Below are an exam-style inference question, the source and a series of statements. Decide which of the statements:

- make(s) inferences from the source (I)
- describes what can be seen in the source (D)
- cannot be justified from the source (X).

**Give two things you can infer from Source A about the treatment of the Jews in Nazi Germany in the years 1936–39.**

### SOURCE A

*A photograph taken in March 1933. It shows members of the SA forcing a Jewish lawyer to walk barefoot through the streets of Munich wearing a sign that says 'I will never again complain to the police'.*

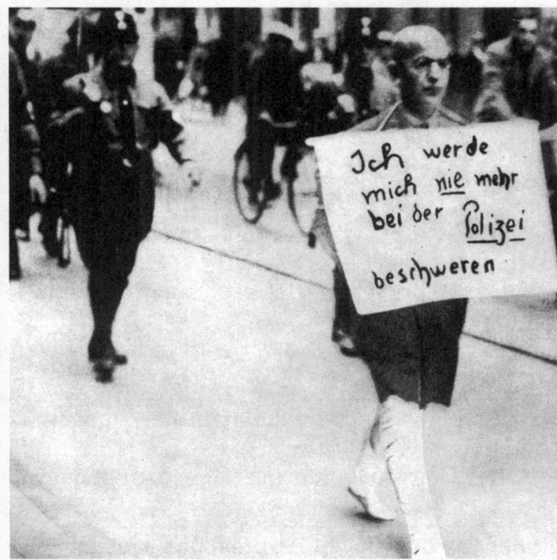


| Statements | I | D | X |
|---|---|---|---|
| The photograph shows a Jewish man walking barefoot down a street | | | |
| Jewish shops were boycotted by the SA | | | |
| The Jews were treated unfairly | | | |
| The Jews were denied German citizenship | | | |
| The Jews were publicly humiliated | | | |
| Jewish shops and synagogues were destroyed by the Nazis | | | |
| The SA played a leading role in persecuting the Jews | | | |
| Members of the SA are forcing the Jewish man to walk down the street | | | |

## You're the examiner

Below is an exam-style question.

**Give two things you can infer about the treatment of the Jews in Nazi Germany.**

1 Below are a mark scheme and a paragraph which is part of an answer to the question. Read the paragraph and the mark scheme. First decide which mark you would award the paragraph (there are a maximum of four marks available).

| Mark scheme |
|---|
| Award 1 mark for each valid inference up to a maximum of two inferences. The second mark for each example should be awarded for supporting detail selected from the source. |

*The source suggests that the Jews in Nazi Germany were publicly humiliated. This is because the photograph shows a Jewish man being forced to walk down a main street barefooted. The source also suggests that the Jews had no protection from the police.*

2 Next try and improve this answer to get four marks.

# Exam focus

Your History GCSE is made up of three exams:

- Paper 1 on a thematic study and historic environment.
- Paper 2 on a British depth study and a period study.
- Paper 3 on a modern depth study, in your case Weimar and Nazi Germany, 1918–39.

For Paper 3 you have to answer the following types of questions. Each requires you to demonstrate different historical skills:

- **Question 1** is a source inference question in which you have to make two supported inferences.
- **Question 2** is a causation question which asks you to explain why something happened. You should develop at least three clear points.
- **Question 3** includes four sub-questions on an enquiry. For this enquiry you are given two sources and two interpretations.

The table below gives a summary of the question types for Paper 3 and what you need to do.

| Question number | Marks | Key words | You need to... |
|---|---|---|---|
| 1 | 4 | Give **two** things you can infer from Source A about ... | • Make at least two inferences<br>• Use quotes from the source to back up your inference, or describe a specific part of it if it is a picture |
| 2 | 12 | Explain why ... You may use the following in your answer: [two given points]. You **must** also use information of your own | • Explain at least three causes. You can use the points in the question but must also use at least one point of your own<br>• Ensure that you focus these on the question |
| 3(a) | 8 | How useful are sources ... for an enquiry into ... ? | • Ensure that you explain the value of the contents of each of the sources<br>• Explain how the provenance of each source affects the value of the contents<br>• You need to support your answer with your knowledge of the given topic |
| 3(b) | 4 | Study Interpretations 1 and 2. What is the main difference between these views? | • Ensure that you understand the main view of each interpretation<br>• Give the view from each interpretation to support your answer |
| 3(c) | 4 | Suggest **one** reason why Interpretations 1 and 2 give different views | • Remember you only have to explain one reason<br>• Make use of the two sources |
| 3(d) | 20 | How far do you agree with Interpretation 2 about ... ? | • Ensure that you agree and disagree with the view<br>• Use evidence from the interpretations and your own knowledge<br>• Ensure that you write a conclusion giving your final judgement on the question<br>• There are up to 4 marks for spelling, punctuation, grammar and the use of specialist terminology |

## Question 1: Inference

Below is an example of an exam-style inference question which is worth 4 marks.

**Give two things you can infer from Source A about Hitler's meetings.**

### SOURCE A

*Adapted from the diary of Luise Solmitz, 23 March 1932. Solmitz was a schoolteacher writing about attending a meeting in Hamburg at which Hitler spoke.*

There stood Hitler in a simple black coat, looking over the crowd of 120,000 people of all classes and ages ... a forest of swastika flags unfurled, the joy of this moment showed itself in a roaring salute ... The crowd looked up to Hitler with touching faith, as their helper, their saviour, their deliverer from unbearable distress ... He is the rescuer of the scholar, the farmer, the worker and the unemployed.

## How to answer

You have to make two inferences and support each with details from the source. For each of the two inferences you are given the prompts 'What I can infer?' and 'Details in the source that tell me this'.

- **'What I can infer?'** Begin your answer with 'This source suggests …'. This should help you to get the message from the source.
- **'Details in the source that tell me this'** Then quote the detail from the source which supports this message. Begin this part of the answer with 'I know this because the source says/shows …'.

Below is a sample answer to this inference question with comments around it.

What I can infer:

The source suggests that Hitler appealed to many different sections in German society.

The first inference is made. Using the phrase 'the source suggests' encourages this inference.

Details in the source that tell me this:

I know this because the source says 'He is the rescuer of the scholar, the farmer, the worker and the unemployed'.

The first inference is supported with evidence from the source. This is reinforced by using the phrase 'I know this because'.

What I can infer:

The source also suggests the crowd were very enthusiastic about Hitler.

The second inference is made. Using the phrase 'the source suggests' encourages this inference.

Details in the source that tell me this:

I know this because the source says 'the joy of this moment showed itself in a roaring salute ... The crowd looked up to Hitler with touching faith'.

The second inference is supported with evidence from the source. This is reinforced by using the phrase 'I know this because'.

## Visual sources

You could also be asked to make inferences from a visual source.

**Give two things you can infer from Source B about the police state.**

Here is the first part of an answer to this question.

This source suggests that the police had a strong presence in Nazi Germany.

I know this because the source shows several police with rifles who are thoroughly searching people in the street.

1 Highlight the following:
- Where the student has made the inference.
- How this inference has been supported.

2 Now add a second supported inference.

### SOURCE B

*German citizens being searched in the street by Gestapo officers and armed uniformed police, 1933.*

## Question 2: Causation

Below is an example of an exam-style causation question which is worth 12 marks.

**Explain why the Weimar Republic experienced a period of recovery, 1923–29.**

You may use the following in your answer:
- The Dawes Plan
- The Locarno Pact

You **must** also use information of your own.

### How to answer

- You need to explain at least three causes. This could be the two mentioned in the question and one of your own. You don't have to use the points given in the question, you could decide to make more points of your own instead.
- You need to fully explain each cause and support your explanation with precise knowledge, ensuring that each cause is fully focused on the question.

Below is a sample answer to this question with comments around it.

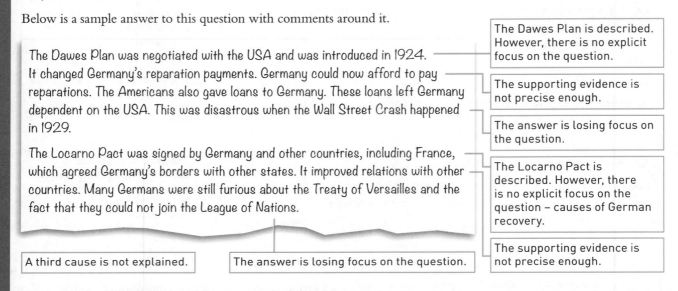

The Dawes Plan was negotiated with the USA and was introduced in 1924. It changed Germany's reparation payments. Germany could now afford to pay reparations. The Americans also gave loans to Germany. These loans left Germany dependent on the USA. This was disastrous when the Wall Street Crash happened in 1929.

The Locarno Pact was signed by Germany and other countries, including France, which agreed Germany's borders with other states. It improved relations with other countries. Many Germans were still furious about the Treaty of Versailles and the fact that they could not join the League of Nations.

The Dawes Plan is described. However, there is no explicit focus on the question.

The supporting evidence is not precise enough.

The answer is losing focus on the question.

The Locarno Pact is described. However, there is no explicit focus on the question – causes of German recovery.

The supporting evidence is not precise enough.

A third cause is not explained.

The answer is losing focus on the question.

### Make an improvement

Try improving the answer. An example of a better answer to this question is on page 41 for you to check your own answer against.

#### Exam tip

Writing a good paragraph to explain an answer to something is as easy as **PEE**ing – Point, Example, Explain.

Your point is a short answer to the question. You then back this up with lots of examples to demonstrate all the knowledge you have learned during your studies: this is the section that proves you have studied and revised, rather than just guessing. Finally, you will link that knowledge to the question by explaining in a final sentence:

- **P**oint: passing my GCSE History exam will be very helpful in the future.
- **E**xample: for example, it will help me to continue my studies next year.
- **E**xplain: this will help me to get the job I want in the future.

Below is a sample answer to the causation question on page 40 with comments around it.

A first cause of German recovery was the Dawes Plan of 1924. This was because this plan reorganised Germany's reparation payments and encouraged further financial support from the USA. German reparations were not reduced but more sensibly staged to match Germany's capacity to pay. Reparations would begin at 1 billion marks for the first year, and would increase over a period of four to five years to 2.5 billion marks. Thereafter, the payments would be linked to Germany's capacity to pay. In return, the French withdrew their troops from the Ruhr. Furthermore, the Dawes Plan included a US loan of 800 million gold marks to Germany. Over the next six years Germany borrowed about $3 billion from US companies and banks, which greatly assisted the growth of German industry as well as the payment of reparations.

> The first cause is introduced and immediately focuses on the question.

> The supporting evidence is precise and relevant to the question.

However, the success of the Dawes Plan was closely linked to a second reason for German recovery, the Rentenmark, which provided the financial stability necessary for economic recovery. The German currency had lost all value due to the hyperinflation of 1923. In November 1923, Stresemann, in order to stabilise the currency, introduced this new currency. This was a temporary measure with its value based on property values. In the following year, the Rentenmark was converted into the Reichsmark, a new currency now backed with gold.

> The second cause is introduced and linked to the first cause and immediately focuses on the question. Notice that this is a cause not mentioned in the question.

> The supporting evidence is precise and relevant to the question.

Economic and financial recovery was supported by improved relations abroad, which was a third reason for recovery. Stresemann greatly improved relations with Britain and France by ending passive resistance in the Ruhr and signing the Locarno Pact of 1925. The Pact also included Italy and Belgium and guaranteed Germany's frontiers with France, Belgium and Italy. In the following year, Stresemann took Germany into the League of Nations. Germany was recognised as a Great Power and given a permanent seat on the League's council alongside France and Britain. This, in turn, encouraged further trade between these countries and greater economic investment in Germany.

> The third cause is introduced and linked to the second cause and immediately focuses on the question.

> The supporting evidence is precise and relevant to the question.

## Have a go

Now have a go at the following causation question:

**Explain why there was increased support for the Nazis in the years 1919–32.**

**You may use the following in your answer:**

- **Hitler**
- **Fear of Communism**

**You must also use information of your own.**

## Question 3(a): Utility

Below is an example of an exam-style utility question. It is worth 8 marks.

**How useful are Sources B and C for an enquiry into Nazi policies towards women in Germany in the years 1933–39?**

### SOURCE B

*From Judith Grunfeld, an American journalist, 1937.*

How many women workers did the Führer send home? According to the statistics of the German Department of Labour, there were in June 1936, 5,470,000 employed women, or 1,200,000 more than in January 1933. The Nazi campaign has not been successful in reducing the numbers of women employed. It has simply squeezed them out of better paid positions into the sweated trades. This type of labour with its miserable wages and long hours is extremely dangerous to the health of women and degrades the family.

### SOURCE C

*A Nazi poster of 1934 which says 'the NSDAP [Nazi Party] protects the national community'.*

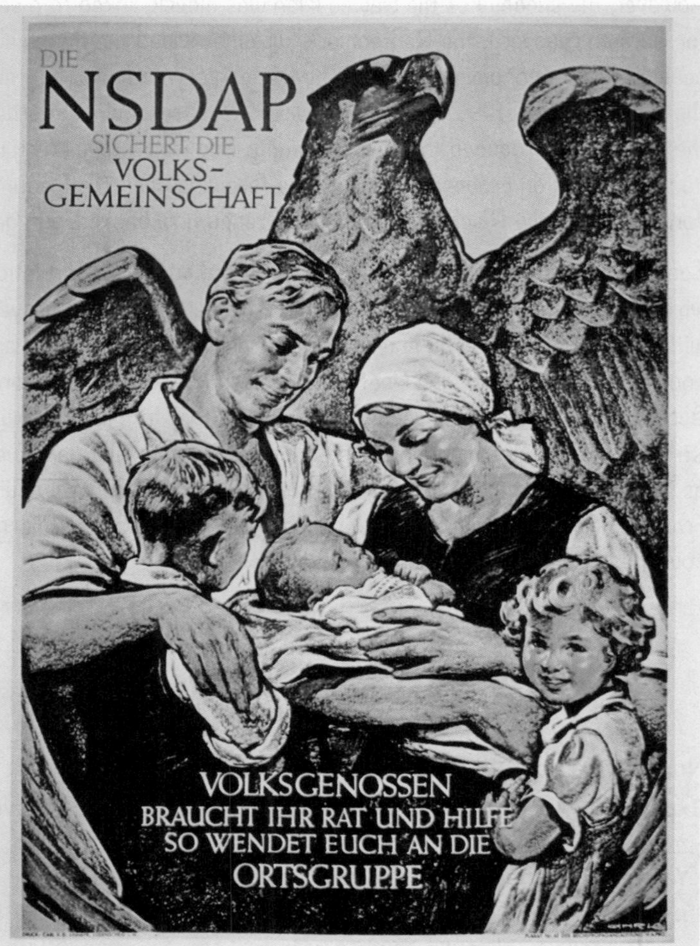


## How to answer

- Explain the value and limitations of the contents of each source and try to add some contextual knowledge when you make a point.
- Explain the value and limitations of the NOP (Nature, Origin and Purpose) of each source and try to add some contextual knowledge when you make a point.
- In your conclusion, give a final judgement on the relative value of each source. For example, one source might provide one view of an event, the other source a different view.

## You're the examiner

1 Below are a mark scheme and a paragraph which is part of an answer to the question on page 42. Read the paragraph and the mark scheme. Decide which level you would award the paragraph. Give a justification for your choice.

**Mark scheme**

| Level | Mark | |
|---|---|---|
| 1 | 1–2 | A simple judgement on utility is given, and supported by undeveloped comment on the content of the sources and/or their provenance |
| 2 | 3–5 | Judgements on source utility for the specified enquiry are given ... related to the content of the sources and/or their provenance |
| 3 | 6–8 | Judgements on source utility for the specified enquiry are given ... with developed reasoning which takes into account how the provenance affects the usefulness of the source content |

Source B is useful because it suggests that the Nazi policies towards women were not successful as there were 1,200,000 more women in employment in Germany in 1936 than there had been in 1933. This was the case because there were labour shortages in certain parts of German industry. It is also useful because it says that the Nazi policies had not been successful because they had forced women out of reasonably paid jobs into those that had poor conditions such as the sweated trades. Source B is also useful because it was written in 1937.

Source C is useful because it suggests that women in Nazi Germany played an important role in the family. The poster shows the woman in the very centre holding and looking after the baby. The Nazis were keen on ensuring that women did all the household duties. It is also useful because it is a Nazi poster which was produced in 1934.

Level ☐ Reason ____________________

____________________

Below is part of a high-level answer to the question on page 42 which explains the utility of Source B. Read it and the comments around it.

Source B is useful because it suggests that the Nazi policies towards women were not successful as there were 1,200,000 more women in employment in Germany in 1936 than there had been in 1933. This was the case because there were labour shortages in certain parts of German industry. It is also useful because it says that the Nazi policies had not been successful because they had forced women out of reasonably paid jobs into those that had poor conditions such as the sweated trades. 'Invisible employment' enabled the Nazis to hide the real extent of unemployment. The usefulness of Source B is further enhanced by its provenance. It was written by an American journalist who will not have been influenced by Nazi propaganda and censorship and would be able to give an objective, independent assessment of the effects of Nazi policies on women. She is able to be critical about these policies.

A judgement is made on the value of the contents of the source.

Own knowledge is used to support this judgement.

The provenance of the source is taken into account when making a judgement on its utility.

2 Now write your own high-level answer on Source C. Remember to take into account how the provenance affects the usefulness of the source content.

## Question 3(b): How interpretations differ

Below is an example of an exam-style question 3(b) on the difference between two interpretations. It is worth 4 marks.

**Study Interpretations 1 and 2. They give different views of Nazi policies towards women in the years 1933–39. What is the main difference between these views? Explain your answer, using details from both interpretations.**

### INTERPRETATION 1

*From* Germany 1918–45 *by J. Brooman, published in 1996.*

Women were soon brought in line. Shortly after the Nazi seizure of power, thousands of married women doctors and civil servants were sacked from their jobs. Over the next few years, the number of women teachers was gradually reduced. From 1936 onwards women could no longer be judges or prosecutors, nor could they serve on juries.

### INTERPRETATION 2

*From* Weimar and Nazi Germany *by E. Wilmot, published in 1993.*

In 1933 there were 4.85 million women in paid employment. This increased to 7.14 million in 1939. Economic reality forced Nazi ideology to do a U-turn. A labour shortage began to develop from 1936 and the government looked to women to plug the gap. In 1937, the Nazis overturned a clause in the marriage loans scheme to permit married women who had a loan to take up employment.

### How to answer

You need to identify the main view that each interpretation has about the Nazi policies towards women in the years 1933–39 and explain each view. Below is an answer to this question which explains how the interpretations differ.

## Question 3(c): Why interpretations differ

A main difference is that Interpretation 1 emphasises the success of Nazi policies towards women in Germany in the years 1933–39, especially in removing married women from employment. Interpretation 2 emphasises the failure of Nazis policies towards women in Germany in the years 1933–39, especially in employment – with more women in employment by 1939.

> The main view of Interpretation 1 is identified and explained.

> The main view of Interpretation 2 is identified and explained.

Below is an example of question 3(c) on the reasons why the two interpretations differ. It is worth 4 marks.

**Suggest one reason why Interpretations 1 and 2 give different views about the achievements of Nazi policies towards women in the years 1933–39. You may use Sources B and C (see page 166) to help explain your answer.**

### How to answer

There are three reasons as to why the two interpretations differ. You only need to give one of these.

- The interpretations may differ because they have given weight to the two different sources. You need to identify the views given in the two sources and match these to the different interpretations.
- The interpretations may differ because they are partial extracts and in this case they do not actually contradict one another.
- They may differ because the authors have a different emphasis.

Below is part of an answer to this question in which the student uses the first option – they give different weight to different sources.

The interpretations may differ because they give different weight to different sources. For example, Source B provides some support for Interpretation 1, which stresses the failure of Nazi policies in removing women from employment.

> Interpretation 1 is matched to Source B.

> The view given in Source C is explained.

## Have a go

Now, on a separate piece of paper, complete this answer by matching Interpretation 2 to one of the sources.

## Question 3(d): How far do you agree with one of the interpretations?

Below is an example of an exam-style question 3(d) which asks you to make a judgement about how far you agree with one of the interpretations. It is worth 20 marks.

**How far do you agree with Interpretation 2 about Nazi policies towards women in the years 1933–39? Explain your answer, using both interpretations and your knowledge of the historical context.**

### How to answer

You need to give a balanced answer which agrees and disagrees with the interpretation using evidence from the two interpretations as well as your own knowledge. Here is one way you could approach this:

- agree with the view with evidence from Interpretation 2
- agree with the view with evidence from your own knowledge
- disagree with the view with evidence from Interpretation 1
- disagree with the view with evidence from your own knowledge
- make a final judgement on the view.

Below is part of an answer to this question in which the student agrees with the view given in Interpretation 2.

I agree with the view given in Interpretation 2 about the achievements of Nazi policies towards women in the years 1933–39. The interpretation suggests that these policies, especially in the area of employment, were not successful. The Nazis' original aim was to remove as many women as possible from the work force to help with their other policy of reducing unemployment and also to ensure that married women could focus on their domestic role as wives and mothers.

However, as Wilmot suggests, the Nazis had to do a U-turn in the mid-1930s as there were labour shortages so that the number of women employed actually increased from 4.85 million in 1933 to 7.14 million in 1939. In addition, the numbers increased because many employers preferred women workers as they were cheaper. Women's wages remained only two-thirds of men's. The Nazis did force women out of the better paid and more professional jobs. However, more and more employed women were employed in lower paid jobs with poor working conditions such as the sweated trades. Some women resented the loss of these more professional jobs such as doctors, lawyers and schoolteachers.

The answer immediately focuses on the question.

Support is provided from Interpretation 2 for this view.

Own knowledge is used to provide support for the view.

## Have a go

Now, on a separate piece of paper, have a go at writing the rest of the answer by disagreeing with the view given in Interpretation 2.

Remember to write a conclusion giving your final judgement on the question. Here is an example of a good conclusion.

Overall, I only partly agree with Interpretation 2 about Nazi policies towards women. As suggested by Wilmot, the Nazis did eventually have to change their employment policies and allow more women to work in industry. However, as Brooman suggests in Interpretation 1, the Nazis did achieve one of their aims in female employment which was to reduce the number of women in professional jobs.

# Revision techniques

We all learn in different ways and if you're going to be successful in your revision you need to work out the ways that work best for you. Remember that revision doesn't have to be dull and last for hours at a time – but it is really important you do it! The highest grades are awarded to students who have consistently excellent subject knowledge and this only comes with solid revision.

## Method 1: 'Brain dumps'

These are particularly useful when done every so often – it's never too early to start! Take a big piece of paper or even a whiteboard and write down everything you can remember about the topic you are revising, one of the units or even the whole History course. You could write down:

- dates
- names of key individuals
- key events
- important place names
- anything else you can remember.

Once you're satisfied you can't remember any more, use different colours to highlight or underline the words in groups. For example, you might choose to underline all the mentions that relate to causes of the Depression in Germany in 1929 in red and effects in blue.

You could extend this task by comparing your brain dump with that of a friend. The next time you do it, try setting yourself a shorter time limit and see if you can write down more.

## Method 2: Learning walks

Make use of your space! Write down key facts and place them around your home, where you will see them every day. Make an effort to read the facts whenever you walk past them. You might decide to put information on Hitler's rise to power on the stairs, with the idea of steadily achieving his dictatorship.

Studies have shown that identifying certain facts with a certain place can help them stick in your mind. So, when you get into the exam room and you find you have a question on the recovery of the Weimar Republic, 1924–29, you can close your eyes and picture that factsheet on your living-room wall ... what does it say?

## Method 3: 'Distilling'

Memory studies show that we retain information better if we revisit it regularly. This means that revising the information once is not necessarily going to help it stay in your brain. Going back over the facts at intervals of less than a week leads to the highest retention of facts.

To make this process streamlined, try 'distilling' your notes. Start by reading over the notes you've completed in class or in this revision guide; two days later, read over them again, and this time write down everything you didn't remember. If you repeat this process enough you will end up with hardly any facts left to write down, because they will all be stored in your brain, ready for the exam!

## Method 4: Using your downtime

There are always little pockets of time through the day which aren't much good for anything: bus journeys, queues, ad breaks in TV programmes, waiting for the bath to run and so on. If you added all these minutes up it would probably amount to quite a lot of time, and it can be put to good use for revision.

Instead of having to carry around your notes, though, make use of something you carry around with you already. Most of us have a phone that can take pictures and record voice memos, or an iPod or something similar:

- Photograph key sections of this book and read over them.
- Record yourself reading information so that you can listen back over it – while you're playing football, before you go to sleep, or at any other time.
- Access the quizzes that go with this book: www.hoddereducation.co.uk/myrevisionnotes

# Notes

# Notes

# Notes

# Notes